YALE HISTORICAL PUBLICATIONS, MISCELLANY, 114

PREPARING FOR THE NEXT WAR

AMERICAN PLANS FOR POSTWAR DEFENSE, 1941–45

MICHAEL S. SHERRY

NEW HAVEN AND LONDON / YALE UNIVERSITY PRESS / 1977

Published under direction of the Department
of History of Yale University with assistance
from the income of the Frederick John Kingsbury
Memorial Fund.

Designed by Sally Sullivan
and set in Times Roman type.
Printed in the United States of America by
The Murray Printing Company, Inc.,
Westford, Massachusetts.

Published in Great Britain, Europe, Africa, and Asia
(except Japan) by Yale University Press, Ltd., London.
Distributed in Latin America by Kaiman & Polon, Inc.,
New York City; in Australia and New Zealand by
Book & Film Services, Artarmon, N.S.W., Australia;
and in Japan by Harper & Row, Publishers, Tokyo Office.

Library of Congress Cataloging in Publication Data

Sherry, Michael S   1945–
    Preparing for the next war.

    (Yale historical publications: Miscellany; 114)
    Originally presented as the author's thesis, Yale,
1975.
    Bibliography: p.
    Includes index.
    1. United States—Military policy.   2. United
States—Armed Forces.   I. Title.   II. Series.
UA23.S47 1977   355.03'307'3   76-27853
ISBN 0-300-02031-7

CONTENTS

PREFACE

This study arose from a need, personal and intellectual, to understand better the origins of the cold war. Like many Americans who came of age during the 1950s and 1960s, I was bewildered by the conflict between "communism" and the "free world" and, as the Vietnam War unfolded, frightened for both self and country. I was puzzled by the nation's extraordinary faith in military solutions to political problems and in technological solutions to military problems. Most of all I was perplexed by the rhetoric used to justify so many of America's cold war endeavors: the insistence that the nation faced the same enemy that it had in the 1930s and 1940s, that Ho Chi Minh was a Hitler, that national irresolution would unleash the totalitarian hordes. No one who grew up in the shadow of World War II could brush aside such warnings. But their credibility waned as the struggle in Southeast Asia dragged on, and the persistence with which they were issued only invited curiosity.

Existing scholarship did not adequately explain the cold war mentality and the central role in it played by faith in military force. The conventional view held that Soviet expansion sparked a defensive American reaction. Americans rose up to defend the free world from another totalitarian threat. In the cold war that ensued, the United States was largely innocent—guilty, maybe, of an early naivete and of erratic or overzealous behavior later, but in any case more sinned against than sinning. Supposedly, a naive and narrow outlook especially characterized American military leaders during World War II. "Military considerations" allegedly governed their policy almost to the total exclusion of postwar aims.[1] This interpretation fit comfortably with the country's popular image of its wartime heroes. Surely such guileless types as Eisenhower, Bradley, and Marshall—men who let the Russians take Berlin—were free of any

---

1. Robert W. Coakley and Richard W. Leighton, *Global Logistics and Strategy, 1943–1945*, p. 820.

hidden, malevolent purpose. Innocents abroad, they fought only to win the war, not to dictate the peace.

In the 1960s revisionist historians began offering some telling arguments against that traditional view. They suggested that because of economic need or greed American policymakers tried to throttle socialism. The rhetoric of freedom and the equation of socialism to fascism masked selfish motives. The more subtle revisionists recognized that economic considerations combined with other factors—historical suspicions of the Soviets and the overconfidence resulting from possession of the bomb—in leading Americans to misperceive and overreact to Russian diplomacy.

The historians, though correct in stressing the problem of American misperception, failed to identify all of its sources. Although World War II was first and foremost a military affair, they ignored its impact on the nation's view of its future security. Few authors studied the role of the military in shaping postwar policies and attitudes. Instead, revisionists and other critics often caricatured the defense leadership either by exaggerating its influence or by belittling the military as the pliant tool of a capitalist elite.[2] Scientists, too, were stereotyped. Historians stressed the aversion of scientists to the role of evil magician and the military's desire to exploit science. "Peace, not preparedness, was their consuming passion," one scholar wrote in describing the outlook of scientists at the end of the war.[3]

Another interpretation of the cold war seemed necessary, and it was suggested by the very rhetoric that had prompted curiosity. Because that rhetoric drew so heavily on the perceptions, images, and experiences of the 1930s and 1940s, it indicated that the model of international relations held by American policymakers took shape during World War II and predated the onset of the cold war. If so, it seemed evident that cold war rhetoric was neither the rational evaluation of the world that its spokesmen believed it to be nor a convenient rationalization for baser instincts that revisionist critics postulated. Instead, the rhetoric of the 1950s and 1960s expressed emotions and preceptions arising from a time when conventional

2. See, for example, Fred J. Cook, *The Warfare State* (New York, 1962), and Gabriel Kolko, *The Roots of American Foreign Policy: An Analysis of Power and Purpose* (Boston, 1969), chap. 2.

3. Clarence G. Lasby, "Science and the Military," in David D. Van Tassel and Michael G. Hall, eds., *Science and Society in the U.S.*, p. 269.

standards of international behavior and traditional guarantees of national safety seemed in collapse. Just as the traumatic events of the 1930s and 1940s shook the nation's faith in its economic health and political isolation, so also did they stir alarm about the country's future security. American policymakers, witnessing Axis aggression and the blitzkrieg campaigns of the war, articulated a new view of the nation's military needs. Military leaders and, often more zealously, civilians urged constant vigilance against surprise attack. Their collective plans and perceptions, which I label the "ideology of national preparedness," became an important component of postwar policy. As such, the ideology encouraged Americans to define the Soviet Union as the nation's next enemy.

My suggestions about the preparedness ideology are meant to complement rather than contradict other revisionist interpretations. We can presume that each source of anxiety about the Soviets—the economic, the political, and the military—reinforced the others. And we can presume that Stalin and his subordinates, even more than Americans the prisoners of narrow experience and suspicions, implemented their own distorted view of the world. No simplistic interpretation of the cold war will do.

In addition to offering new suggestions about the origins of the cold war, a study of the nation's planning for postwar defense simply tells an important story, long neglected because of an understandable fascination with the more dramatic military operations of the war. No systematic study has been made of wartime plans for postwar defense. In the late 1960s, two works broke new ground by examining the plans of the Army Air Forces and the United States Navy.[4] But because each study focused on one service, each stressed the sense of rivalry among the services and failed to see the common perceptions that emerged from a shared experience. My study emphasizes those common perceptions, with its stress, however, on the previously neglected army plans. Because nuclear policy has been over-emphasized and extensively studied elsewhere, this study also focuses on how changes in conventional weaponry affected policy. Likewise, other scholars have examined the controversy over unification of the services. And, obviously, before final judgment on postwar defense planning is made certain plans not treated here (such

4. Vincent Davis, *Postwar Defense Policy and the U.S. Navy, 1943–1946*; Perry McCoy Smith, *The Air Force Plans for Peace, 1943–1945*.

as those on industrial mobilization) deserve examination, as does the course of military planning after 1945.

Scholars who have used military records are familiar with their confused organization and filing systems. Wherever possible, spelling, punctuation, and file symbols are given as they appear in those records, inconsistencies and all. For abbreviations used in citing archival material, the reader should consult the entry on manuscript and archival records in the bibliography. For more detailed discussion of these records and other sources, the reader can consult the bibliographical essay in the author's dissertation, "Preparing for the Next War: American Plans for Postwar Defense, 1941–1945" (Yale University, 1975).

In the preparation of this study my greatest debt has been to archivists. Dozens were helpful, but especially two at the National Archives, Hazel Ward and William Cunliffe, who guided me through the maze of military records and security regulations, searched for documents, and offered insight, information, and encouragement. At the National Academy of Sciences, Jean St. Clair and Paul McClure were extremely helpful. Daniel Kevles helped me understand scientists better. Gaddis Smith helped me see how much the World War II generation acted on its perceptions of the past. Though not by title a teacher, Forrest Pogue is a superb one, providing much encouragement and knowledge. John Morton Blum, my dissertation advisor, guided me in developing a manageable topic, organizing my presentation, and refining my prose. Friends and family provided critical personal and intellectual support: Suzanne and Derich Becker, John Buell, Marilyn and Richard Chapman, Ellen Dwyer, Gail Evans, Charles Grench, David Pace, Leo Ribuffo, Abby Solomon, Jack Teahan, and Allan Winkler.

Branford, Connecticut
May 1976

1 ORGANIZATION AND ASPIRATIONS

The end of World War II could not have appeared more remote than in November 1941. Utilizing fearsome advances in the tank and the airplane, the Nazis had swept over most of Europe and struck deep into the Soviet Union. As German armies snuffed out the life of Europe, in Asia Japanese forces, proceeding at a more deliberate pace, had occupied much of China and now stood poised to seize the colonial remains of Europe's moribund imperialism. To American military leaders, the mounting intensity of the submarine war in the Atlantic and a deadlock in Japanese-American negotiations made the country's entry into the war seem imminent. Alarmed by the speed of the Axis advance, the American army and navy struggled to equip the nation's allies and to mobilize and deploy an American fighting force.

Despite the crisis, the services were worried over what would happen to them and the nation when the war ended. On November 12, still almost a month before Pearl Harbor, Army General George C. Marshall recalled to active duty Brigadier General John McAuley Palmer to advise him on postwar plans. Not yet officially at war, the United States was already preparing for peace, and the next war to follow it.[1]

For that haste, the two generals' sense of history was partly to blame. Marshall and Palmer shared bitter memories of demobilization after World War I. Failing to anticipate a sudden end to the war, belatedly assigning only one officer to prepare for demobilization, the army was not ready in 1918 to transport and muster out nearly three million men. The subsequent confusion invited restlessness among the troops, whose anger Marshall himself, on orders from General John J. Pershing, had to still. The delays quickly

1. Marshall to Palmer, 13 November 1941, World War II File, Box 14, Papers of John McAuley Palmer, Library of Congress; Palmer to Major General I. H. Edwards, 3 March 1943, Chronological Files 1942–43, Box 10, Palmer Papers; John C. Sparrow, *History of Personnel Demobilization in the United States Army*, p. 30.

tarnished the glory of the newly victorious United States Army, and aggravated long-standing suspicions among some politicians that the regular army sought to aggrandize itself.[2]

Worse, Congress defeated the War Department's grandiose plans for the postwar army. Waiting until after the Armistice to develop those plans, the army did not submit them to Congress until January 1919, when discontent over demobilization had helped dissipate the department's political strength. A split in ranks further eroded that strength. Peyton March, the chief of staff, and Secretary of War Newton Baker argued for a permanent force of 500,000 men backed by a system of universal military training. Congress, accustomed to a peacetime army scarcely a fifth that size, balked at the plan. More extraordinary, so did General Pershing, backed by Marshall, now his aide, and Palmer, sent home from France by Pershing to help the Senate Military Affairs Committee draft legislation for the peacetime army. The three considered the Baker-March plan destructive of democratic values and politically unattainable. They advocated instead a smaller professional army of 300,000 men which, when reinforced by citizen reservists with a year's training, would be capable of speedily mobilization to war strength. As finally written, the National Defense Act of 1920, the basic law governing the army between the two world wars, incorporated two key principles of the Pershing group: a standing force of 280,000 men and universal military training (UMT). But to gain passage of the bill against intense opposition, Palmer and his congressional allies compromised the critical provision of the bill: compulsory training became "voluntary." Even that legislation was never implemented. After 1920, Congress funded an army of barely half the size it had authorized that year. Congress as well as the President and the regular army also neglected the voluntary training program.[3]

More than twenty years later the disappointments of 1919 and 1920 still nagged at Palmer and Marshall, now the army's chief of staff and supreme military commander. Those years served as

2. Russell F. Weigley, *Towards an American Army: Military Thought from Washington to Marshall*, pp. 225–27; Forrest Pogue, *George C. Marshall: Education of a General, 1880–1939*, pp. 193–96, 204, 206, 213.

3. On planning and financing the post–World War I army, see Pogue, *Education of a General*, pp. 203–14, 219–21; Weigley, *Towards an American Army*, pp. 225–27; Russell F. Weigley, *History of the United States Army*, pp. 395–403; John McAuley Palmer, *America in Arms*, chap. 18.

the touchstone of their efforts to design the post-World War II army. The blunders of the War Department, they believed, had helped turn the victory of 1918 into disaster. In their view, the army had so mishandled its troops after the Armistice that it squandered the political support and popular approbation lavished on it during war and triumph. Tardy in preparing its peace plans, given to extravagant schemes, and divided within its ranks, the War Department delayed securing from Congress a sound peacetime defense program. By the time the army acted, the legislators had tired of talk of defense and turned against the military.[4]

The years after 1920 were, in Marshall's recollection, the "Dark Ages" of the army.[5] His own career progressed slowly, despite the early promise which came with graduation from the Virginia Military Institute and service with Pershing during World War I. Even Pershing's patronage in the 1920s and 1930s did Marshall little good. He and his fellow officers found their path to promotion choked off by a surfeit of senior officers left over from the Spanish-American War and World War I. Shuffling from one mediocre post to another, Marshall trained National Guard troops and supervised Civilian Conservation Camp boys, among other assignments. Only late in the 1930s did promotion come more rapidly for him, and on September 1, 1939, he finally became chief of staff, the title he held until November 1945.[6]

Unlike many lower-ranking officers, Marshall doubtless steeled himself against resentment over the pace of his advancement. He had that kind of self-control and, as the army's top officer, no incentive for further promotion. Yet the interwar experience embittered Marshall for professional if not personal reasons. In the 1930s, lack of funds seemed to turn army maneuvers into a joke. Trucks painted "tank" replaced the real thing; transportation and even

4. Palmer, "Notes on the War Plans Division Plan of April 1, 1919," 17 July 1942, file 380, Records of the Special Planning Division, Records of the War Department General and Special Staffs, Record Group 165, National Archives Building; Palmer to President of the Post-War Planning Board, 14 January 1943, Chronological Files 1942–43, Box 10, Palmer Papers; Palmer, American in Arms, chap. 18; personal communication from Forrest Pogue.

5. Transcript, "Comments on Universal Military Training at the Meeting of Religious Leaders—3 May 1945 by General George C. Marshall, Chief of Staff," Plans and Policy Office UMT Decimal File (1944–48) 020 Chief of Staff, Records of the Legislative and Liaison Division, RG 165.

6. On Marshall's career and the slowness of promotions in the interwar army, see Pogue, Education of a General, chaps. 13–18.

small arms were inadequate. Other aspects of army preparedness also suffered. After September 1, 1939, when Germany invaded Poland, the new chief of staff found himself the arbiter of innumerable claims for war materiel far beyond his capacity to provide. Shortages of men forced him to take risks which he believed unconscionable in the face of Axis threats. Confronted in 1940 and 1941 with the need to divert regular army troops from operational duties to the training of guardsmen and draftees, he had to gamble sacrificing either immediate defense or long-run preparedness.[7]

Throughout the war Marshall neither forgot the desperation of those months nor forgave those who had questioned preparedness. For the supposed "emasculation of the Army" in the 1920s and 1930s, he blamed the nation and its politicians. Had the country only "followed through" with the 1920 Defense Act, he asserted in 1942, "Germany would not have dared to involve herself in a war that would draw the United States into the conflict." Instead the United States fell prey to "the immediate postwar aversion of the people to everything military," and to "the imperative demand of the taxpayer for relief from the burden imposed by the huge war debt." With the nation again at war, Marshall worried about what he saw as the country's chronic indifference in peacetime to national security and professional military opinion.

> Of course, changes may come, but if there is any one thing I feel reasonably certain of, it is the lack of power and prestige of the Regular Army officer in time of peace. I have had a considerable experience in this. If the history of our post war procedures means anything it would seem clearly to indicate that we must expect an intolerance of military proposals and requirements, along with powerful opposition to all military appropriations. We know what follows, that is, the tragedy of war, which I believe might be avoided, with attendant colossal appropriations and subsequent debts and interest charges.

7. Mark Skinner Watson, *Chief of Staff: Prewar Plans and Preparations,* especially chaps. 2, 7; Weigley, *U.S. Army,* pp. 404–20; Pogue, *Education of a General,* pp. 89–91, 290–92; Forrest Pogue, *George C. Marshall: Ordeal and Hope, 1939–1942,* pp. 46–87, 142–52, 159, 162; Walter Millis, *Arms and Men: A Study of American Military Policy,* p. 247; Richard C. Lukas, *Eagles East: The Army Air Forces and the Soviet Union, 1941–1945,* pp. 18–19, 22–23; U.S. Congress, House Select Committee on Postwar Military Policy, *Hearings, Universal Military Training,* 79/1, 1945 (hereafter cited as Woodrum Committee, *Hearings, UMT*), p. 549; Marshall, "Comments ... 3 May 1945 ... ," Plans and Policy Office UMT Decimal File (1944–48) 020 Chief of Staff, L&LD.

Like Walter Lippmann and others, Marshall deplored a feast-or-famine pattern of defense whereby the United States assembled a powerful military machine in the passion of war only to dismantle it abruptly afterward.[8]

Marshall's interpretation of American preparedness was misleading. The United States demobilized its armed forces rapidly after each war it had fought, but not since the years after the War of 1812 had Congress allowed postwar strengths to sink to prewar levels. After each later war, permanent army strength, mirroring but more often outstripping population growth, increased fifty to one hundred percent. The growth of the peacetime navy and Marine Corps was just as rapid. The army and navy, which together numbered only about 40,000 men in the years before the Spanish-American War, more than trebled in size by the time of the Taft administration, and nearly doubled again in peacetime strength by the 1920s. Despite the Budget Bureau's efforts at economizing, the army's personnel in the 1920s and 1930s numbered from 135,000 to 185,000, far above the average figure of 81,000 during the 1902–14 period. Whatever the "powerful opposition to all military appropriations" which Marshall believed had reigned before World War II, the nation chose to strengthen its peacetime military power after each war it fought.[9]

Undoubtedly Marshall knew those statistics. He would have argued that raw strength figures were significant only in relation to the nation's security needs. He believed that army strengths after World War I fell far short of providing a force capable of defending a nation with global interests and declining geographical isolation. For evidence he could cite, as he frequently did during the war, the perilously narrow margin of Allied victory in World War II. His insistence on relating the size of the army to security needs was obviously sound. But the standards for "security" depended

8. Marshall's remarks to the Annual Conference of Supervisory Chaplains, 5 April 1945, transcript (unedited version) in file 353 (197), Records of the Chief of Staff, RG 165; Marshall's remarks to the Academy of Political Science in New York City, 10 November 1942, excerpts attached to memorandum, Marshall to General Ray Porter, 21 October 1945, file 353 (219), Chief of Staff; Marshall's comments in "Transcript of Committee Meeting Conference of The Secretary of War and The Secretary of the Navy and Their Staffs with Leading Educators of the Country, 29 December 1944," pp. 15–16, file 353 (Dec 1944), SPD. On Lippmann, see Walter Lippmann, *U.S. Foreign Policy: Shield of the Republic* and *U.S. War Aims*.

9. U.S. Bureau of the Census, *Historical Statistics of the United States: Colonial Times to 1957*, pp. 736–37; Elias Huzar, *The Purse and the Sword: Control of the Army by Congress through Military Appropriations, 1933–1950*, pp. 133–56.

upon perceived needs for implementing foreign policy. Marshall's accusations overlooked the substantial expansion of the armed forces which occurred after each of America's many wars.

However distorted, perceptions about the past nonetheless guided Marshall and other military leaders as they considered future defense needs. Even during the war they thought they saw the signs that the old pattern of neglect of defense was returning. Speaking in April 1945, Marshall complained about "the sophistry that was preached" in the 1930s and about how he "had to take the brunt of the results of 20 years of neglectfulness." Under fire that spring for sending eighteen-year-olds to battle with as little as four months' training, he found that criticisms bitterly ironic and familiar:

> I am ... still in the middle of the spiral of criticism which comes, incidentally, from the same people who prevented the building of an adequate Army in the 1920's and 1930's. I believe I can rightly feel that in some respects I have had to suffer more from war than anybody else. It concentrates, focuses and descends heavily upon me.[10]

This self-righteousness and self-pity, rare for Marshall, measured the magnitude of his bitterness over the neglect of national defense before World War II.

Determined to prevent a recurrence of that neglect, Marshall urged his staff to prepare for the coming of peace. The War Department, he was convinced, must ready its plans for peace before victory turned the nation against it. Should the army once more conduct a chaotic demobilization, he argued in 1942, it would again alienate soldiers and jeopardize public support for a strong postwar army.[11]

To Secretary of War Henry L. Stimson, Marshall described the stakes more graphically. If the army failed to shoulder the "hideous responsibility" of mustering out its men efficiently, he said, "we are going to wreck our reputation on the heels of what we hope is victory." "This will be the final triumph if we put this over, and if it isn't, then it will damn us and ruin all that we have done." Stimson understood Marshall's point perfectly.[12]

10. Marshall, remarks before the Annual Conference of Supervisory Chaplains, 5 April 1945, unedited transcript, file 353 (197), Chief of Staff. In his edited version of these remarks, Marshall deleted the comments quoted here.
11. Palmer to President of the Post-War Planning Board, 14 January 1943, Chronological Files 1942–43, Box 10, Palmer Papers.
12. Marshall, Statement to HLS [Henry L. Stimson] re Single Department of Defense, 18 April 1944, Stimson Memos, Papers of Henry L. Stimson, Yale University Library.

Marshall's choice of Palmer as advisor indicated the importance he attached to postwar planning and its early commencement. Palmer's distinguished family included a grandfather who served as a Republican governor and senator for Illinois and as the Gold Democrats' nominee for president in 1896. One of Marshall's few close friends, Palmer (West Point, 1892) was older and in many respects the mentor of Marshall. The two often served together until in the 1920s Palmer, by that time Pershing's aide-de-camp, found his promising career terminated by poor health. He then turned to proselytizing his notions of a citizen army and universal military training. In an army where few officers wrote books, Palmer's authorship of several gave him a considerable reputation as an intellectual. Marshall, impressed by his ideas, afforded Palmer ready access to him during World War II. Although seventy-one years old in 1941, declining in energy, and remote from younger officers, Palmer exercised a powerful influence on the army's preparations for peace.[13]

Palmer, aware of his limitations, knew he "was in no sense qualified to advise on purely military aspects of Army organization as affected by the enormous changes in weapons and tactics which had taken place since my retirement from active service." He realized that Marshall recalled him for his political advice, his contacts with congressmen, his familiarity with the army's blunders after World War I, and his ability to devise a postwar program which would meet congressional approval.[14] Together, the two generals would help the army and the nation avoid their past errors.

Objectives and Obstacles

Only days after Marshall appointed Palmer, Pearl Harbor ended the false peace. Now the training of draftess, halting the Japanese advance, and other operations became so pressing that for over a

13. See John McAuley Palmer, *Statesmanship or War; Washington, Lincoln, Wilson: Three War Statesmen*; and *America in Arms*. On Palmer and his relationship to Marshall, see Pogue, *Education of a General*, pp. 107, 149, 204–13; Allen Johnson and Dumas Malone, eds., *Dictionary of American Biography*, 22 vols. (New York, 1928–44), 14: 187–88; *The National Cyclopaedia of American Biography* (New York, 1962), vol. 44, pp. 70–71; Weigley, *Towards an American Army*, chap. 13. Forrest Pogue provided the author insights into the Palmer-Marshall friendship.

14. Sparrow, *History of Personnel Demobilization*, p. 30.

year the army made slow progress on its postwar plans. What momentum it maintained came principally from Palmer. Aided by a Post-War Planning Board, he worked for early congressional action on UMT, established liaison with the National Resources Planning Board, and reminded Marshall of the need for early action on peacetime policy. Meanwhile the three major commands of the army—Ground Forces, Service Forces, and Air Forces—began their own studies of postvictory needs.[15]

Marshall had not forgotten the urgency of action. On April 14, 1943, as his forces in North Africa were completing the army's first major campaign in the European theater, he directed General Brehon Somervell, commanding general of the Army Service Forces, to "initiate preliminary studies" on demobilization. The chief of staff, believing the army's challenge at war's end would be "largely logistical," emphasized preparations for "the return of industry to a peacetime basis and the orderly demobilization of our military manpower." He also directed Somervell to estimate the size of forces needed in the interim between the end of the war and the advent of a "permanent post-war military establishment."[16]

Somervell followed up Marshall's directive by establishing the Project Planning Division within the Army Service Forces. He named Brigadier (later Major) General William F. Tompkins as its director. The Project Planning Division lasted only until July 1943. It drafted no plans, but its final report did enumerate the obstacles facing the army in preparing for peace and emphasize the danger of repeating the errors in demobilization committed after World War I.[17]

The report met the approval of Marshall, Stimson, and Under Secretary Robert Patterson, who replaced the Project Planning Division with a new agency, one with a higher status in the War Department bureaucracy. On July 22, 1943, Patterson, as acting secretary of war, established the Special Planning Division and appointed General Tompkins its director.[18] The Special Planning

15. Ibid., pp. 31–32; Major General I. H. Edwards to Marshall, 8 April 1943, file 370.9, Chief of Staff; folder "Delano Board–1942 Nov 4," Chronological Files 1942–43, Box 10, Palmer Papers. See also file 380 (Postwar Planning, June 24, 1942), SPD.
16. Marshall to Commanding General, Army Service Forces, 14 April 1943, file 310 (Organizational History), SPD.
17. Sparrow, *History of Personnel Demobilization*, pp. 32–33; Project Planning Division, "Survey of Demobilization Planning," 18 June 1943, file 310 (Organizational History), SPD.
18. Sparrow, *History of Personnel Demobilization*, pp. 34–35.

Division (SPD), established two years before the fighting ended, served for the rest of the war as the main agency charged with planning the postwar army.

The Special Planning Division had weighty responsibilities, especially for the politically sensitive task of demobilizing personnel. SPD developed a point system by which some eight million soldiers received credit for length of service, combat duty, decorations, dependent children, and other factors. Men with the highest point totals were to receive early release from the army once demobilization began. The system, fairly simple in its final form, required an enormous amount of preparation.[19]

Many other problems, especially logistical ones, arose. They ranged from such touchy matters as industrial demobilization to mundane or obscure chores: overhauling the army's postal system, determining what military hospitals to retain, or arranging for the burial of dead servicemen after hostilities. During the war the army and navy built giant military machines heedless of cost or future needs. The leftovers abounded, and SPD had to decide what the army would keep and what it would throw away.

SPD was also charged with shaping strategy and policy for the peacetime army. In this regard it faced numerous imponderables. What threats might the United States confront after the war? What strategy and weaponry would other nations utilize in future wars? What policies should the army follow in a future struggle? Since the regular army could never provide full war strength, SPD had to determine War Department policy on reserve forces, especially the feasibility of universal military training and the relationship among the regular army, the Organized Reserves, and the National Guard. It had to suggest how the nation might mobilize its economy in future emergencies, to plan for the development of new weapons, and to determine how changing technology would affect the army. Not least, SPD needed to define the army's future relationship to the Army Air Forces and the navy. The growth of air power and controversy over the failure of interservice cooperation at and after Pearl Harbor made that question a matter of continuing public debate. In one sense, SPD had an impossible assignment. No matter how refined its techniques, prediction about the contingencies and

---

19. A thorough account of army plans for personnel demobilization is Sparrow, *History of Personnel Demobilization*.

questions it faced could rarely be reliable. Yet assumptions had to be made. No army could simply wait passively for the future to unfold. SPD's challenge was to speculate boldly.

At the same time, it needed to recognize the hazards of planning. Since the future was so unpredictable, the planner could easily fall back on what he best knew, his experience, and fall victim to the most common fault of his profession, preparing for the future solely in terms of the past. SPD officers were at least aware of such dangers. Still, like other planners, they often committed the errors they tried to guard against.

Another obstacle to effective planning was the temptation to focus on the army's most immediate exigencies, those of demobilization, to the neglect of long-term needs. Very early in the war General Palmer and other officials recognized demobilization as a continuous process leading to a permanent force. The army would pass through several stages: (1) the wartime force (redeployed and partially demobilized for the defeat of Japan); (2) "temporary emergency forces" to occupy the Axis lands and maintain peace in the immediate postwar years; (3) the permanent army. The concept of a phased demobilization quickly became doctrine.[20] Its acceptance indicated that department leaders knew that the distinction between "demobilization" and "postwar" was only an arbitrary device for sorting out the planning tasks which lay ahead. They recognized that demobilization was no simple logistical process. The army could determine how "far" to demobilize only when it knew how large would be its permanent force, and thus only when it made assumptions about the strategic and diplomatic environment in which the peacetime army would operate.

Marshall and Stimson never forgot the political implications of logistics. Failure to develop a sound scheme for demobilization, Marshall explained to the Joint Chiefs of Staff in August 1943, would cause "a terrific problem of morale" at the war's end and subvert the military's pursuit of its postwar program. The "only hope" Stimson saw for winning that program was "to gradually slide our plan of demobilization into the permanent plan. There

---

20. Palmer memorandum, "Proposed Legislation for Universal Military Training," n.d. [probably August 1942], file 380 (Postwar Planning, June 24, 1942), SPD; Palmer to Marshall, 5 April 1943, file 370.9, Chief of Staff; Marshall to Somervell, 14 April 1943, and "Survey of Demobilization Planning," both in file 310 (Organizational History), SPD.

must be no general complete demobilization, leaving it necessary to make a fresh start on the peace time plan. Perhaps I sh'd [should] say: there must be no sudden recognition of general Peace!"[21]

But subordinates did not always grasp or act on the point Stimson and Marshall were making, nor did those two have the chance to impress it on them. In practice, the War Department often divorced postwar planning from redeployment and demobilization, always the more pressing, if not more important, tasks. The services, having elected to defeat Germany first, wanted to transfer their forces to the Pacific as quickly as possible after V-E day, lest a long war overtax the patience of Americans.[22] Anticipating a reversal of the policy followed after World War I, the army had to prepare to govern the defeated Axis powers for a prolonged period.[23] SPD did not formulate occupation policy, but it did have to schedule demobilization so that troops were available for occupation and peace-keeping duties until the Allies pacified the Axis, rehabilitated war-torn areas, and established an effective United Nations organization. Knowing that business and labor would demand rapid conversion to civilian production, SPD also had to plan how to close defense plants, terminate or renegotiate contracts, and dispose of surplus war materiel. With soldiers and their families agitating for assurances of a speedy return home for the boys, SPD needed to prepare to mothball equipment, phase out bases, and, most critically, return home and muster out the troops. Too, government agencies like the Office of War Mobilization and Reconversion wanted the army's production and manpower schedules, and Congress could be counted on to demand that the military return promptly to peacetime status. Since the army could not retrench without knowing what equipment to keep, the pressure to demobilize did compel some attention to long-term strategy and force levels. Just as often, the War Department's mammoth resources became ends in themselves, the masters rather than the servants of strategy.

21. Extract from minutes of the 99th meeting of the Joint Chiefs of Staff, 3 August 1943, file ABC 321 (30 July 1943), Records of the Operations Division, RG 165; HLS [Henry L. Stimson] to Marshall, note in Stimson's handwriting, n.d. [fall 1943], file 350.06 (Study 64), SPD.
22. As one high-level army committee reported in March 1943, "the American public will not countenance a long war of attrition and hence every effort must be made to speed the defeat of our enemies." Special Army Committee, "Survey of Current Military Program," 15 March 1943 (revised 28 April 1943), file 320.2 (1576), OPD. See also Russell F. Weigley, *The American Way of War*, p. 281.
23. Forrest Pogue, *George C. Marshall: Organizer of Victory, 1943–1945*, pp. 465–66.

Strategic, logistical, and political pressures, then, all dictated the army's concentration of its energies on demobilization to the neglect of postwar planning. Though demobilization ultimately led to the permanent army, the end was sometimes lost from sight, especially by lower-level officers.

Personnel limitations further hampered SPD's planning effort. For its large task, SPD assembled an obscure staff. As Forrest Pogue put it, "few officers ... are more faceless than those who 'plan.'" The SPD staff was small in both size and reputation. It numbered only some twenty officers in April 1944, as well as General William Tompkins as director and General Palmer as advisor. Only six were West Point graduates. In contrast, the Operations Division, the central command post for the army during the war, utilized up to two hundred officers at a time. Many Operations Division personnel (Dwight Eisenhower, Albert Wedemeyer, Thomas Handy, Dean Rusk) achieved fame or high responsibility during or after the war, but of the SPD staff only Palmer had a reputation extending beyond army circles. SPD was no prized billet; nor were the equivalent positions in the other services. No matter what the importance of postwar planning, few officers desired a post far removed from both combat planning and operations, the assignments regarded as stepping-stones to higher position. As a result, SPD officers generally lacked imagination even though they were assigned to the one type of planning which, perhaps more than any other, required that quality. Except for Palmer, they also lacked the prestige to commend attention for the ideas they did have.[24]

Tompkins, the SPD director until July 1945, typified some of the strengths and weaknesses of his staff. From an old army family, Tompkins, whose grandfather was a West Pointer, graduated from the U.S. Military Academy sixteenth in the exceptional class of 1915, which produced Eisenhower, Omar Bradley, and fifty-seven other general officers. He moved up through the ranks of the Army Corps of Engineers, attended the Command and General Staff School and the Army War College, served on the General Staff in 1934 and

---

24. Pogue, *Ordeal and Hope*, p. 122; U.S. Congress, House Select Committee on Postwar Military Policy, *Hearings, Proposal to Establish a Single Department of Armed Forces*, 78/2, 1944, p. 18; U.S. Military Academy, West Point, The West Point Alumni Foundation, *Register of Graduates and Former Cadets of the United States Military Academy* (West Point, 1971); Ray S. Cline, *Washington Command Post: The Operations Division*, pp. 195, 363–71; Perry McCoy Smith, *The Air Force Plans for Peace, 1943–1945*, p. 11.

1935, and later was attached briefly to the Works Progress Administration. By World War II Tompkins was in his fifties, with three sons also in service, two of whom were later killed in action. If his engineering background provided poor preparation for long-range strategic planning, it did sensitize him to the role of technology in the postwar army, the area of policy in which he played his most personal and creative role. Aside from his work on military technology, Tompkins was not an innovator. A competent writer and administrator, at times he pushed for action on a particular problem. But he did not often leave his personal stamp on policy.[25]

SPD's mode of operation and place in the War Department bureaucracy also minimized its power. Within the War Department, SPD was a Special Staff division directly responsible to the chief of staff (see diagram). It was the only staff division divorced from war-

War Department Lines of Command, 1942–45

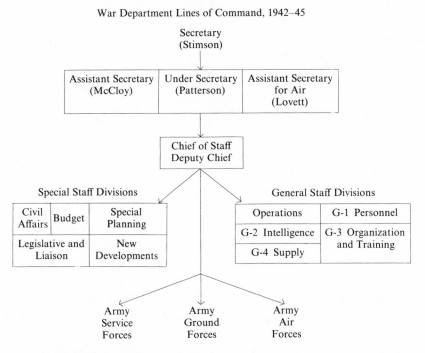

25. West Point Alumni Foundation, *Register of Graduates* (1971), p. 337; Stephen Ambrose, *Duty, Honor, Country: A History of West Point*, p. 252; George W. Cullum, *Biographical Register of the Officers and Graduates of the U.S. Military Academy at West Point Since Its Establishment in 1802*, Supplement, ed. W. M. Donaldson, vol. 7 (Chicago and Crawfordsville, Ind., 1930), p. 1055; *Who's Who in America, 1950–51*, vol. 26 (Chicago, 1950); *New York Times*, 30 March 1945; *Washington Post*, 28 October 1969.

time operations, for Marshall insisted that the postwar planners give their attention solely to the transition to peace.[26] But SPD did not have exclusive responsibility for planning that transition. Army Air Forces, increasingly autonomous from the War Department despite its position in the hierarchy, maintained its own independent-mined postwar staff, and the General Staff divisions, older and larger than SPD, also had a voice in planning.

Special Planning served primarily as the coordinator, rather than the author, of postwar plans. In the customary procedure for developing a plan, SPD first ascertained the need for a policy, either on its own initiative or under prodding from other agencies or superior officers in the War Department. SPD then usually assigned preparation of the plan to the War Department bureau or command most knowledgeable about the problem under study— Army Service Forces would handle logistical problems, for example, and the judge advocate general would be assigned policy on prisoners of war. When farming out the preparation of plans, SPD provided policy guidelines, reviewed the completed plan for conformance to established army policies, and circulated it to other interested agencies and staff divisions for their "concurrence" or "coordination" (agreement or criticism). Only after getting the consent of all interested parties would SPD usually dispatch the plan to Marshall, Patterson, or Stimson for their final approval.

The "concurrence system" was designed to insure painstaking review of plans, and it was valuable in that one office often spied a blunder that another overlooked.[27] As a device for developing highly technical policies it proved efficient. But since the process required SPD to reconcile divergent interests and opinions, it encouraged compromise and blandness, the reduction of policy to the lowest common denominator acceptable to the concerned parties. Further, the delegation of planning to the most knowledgeable agency gave vested interests the chance to plot their own future, a practice hardly conducive to a fresh look at past policies. The procedure also ignored combat commanders, whom SPD rarely consulted despite their familiarity with the latest techniques of war,[28] and G-2 (Intelligence),

26. Marshall to Somervell, 14 April 1945, file 310 (Organizational History), SPD.
27. See also the discussion of the concurrence system in Cline, *Washington Command Post*, pp. 113, 127, 139–40.
28. Numerous obstacles existed to effective consultation with theater and combat commanders. SPD's failure to consult those commanders not rotated back to Washington weakened its planning. Once hostilities ended, the combat theaters established procedures for analyzing the lessons of their war experience, but most theater studies came too late to help SPD.

with which SPD apparently did not work closely. SPD's system for planning smoothed bureaucratic conflicts and soothed wounded sensibilities. But it penalized boldness or imagination in planning.

The slow passage of plans through channels of concurrence also undermined Marshall's goal of having a postwar program ready on the day of victory. Some of the most important plans, including the War Department Plan for the Post-War Army—the basic statement of policy on the size, composition, and mission of the postwar army—were far from complete at the war's end. Sometimes the Office of Chief of Staff upbraided the General Staff for its failure to assist SPD to a speedy completion of its work,[29] but to little avail, since the fault lay as much with the system as with individuals. Bureaucratic politics were not the only cause of delay, but they were important. Significantly, the few times that SPD bypassed orthodox channels, it produced quicker and more creative results. Such was the case when General Tompkins took personal command of planning for research and development, and substituted informal consultation for the rigid concurrence system.

SPD could do little to embolden or hasten the planning process. Its staff did not possess the prestige, authority, or inclination to strike out in new directions, and competing interests were powerful. Of the many staff divisions only Operations, during the war a sort of inner general staff for the General Staff, had the power frequently to defy orthodox procedure. SPD was set up to coordinate the preparation of blueprints for the future army, not to speculate in isolation on postwar needs. In those terms SPD saw its job, and in those terms SPD performed it. The Special Planning Division would make few waves.

Rivals and Partners

While the army was establishing the Special Planning Division, the Army Air Forces and the navy were also organizing agencies to formulate peacetime plans. But the AAF and the navy inaugurated planning for reasons of their own. General H. H. Arnold, commanding general of the Army Air Forces, and Admiral Ernest J. King, chief of naval operations and commander-in-chief of the navy, did share

29. See the remarks of Deputy Chief of Staff General Thomas Handy, in Minutes of the War Department General Council, 13 November 1944, Document 262, Reference Collection, Modern Military Branch, National Archives Building.

Marshall's concern about public indifference to defense. But since federal budgets traditionally favored the navy, "the first line of defense," its sense of historical neglect was less acute. Instead, bitter interservice rivalries helped push the navy and the AAF into planning.

Since the 1920s, when Billy Mitchell led insurgent flyers in a campaign for a strategic air force, army aviators had demanded independence from the War Department, whose control of the Army Air Corps, so they alleged, crippled its growth. Air enthusiasts seized on the agitation for unifying the armed services, an idea first advanced by advocates of economy and efficiency in military affairs, and argued that in any unification scheme air power should receive status equal to that of the ground and naval forces. Unification, they hoped, would also mean "triplification," a freeing of the air corps from its subordinate position. During the 1920s and 1930s the army and navy fought off the air corps' unification scheme. They regarded merger of the armed forces as little more than a ruse by which air power would capture a favored place in the military establishment and rob the army and navy of their land- and carrier-based planes. Antagonisms among the services over the unification issue remained intense as World War II began.

By 1943 the army had recanted its opposition to unification, in part because successful prosecution of the war demanded that the army and AAF make peace. Marshall was compelled to grant the AAF virtual autonomy within the War Department and to make an implied promise of eventual independence before Arnold and his congressional backers would suspend their campaign for independence.[30] Marshall's recognition of the utility of strategic air power increased his willingness to see the AAF become a separate force. Public criticism accelerated the army's reassessment of its stance on unification. Coming on the heels of Pearl Harbor, the spectacle of feuding among the services over the command of Pacific operations and control of antisubmarine warfare in the Atlantic generated popular and congressional pressures to unify the armed forces. Partly converted to the cause, partly sensing its eventual triumph, Marshall and Stimson endorsed unification. Though SPD chief Tompkins believed that realistic planning was impossible until

30. Pogue, *Organizer of Victory*, p. 71; personal communication from Forrest Pogue.

the unification issue was settled,[31] that issue did not preoccupy the army staff. Having reconciled itself to the independence of air power, the army had little to gain or lose in a struggle in which the AAF and the navy became the main contestants.

Army Air Forces wanted total political victory. To that end Arnold in 1943 directed his staff to begin postwar planning. Because the best argument for an independent air force was an independent strategic mission, architects of the AAF's postwar plans concentrated on strategic air power doctrine. "Since Air Force autonomy was the primary concern for the planners," the historian of AAF plans has commented, "other factors such as doctrine, base requirements, and weapons forecasts were secondary considerations which could be modified in the interest of strengthening the AAF aim." Like the army, the AAF also started its planning early because it faced logistical and personnel problems and feared cutbacks in military appropriations after the war.[32]

With the army's defection from the antiunification ranks, the navy stood alone. The admirals worried that in a unified defense department the army and air force would team up to strip the navy of its land- and carrier-based air power and its ground forces, the marines. A rump navy would remain where once there had been the preeminent service. Despite their quarrels with the battleship admirals, even naval aviators opposed the army and the AAF.[33]

Determination to preserve its traditional position goaded the navy into planning. In August 1943, after learning that the army had set up its Special Planning Division, King and his staff ordered the drafting of navy plans. Apparently they feared that the army had gotten a head start in the race for postwar favor. As the war progressed the navy's jealousy of the army and the AAF mounted. "The Air Forces," lamented a key naval aide, have "built themselves into the public's darling" and "now are systematically selling the idea that they alone can keep the peace!" Navy Secretary Frank Knox bolted ranks and endorsed unification, but with his death in April 1944 the

31. Tompkins, letter to Vincent Davis, 19 April 1960, copy provided the author by Colonel William Wix.
32. Smith, *Air Force Plans*, pp. 6, 11, 14.
33. For the navy's attitude toward unification, see Vincent Davis, *Postwar Defense Policy and the U.S. Navy, 1943–1946.*

new secretary, James Forrestal, inaugurated a resourceful campaign against the army and the AAF. Simultaneously the House Committee on Postwar Military Policy began hearings on unification. Those hearings, and an acrimonious debate within the Joint Chiefs of Staff over the question, stiffened the navy's opposition to unification.[34]

Contrasts in leadership widened the differences among the services, though the leaders did have one common denominator: advancing age. Except for Forrestal, all were born before 1890, and educated and initiated into military affairs before World War I. Presiding over the War Department was the oldest of all, Henry L. Stimson, in his second tour as secretary of war and his eighth decade of life. Certain matters of long-range policy—control of nuclear weapons, occupation policy for Germany, universal military training—could fire the old man's passion. But he found that he could not get himself "churned up" about many problems of the peacetime army. "In the first place I can't take my attention off the winning of the war; in the second place, I went through such a period of disillusionment twenty-five years ago in respect to war patriotism after the war was over that I can't help feeling very pessimistic about it now."[35] In the third place, he was too old and tired. More a chairman of the board for the department than its chief operating officer, Stimson often deferred to Marshall, who shared most of the secretary's views on postwar military policy.

Marshall, though not a glamorous public figure, was the dominant American military personality of his time.[36] Among those in high office, he enjoyed enormous respect for his toughness and integrity. More than his colleagues, he rose above at least the pettier forms of interservice bickering. With Congress and the press he was persuasive and resourceful without being pushy or disingenuous. His lack of arrogance, distaste for military pomp, and scrupulous personal integrity completed the qualities that reassured civilian sensibilities.

34. Ibid., pp. 10–13, 50–67, 138–56. Quotation from Eugene Duffield to Secretary of the Navy, 31 July 1944, folder marked "Memorandum from the Secretary of Navy, 1944," Subject File, Box 22, Papers of Ernest J. King, Library of Congress. See also Duffield to Forrestal, 28 August 1943, folder "Air Power," Eugene Duffield Files 1942–1944, Records of the Secretary of the Navy James Forrestal, General Records of the Department of the Navy, RG 80, National Archives Building.

35. Stimson Diary, 15 March 1944, Stimson Papers.

36. The following sketch draws on Forrest Pogue's three volumes of biography of Marshall and on conversations with Pogue, as well as on examination of War Department records. On Marshall's influence on those around him, see also David Halberstam, *The Best and the Brightest,* pp. 131, 388–95, 572.

Like Eisenhower, whose career he promoted, he seemed, and in many respects was, a democrat's ideal general.

Marshall not only dominated the army. Unwittingly, he sometimes overwhelmed it. Quick and devastating as a critic of staff papers, he slashed up a draft with deletions, pointed questions, and revisions that boiled it down to a simple, forceful statement. He was brilliant at that sort of thing, but overpowering as well. Wary of his capacity to intimidate independent thinking, he usually hid his thoughts on controversial matters while policy was undergoing development. But far from concealing his views on postwar policy, he intervened decisively in postwar planning. His directives were sweeping, his opinions unchallenged. While Palmer and Tompkins shared his views, others perhaps did not. They were not about to say so.

The AAF chief, General Arnold, cast a different image, one of amiability befitting his nickname "Hap." He did not dominate his postwar planners as Marshall did. He did not have to: the doctrine of strategic air power so infected the air staff that no one had to kindle its ambition or coerce it into action. Behind his affability, Arnold, a pioneer army aviator jealous of his calling, was a relentless prophet and proponent of the most terrifying technologies of war, a master of lurid prophecy and alarmist prose. "War may descend upon us by thousands of robots passing unannounced across our shorelines—unless we act now to prevent them," he warned in a typical statement late in 1945. He pushed scientists hard to develop new instruments of destruction, "explosives more terrible and more horrible than anyone has any idea of." Advised of Stimson's doubts about the bombing of Dresden, he complained that "we must not get soft. War must be destructive and to a certain extent inhuman and ruthless." He got along well with Marshall, who indulged challenges from Arnold that few others in the War Department dared offer.[37]

No one personality dominated navy planning. Admiral King, cold

37. Quotations from General Henry Harley Arnold, *Third Report of the Commanding General of the Army Air Forces, November 12, 1945, to the Secretary of War*, in *The War Reports of General of the Army George C. Marshall . . . General of the Army H. H. Arnold . . . Fleet Admiral Ernest J. King*, foreword by Walter Millis, (hereafter cited as *War Reports*), p. 454; transcript, "Conference between General Arnold, Dr. Bowles and Dr. Ridenour—August 9, 1944," Jacket 147, Box 45, Official Files (1932–1946), Papers of Henry Harley Arnold, Library of Congress; handwritten comment on memorandum, Giles to Arnold, 7 March 1945, Diary of Events and Decisions Made in Absence of Arnold, Subject File (1918–1949), Box 223, Arnold Papers.

to the point of rudeness, ruthless when he chose to be, was a powerful leader and a tenacious advocate of navy interests. But unlike Arnold, he shared no striking vision of the future of warfare. His views on the conduct of the current war could be rigid, but his ideas on postwar strategy were not as dogmatic as the other chiefs', and his interest in postwar policy not as keen.

Secretary Knox, a heretic because of his advocacy of unification, did not otherwise impress himself on the navy, but his successor, James Forrestal, projected a more decisive personality. A New York investment banker with an establishment background, Forrestal entered the Navy Department in 1940 as one of the Roosevelt administration's recruits from the business world. As under secretary of the navy, he gained respect for his management of the navy's massive procurement effort. Possessed of wide-ranging if superficial interests, he masked his ambition and strong passion by a cult of rationality, managerial efficiency, and self-effacement. Deeply suspicious of the Soviet Union's postwar intentions, Forrestal held strong convictions about postwar defense needs. He could not quickly translate those convictions into policy. He became secretary only in May 1944 and required time to influence the planning machinery. Further, he, King, and their senior associates did not share the identity of viewpoint enjoyed by Stimson and Marshall. Deprived of consistently strong leadership and disrupted by frequent shakeups in organization and personnel, the navy's postwar planning drifted during much of the war and lacked the painstaking thoroughness which characterized SPD's endeavors. Desire to secure a strong peacetime navy provided the continuing focus for the navy's efforts.[38]

Begotten in rivalry, led by contrasting personalities, and exposed to sharp conflicts among the Joint Chiefs over the spoils and conduct of the war, the postwar staffs of the army, AAF, and navy often refused to cooperate with each other. Postwar plans touched on such vital interests that the three services hesitated to divulge their separate plans for fear of tipping off their rivals to the political goals they sought. The navy was especially tight-lipped. Still a part of the War Department, the AAF could not long keep secrets from the army,

38. On the frequent changes and shakeups in navy planning, see Davis, *Postwar Defense Policy and the U.S. Navy*, pp. 10–13, 20–21, 101–05.

but it resisted close collaboration with either of the other services. Less parochial in outlook, the army's Special Planning Division shared its ideas on postwar policy somewhat more willingly.[39]

The problem of interservice cooperation was institutional as well as political. As it had been since the nation's infancy, the defense establishment was split into the War and Navy Departments. The president alone provided statutory authority over them. Only the Joint Chiefs, established without any formal legislative or executive sanction in the weeks after Pearl Harbor, exercised united command. During the war the JCS consisted of Marshall, Arnold, King, and Admiral William Leahy, chief of staff to President Franklin D. Roosevelt.

The JCS gave scant guidance on postwar policies to the three services. Leahy might have served as a strong link between the President and the armed forces on postwar matters. But Roosevelt hesitated to delegate much authority to him. "He keeps Leahy with him but he is still giving him trash," Marshall remarked to Stimson in 1944.[40] The committee structure of the JCS and its unwritten rule of unanimity before action made decisions on controversial matters difficult. Secretiveness about postwar plans made the services reluctant to use the JCS for joint planning. Most important, the unyielding pressure of current operations tended to crowd out more distant needs. While Marshall, King, Leahy, and Arnold all held strong convictions on peacetime military requirements, during the war they had little chance to reflect on those needs or to work out a collective statement of postwar policy.

Staff committees of the Joint Chiefs did study several specific problems of postwar policy, among them occupation of the Axis powers, unification of the armed forces, and location of postwar bases. But only once during the war, in 1943, did the JCS attempt to

39. Ibid., pp. 15, 22, 68–72, 109; Horne to Cominch, 30 August 1944, Secret Serial 024405-D, and King to Horne, 6 September 1944, Serial 002580, both in file A16-3/EN (Sept–Dec 1944), Records of the Chief of Naval Operations—Commander-in-Chief, Naval History Division, Washington, D.C.; Smith, *Air Force Plans*, p. 65. For the army's openness, see the extended description of the army's plans by SPD's deputy director in a meeting with Forrestal, King, and other high naval officials, in Minutes of Top Policy Group Meeting 10, 15 January 1945, file Minutes of the Top Policy Group Meetings, SecNav.

40. Marshall, Statement to HLS [Henry L. Stimson] re Single Department of Defense, 18 April 1944, Stimson Memos, Stimson Papers.

establish broad guidelines for demobilization and peacetime. In July, Marshall, observing the military's mistakes in 1919, submitted for JCS approval a list of assumptions to guide postwar planning, a list he may originally have intended to give Roosevelt.[41]

On September 28 the JCS accepted Marshall's list with some alterations. They approved the notion of a phased demobilization beginning with victory over Germany and continuing through Japan's defeat (assumed to occur about a year later) and the occupation period. They assented to Marshall's suggestion that the United States would "furnish a share of the emergency interim forces required to maintain order and to guarantee adequate consideration of American peace aims." They accepted the premise that the United States would adopt some form of universal military training. On the recommendation of a staff committee, they rejected as premature Marshall's assumption that the United States would "furnish a share of an international Police Force (probably largely air)" after the war. Little reflection or staff study went into those decisions. And though the JCS gave lip service to the need for genuine joint planning, not until the end of the war did they try to draft a more complete statement of postwar military policy.[42]

The Joint Chiefs were not alone to blame for the absence of central direction in military planning. As in other matters, Roosevelt was disdainful of organizational niceties and wary of centralized authority that might divert decision-making from him. He authorized no person or agency to oversee the government's many efforts at planning for peace. Consequently, the armed services, like other agencies during the war, looked to the future with only the sketchiest idea of the policies he and the Congress intended to pursue. But the services were also responsible for their ignorance. When the army established SPD in the summer of 1943, Marshall received warnings of the need for "an overall plan by the Federal Government" and of the dependence of army policies on the decisions of countless other government

41. Marshall to JCS, 30 July 1943; "Notes on JCS 99th Meeting," 3 August 1943; extract from minutes of the 99th meeting of the JCS, 3 August 1943, all in file ABC 321 (30 July 1943), OPD; Sparrow, *History of Personnel Demobilization*, p. 45.

42. Quotations from Sparrow, *History of Personnel Demobilization*, pp. 44–47. See also JCS 431/1 (Report by the Joint Strategic Survey Committee), 21 September 1943, and extract from minutes of the JCS 116 meeting, 26 September 1943, both in file ABC 321 (30 July 1943), OPD; "Policy on Post-War Military Problems," attached to Leahy to President, 15 November 1943, Leahy File 126, Records of the United States Joint Chiefs of Staff, Record Group 218, National Archives Building.

agencies. General Somervell wrote the chief of staff deploring the army's failure to press for a central planning agency and recommending that the Office of War Mobilization perform that function. Marshall rejected that advice without written explanation.[43]

Marshall did not reject informal cooperation with other governmental agencies. He informed Roosevelt, Leahy, the State Department, and the Joint Chiefs about the establishment of SPD. In June 1943 he advised FDR that he sought to get purely military requirements for postwar planning determined "before the larger aspects of the demobilization questions were undertaken." That counsel implied that the War Department might later approve centralized planning or assumptions. Shortly thereafter a staff officer advised the White House of "the need for an overall plan by higher authority." Although Marshall discussed the problem with the JCS, apparently neither the military nor the White House took further steps to institute centralized control. Given his tendency to keep large decisions in his own hands, FDR would probably have rejected the delegation of overall authority to a subordinate body. But Marshall's decision not to press for top-level direction left the services and the other concerned agencies free to plan independently of each other, as they preferred to do.[44]

Congress did little to improve the situation. Partisan differences and the fragmentation caused by the committee system made it impossible for either house to offer a unified view of postwar needs. Military secrecy limited congressional knowledge of developments in the art of war. The House Select Committee on Postwar Military Policy did conduct useful hearings in the last year and a half of the war. But it focused on specifics—the unification question, UMT, weapons research—rather than on broad principles for peacetime defense.

Likewise the State Department offered little leadership in planning.

43. Project Planning Division, "Survey of Demobilization Planning," 18 June 1943, file 310 (Organizational History), SPD; Major General George Grunert to Somervell, 17 June 1943, with addendum by Somervell dated 19 June 1943, file 370.9 (17 June 1943), Chief of Staff; Marshall to Somervell, 2 July 1943, file 370.9 (19 June 1943), Chief of Staff; McNarney to Chief of Staff, 2 July 1943, file 370.9, Chief of Staff. McNarney's memo argued that "an agency such as the one described, even if approved by the President, would create such bitterness in Congress that the war effort would be definitely hindered." Marshall may have accepted McNarney's reasoning on this matter.

44. Marshall to President, 21 June 1943, file 370.9 (21 June 1943), Chief of Staff; Marshall to Norman Davis, 28 July 1943, file 370.9 (28 July 1943), Chief of Staff; Marshall to JCS, 30 July 1943, and "Notes on JCS 99th Meeting," 3 August 1943, both in file ABC 321 (30 July 1943), OPD; Brigadier General Edward S. Greenbaum to Samuel Rosenman, 20 August 1943, file Demobilization 1, Box 4, Papers of Samuel Rosenman, Franklin D. Roosevelt Library.

Contact between it and the Special Planning Division was infrequent and often unproductive. Early in 1944 SPD established liaison with Leo Pasvolksy, special assistant on postwar planning to the secretary of state, and inquired of him whether the administration had made any long-range policies which might bear on War Department planning. Pasvolksy sympathized with the army's need for a "firm definition of our international commitments" in order to estimate the size and policies of the postwar army. But, he explained, those commitments were too fluid for him to specify. He did advise the army "that our post-war military obligations will be more comprehensive than ever before in the history of the country," and that the United States would enter "some form of arrangement for international security," probably one with a regional division of peacekeeping responsibilities.[45]

Beyond such rather obvious generalities, the State Department could not go. It lacked both the internal leadership and the mandate from Roosevelt to play a more aggressive role in planning. It lacked the prestige as well. The military was now the ascendant bureaucracy as a result of the attention and authority it received for the conduct of the war. Encroaching on State's domain, military officials increasingly undertook tasks more diplomatic than military in nature. The State Department was eclipsed, its shortsightedness, as members of the Council on Foreign Relations complained, contrasting with the "uniformly enthusiastic" attitude of military officials toward long-range planning.[46]

Given the State Department's lassitude about postwar issues, there was no point in the military pushing State hard for guidelines, nor were Tompkins and other officers, especially those in the navy, always inclined to seek them.[47] The armed services and the State Department worked together on immediate diplomatic and military problems such as occupation policy, planning for an international peacekeeping organization, and the services' campaign for UMT. But that piecemeal approach fell far short of a broad definition of policy for postwar security.

45. General Council Minutes, 14 February 1944; Colonel William E. Carpenter to Tompkins, 30 May 1944, file 040 State Department, SPD.

46. Comment by Hanson Baldwin in Digest of Discussion, 50th Meeting, Security and Armaments Series, "War and Peace Studies," Council on Foreign Relations, folder 2, Box 115, Papers of Hanson Baldwin, Yale University Library.

47. Smith, *Air Force Plans*, p. 42; Davis, *Postwar Defense Policy and the U.S. Navy*, pp. 15, 109, 183.

Now unwilling, now unable to obtain guidance from Congress or the executive, the armed forces had to plan in a vacuum or devise their own assumptions about the postwar world. Either option posed the risks of unrealistic planning and creating the appearance of infringing upon traditional civilian prerogatives in the making of foreign policy. To minimize those risks, military authorities attempted to cull from the speeches and writings of national leaders key passages indicating the foreign policy they might pursue after the war. The services knew that such guesswork could not replace direct information.

Outside the government there existed further sources of assistance to the planners. Marshall had originally insisted on the utmost secrecy for postwar plans, probably for fear of encouraging public complacency about victory.[48] Secrecy could not last. SPD needed the collaboration of organizations with a stake in demobilization and postwar policy. Tompkins and his staff developed close ties with business and industrial groups. They also consulted with a host of other private lobbies, from the American Legion to Ivy League presidents, liberal academicians, and the foreign policy groups which flourished during the war.

Special Planning's contacts with these groups were numerous but irregular. Cooperation was most effective in technical matters where civilian expertise appeared indispensable. Industrial and personnel demobilization were prime examples. The military also went to extraordinary lengths to secure the participation of civilian scientists in arrangements for peacetime weapons research. Because of its volatile political nature, UMT was likewise subject to strong civilian pressures. SPD had far less use for civilian opinion on matters of postwar strategy, despite the rapid wartime growth of academic expertise on national security affairs. From groups like the Council on Foreign Relations, whose meetings Army officers frequently attended, Special Planning solicited advice about public opinion on postwar policy and the course of future international relations.[49] But it did not draw outside specialists directly into the shaping of strategy. Custom and a penchant for secrecy were probably more responsible for that distance than was overt hostility.

48. Marshall to Somervell, 14 April 1943, file 310 (Organizational History), SPD.
49. See materials in the SPD file, 334 (Council on Foreign Relations); Digests of Discussion of the Security and Armament Groups of the Council on Foreign Relations, folder 2, Box 115, Baldwin Papers; History (October 1944), "War and Peace Studies Project," Council on Foreign Relations, folder 1, Box 115, Baldwin Papers.

All in all, the fruits of the armed services' contacts with civilians were not impressive. Too often the three services worked in isolation from each other, from other agencies of government, and from outside groups. Poor communication among these organizations did not necessarily mean a divergence of goals among them, however. Haphazard as their collaboration on broad policy was, Congress, the State Department, the White House, and the armed services frequently saw eye to eye when they discussed specifics.

Likewise, much as the services appeared to fight each other more than the Axis, shared fears and experiences often pushed them together. All military men remembered the desperation of getting ready for battle with the Axis, the time when only forty-five fighter planes guarded all the west coast and the fleet lay crippled at Pearl Harbor. War and Navy Department leaders expected the cycle of weakness to repeat itself after World War II. As they saw it, Congress and the public would refuse to support adequate defense. While anticipation of meager budgets intensified competition for limited funds, it also provided cause for a common effort to increase those budgets.

Despite their secretiveness, military leaders found they had the same goals and worked together to secure them. They shared a similar past and believed they faced a common future of international uncertainty, explosive technology, and public neglect. As one naval officer wrote in 1943:

> It would be well for any naval officer who is going to assist in the demo-bilization of the navy after this war to recall the demobilization of the last war, and the insistent demand for economy that came from practically every American citizen. Even staunch advocates of a big navy in Congress were unable to resist this insistent demand. The Navy will be required to cut its expenditures to the bone.

Miserly appropriations, he concluded, were "the most difficult obstacle the navy will have to surmount."[50] On that point all the services agreed.

50. Davis, *Postwar Defense Policy and the U.S. Navy*, pp. 30–31.

2 FIRST PLANS

All postwar planners worked in the shadow of Pearl Harbor. The startling advances in military technology demonstrated by the Japanese attack there became their chief worry. The long-range bombers, rockets, and other new weapons of the war threw into question every comfortable tenet about America's isolation from attack. Yet the armed forces could not fashion a new national strategy out of whole cloth. Largely trained at the start of the century, the military leadership had served far too long and venerated strategic tradition far too much to make a sudden break with the past. Furthermore, the changes in warfare which alarmed the men of the 1940s were hardly new, though their effect on military thinking heretofore had been marginal.

Even before World War I, the mechanization and increasing destructiveness of weaponry threatened the nation's traditional concepts of preparedness and security. In language that would be the common coin of strategists a half century later, Navy Secretary Benjamin Tracy warned in 1889 that "the nation that is ready to strike the first blow will . . . inflict an injury from which he [the enemy] can never recover." Partly because of changes in military technology, the armed forces underwent modernization, capped by the creation of the Army General Staff in 1903 and the construction of a battleship navy. But no revolution in world view accompanied modernization. Reformers concentrated on organization, weaponry, and tactics. North America still seemed safe behind ocean barriers and the navies of the United States and Great Britain. The two services regarded continental defense and the protection of the Pacific possessions of the United States as their primary objectives. Involvement in the wars of Europe or Asia seemed to them unlikely. Deterrence and mobilization, two concepts which would dominate American military thinking in the 1940s, received little scrutiny before World War I.[1]

1. Quotation by Tracy from Millis, *Arms and Men*, p. 148. Prewar plans are discussed in John Grenville and George Young, *Politics, Strategy, and American Diplomacy, 1873–1917*, chap. 11. See also Davis, *Postwar Defense Policy and the U.S. Navy*, pp. 3–4.

Preparedness advocates challenged the complacency of the prevailing outlook. Theodore Roosevelt stressed that technological changes had eroded America's natural defenses. At the onset of the war in Europe, proponents of preparedness worried about the speed with which American forces could mobilize for battle. "Modern war gives no time for preparation," warned General Leonard Wood. "Its approach is that of the avalanche and not of the glacier." Wood, Stimson, the young John McAuley Palmer, and others championed universal military service to provide a ready reserve capable of quick mobilization. Wood and Roosevelt also contended that American strength would discourage other countries from undertaking aggression.[2]

Yet such claims and caveats were peripheral to the preparedness movement before World War I. Defense of American rights on the seas, a muscular nationalism, and visions of postwar military supremacy agitated men like Wood and Roosevelt. So did anxieties over social cleavage and ethnic disloyalties. Roosevelt envisioned universal service as a means to make "the son of the multi-millionaire and the son of the immigrant . . . sleep under the same dog-tent and eat the same grub." On the fringes of the preparedness movement, alarmists sketched lurid scenarios of a European invasion of Latin America or even of the United States. Military planners toyed with the prospect of a German strike against the east coast.[3] But the absurdity of such nightmares, which few officers or other Americans seriously expected to come true, only undercut realistic consideration of how changing technology might undermine the nation's safety from attack. Americans debated national rights and national honor, but not national security.

World War I changed the military outlook surprisingly little. The army busied itself with preparations for a war with a European power. But its plans, postulating a war between the United States and Great Britain, dealt with the worst contingency the army faced, not, to the

2. Quotation from Hermann Hagedorn, *Leonard Wood*, 2 vols. (New York, 1931), 2:152. See also Hagedorn, *Leonard Wood*, 2:149, 171; Hermann Hagedorn, *The Bugle That Woke America* (New York, 1940), p. 30; John Morton Blum, *The Republican Roosevelt* (New York: Atheneum, 1966), pp. 125, 127; Weigley, *U.S. Army*, pp. 339–40; Weigley, *Towards an American Army*, p. 229.

3. Quotation from William E. Harbaugh, *Power and Responsibility* (New York, 1961), p. 490. See also Millis, *Arms and Men*, pp. 192–98; Grenville and Young, *Politics, Strategy, and American Diplomacy*, pp. 305–12; Robert Osgood, *Ideals and Self-Interest in America's Foreign Relations*, pp. 82, 125–33.

staff, a likely occurrence. The plans sprang from an obsession with the World War I experience, not from a conviction that it would recur. Not until the late 1930s did Germany appear to planners as a possible antagonist. Until then, a return of American soldiers to Europe seemed a farfetched prospect. A clash with Japan appeared far more probable, though of little concern to army planners since a Pacific war would supposedly be the navy's show. To the army and navy, the primary concern remained continental and later hemispheric defense, and preservation of American interests in the Pacific.[4]

Believing that wars most often resulted from a clash of economic interests, the army criticized American commercial and military commitments outside the hemisphere as impossible to uphold, provocative of war, and unnecessary to national well-being. As late as 1935 one army planner, like Theodore Roosevelt years earlier, viewed acquisition of the Philippines as a "departure" from America's chosen destiny likely to "produce a clash with a power [Japan] into whose natural domain of expansion we had accidentally strayed." Recommending that the United States abandon its interests in the Far East rather than risk war over them, the officer argued that "the energies of our people can be fully absorbed in that [Western] hemisphere for many generations to come. It is practically self-supporting," and given "reasonable naval and military preparedness on our part, it is virtually invulnerable." Other army planners endorsed that view. The navy, on the other hand, rejected it.[5]

The army's arguments revealed a persisting sense of geographical isolation. Awesome weapons had received a preview in World War I, but their imminence disturbed few military policymakers. New technologies of war in the twenties and thirties generated no concurrent revolution in the military view of America's security needs. The Morrow Board could argue, perhaps still with justification in 1925, that American air power should be seen

---

4. Maurice Matloff, "The American Approach to War, 1919–1945," in *The Theory and Practice of War*, ed. Michael Howard, pp. 215–23; Fred Greene, "The Military View of American Foreign Policy, 1904–1940," *American Historical Review* 66 (January 1966): 354–77; Robert A. Miller, "The United States Army During the 1930s" (Ph.D. dissertation, Princeton University, 1973), pp. 4–6, 64–65, 70–73, 77–82, 88–90, 97–106; Ronald Schaffer, "General Stanley D. Embick: Military Dissenter," *Military Affairs* 37 (October 1973): 89–95.

5. Quotations from Greene, "The Military View of American Foreign Policy," pp. 370–74. See also Schaffer, "General Stanley D. Embick," pp. 90–91; Miller, "The United States Army During the 1930s," pp. 88–96.

primarily as an agency of defense. Protected, as the United States is, by broad oceans from possible enemies ... there is no present reason for apprehension of any invasion from overseas directly by way of air; nor indeed is there any apparent probability of such an invasion in any future which can be foreseen.[6]

The seas still seemed to be unbridgeable moats.

At the same time, some military thinkers propounded new concepts of deterrence, mobilization, and offensive warfare. In the 1920s Palmer suggested that American adoption of universal military training would have made the Kaiser's Germany shrink from war and could force future aggressors to do likewise. UMT was also important to Palmer because it would facilitate speedy mobilization of the army in the event of another war. Other army officials, in cooperation with business leaders, developed primitive plans for economic mobilization in case of another war.[7]

Air power enthusiasts struck out in a different direction. Billy Mitchell argued for strategic bombing as a quick, cheap, and therefore humane alternative to the mass carnage of the land battles fought in World War I.

> Air power can attack the vital centers of the opposing country directly, completely destroying or paralyzing them.... A few men and comparatively few dollars can be used for bringing about the most terrific effect ever known against opposing vital centers.

A strong air force would also provide a cheap deterrent to Japanese aggression, Mitchell believed. Other officers puzzled over different ways to restore offensive capability to war-making: motorized and mechanized land armies; carrier and amphibious task forces; doctrines of concentration and mass; and new theories of total war.[8]

---

6. Quoted in George H. Quester, *Deterrence before Hiroshima: The Background of Modern Strategy*, p. 71. See also Millis, *Arms and Men*, pp. 229, 231.

7. Weigley, *Towards an American Army*, pp. 233–34; Weigley, *The American Way of War*, pp. 203–09; Weigley, *U.S. Army*, pp. 404–09; Paul A. C. Koistinen, "The 'Industrial Military Complex' in Historical Perspective: The InterWar Years," *Journal of American History* 56 (March 1970): 819–39.

8. Quotation from William Mitchell, *Skyways: A Book on Aeronautics* (1930), as quoted in Weigley, *American Way of War*, pp. 234–35. See also Weigley, *American Way of War*, chap. 11, pp. 203–22, 248–52, 254–64; Weigley, *U.S. Army*, pp. 409–11; Matloff, "The American Approach to War, 1919–1945," pp. 217–29; Miller, "The United States Army During the 1930s," chaps. 3–4.

Advocates of such ideas waited in the wings for acceptance by the military hierarchy and the nation. The strongest promoters of UMT were influential eastern conservatives like Stimson and Elihu Root or unconventional officers like Palmer and Wood, not General Staff officers, many of whom were skeptical of the value of citizen soldiers. Politically, the movement for UMT was dormant in the 1920s and 1930s.[9] The air corps was still a sideshow in the army. The corps itself, and Mitchell until after his court-martial, rejected the more extravagant claims for air power advanced by British and Italian theorists. American officers were slow to develop the new equipment necessary for mechanization and lagged behind their European brethren in incorporating the principles of mechanized warfare into their tactics and strategy. Battleship admirals kept a tight grip on the navy, although naval aviators made greater progress than their army counterparts and submariners gained in influence as well.[10]

But the reigning military orthodoxies crumbled as World War II approached. The President himself, in his public addresses, signaled the change. He illustrated the uselessness of the oceans as defensive barriers by ticking off in almost monotonous repetition the flying times from possible enemy bases to dozens of points in the Western Hemisphere. Hammering at the impact of science on geographical relationships, Roosevelt warned of "the amazing speed" of modern warfare, the danger of "lightning attacks," and the futility of mobilizing for war after the start of hostilities.[11] Mobilization suddenly became the paramount military problem, while the rapidity of Axis expansion lent a credibility to fears for hemisphere security never attached to the prophecies of invasion made in 1914–16. The ascension to power of Marshall in 1939, the continued employment of mass armies in warfare, and the need to strengthen American defense led to greater acceptance of UMT by the officer corps. In 1941, the army

9. Robert David Ward, "The Movement for Universal Military Training in the United States, 1942–1952" (Ph.D. dissertation, University of North Carolina, 1957), pp. 1–36; Weigley, *Towards an American Army*, chaps. 12–13; Weigley, *U.S. Army*, pp. 409–10; Pogue, *Education of a General*, pp. 209–10.

10. Weigley, *American Way of War*, pp. 215–20, 226–36, 253–54, 264–65; Quester, *Deterrence before Hiroshima*, pp. 71–74, 127–29; Watson, *Chief of Staff*, pp. 35–36; Millis, *Arms and Men*, p. 232; Miller, "The United States Army During the 1930s," chaps. 3–4.

11. Samuel I. Rosenman, ed., *The Public Papers and Addresses of Franklin D. Roosevelt*, 13 vols., 9: 198–200, 251, 636.

staff began consideration of how to convert selective service into a permanent program of universal training after hostilities.[12]

During the crisis before Pearl Harbor, policymakers attached new hope to deterrence. After Munich, Roosevelt, searching for some means to ward off war, grasped at air power. In the face of a vast fleet of bombers, he believed, Hitler might retreat from further aggression, much as the reputed strength of the Luftwaffe helped overawe Britain and France at Munich. War broke out before the United States could construct an air armada, and in 1940, at the urging of Marshall and other military advisors, FDR accepted a balanced program of rearmament.[13] But Roosevelt's belated gesture to caution Hitler suggested an extension of the idea of deterrence, its application on a global scale. American air power might check aggression not only against the United States but against other nations as well.

In 1941 the Roosevelt administration gave deterrence another try. FDR had previously sent much of the fleet to Pearl Harbor as a measured warning to the Japanese. Now, Marshall and the War Department formulated a new plan to restrain Japan. The AAF would secretly gather a force of 340 B-17s in the Philippines. The bombers might not only block a Japanese advance southward, but through their capacity to bomb Japanese cities they might, when their possession was revealed to moderate Japanese leaders, blackmail Japan out of even making the attempt. The frantic buildup of B-17s, targeted for completion in March 1942, came too late. The United States never completed its trap.[14] Faith in deterrence went untested, but was neither disproven nor discarded. Indeed, it would inspire those who planned the nation's postwar defenses.

The Navy

Even before the navy began its postwar planning, Under Secretary James Forrestal made clear the navy's intention to keep the fleet of

12. Osgood, *Ideals and Self-Interest*, chaps. 16–17; Ward, "Movement for Universal Military Training," pp. 37–41; Brigadier General Harry L. Twaddle, "Plan (In Outline) For Organization of the Army of the United States," and Twaddle to Assistant Chief of Staff, WPD, 17 July 1941, both in file WPD 3674–50, Records of the War Plans Division, RG 165; Marshall to Palmer, 13 November 1941, World War II File, Box 14, Palmer Papers; Palmer to Edwards, 3 March 1943, Chronological Files 1942–43, Box 10, Palmer Papers.

13. Pogue, *Education of a General*, chap. 19; Pogue, *Ordeal and Hope*, pp. 26–32, 76–79; Quester, *Deterrence before Hiroshima*, pp. 129–30.

14. Pogue, *Ordeal and Hope*, pp. 202–03; Quester, *Deterrence before Hiroshima*, pp. 131–35.

powerful warships assembled to fight the Axis and use it to deter future aggressors. After victory "we must not again quit with the job half done," Forrestal proclaimed several weeks before Pearl Harbor. "We must lead toward peace, not war, but with the strength in our hands that gives us the power to implement our desire for peace." The under secretary wanted the navy to have the "police power and adequate strength for men of good will to curb the ruffians of the world. We have the power now. We must resolve to keep it."[15]

The navy's first postwar plans, pieced together between June 1943 and May 1944, did not pinpoint an exact figure for the size of the postwar navy, but they reflected Forrestal's injunction to think big. The first proposal, offered in June 1943, suggested a minimum fleet of a dozen battleships and twelve large carriers, plus twenty smaller carriers, five thousand planes, and lesser craft. Subsequent plans increased those figures, especially the ones for naval aviation. To man such a large peacetime force the navy would require some 550,000 to 825,000 officers and enlisted men.[16]

The initial plans were fuzzy on several issues critical to the postwar navy. Officers were uncertain about how much of the wartime fleet the navy should replace by peacetime construction. They vacillated on how much prominence to attach to naval aviation. Most important, the first proposals lacked a clear notion of the navy's postwar mission. Uncertain about what enemies the United States might face, unable to predict the future of the Grand Alliance, the staff found it difficult to pin down the tasks or the geographical areas for which the future navy might exercise responsibility.[17]

The first plans lacked specificity, but not an embryonic strategic concept. For one thing, the navy, by endorsing universal military training, took note of potential problems in mobilizing for a future war. Since the navy had traditionally considered itself an M-day (mobilization day) force, ready for battle at the onset of hostilities and expanding only modestly thereafter, UMT had not hitherto appeared applicable to its manpower needs. But during World War I and even more during World War II, the navy faced the mobilization

15. Forrestal, speech at Union League Club Navy Day Dinner, Philadelphia, 27 October 1941, Box 5, Papers of James V. Forrestal, Princeton University Library. Forrestal, address before the Maryland Historical Society, 10 May 1943, Box 5, Forrestal Papers.
16. Davis, *Postwar Defense Policy and the U.S. Navy*, pp. 10, 32–35.
17. Ibid., pp. 11, 14–17, chap. 2 passim.

challenges once encountered only by the army. A large trained reserve appeared more and more desirable. In 1940 the navy's General Board advocated adoption of UMT, a recommendation renewed in some, though not all, of the plans made in 1943–44. Secretaries Knox and Forrestal became zealous proponents of the training program.[18]

A new, if uncertain, vision of the navy's responsibilities influenced the first plans. Previously concentrating on the Atlantic and Pacific approaches to the hemisphere, the navy now saw its postwar task as global. Heretofore gathered into a single massive fleet under Mahan's doctrine, the navy would now be dispersed into task forces operating in most of the world's seas. The purpose of such a navy was vague as outlined in early plans, particularly since officers downplayed the role the United States would play in European affairs after the war. But the planners seemed to believe that the navy would perform the policing and preventive functions outlined in Forrestal's addresses. Even preemptive strikes against potential aggressors appeared justifiable. "Defense of our national interests," Vice Admiral Frederick Horne argued, "must envisage the desirability of being able to commence offensive operations without waiting for an assault and setback by any future enemy."[19]

The planners did not elucidate the reasons for their advocacy of UMT and an expanded responsibility for the navy, but indirectly their superiors and fellow officers advanced an explanation. Top naval officials believed that technological change imperiled the nation's security. "Previously," Admiral King explained in a typical warning, "we have looked upon the Atlantic and the Pacific as great natural barriers behind which we could pursue our peaceful ways in detached security. But we have learned—and learned the hard way—that our oceans are both bulwarks of defense and avenues of attack." Another officer expressed that anxiety more vividly. "In future wars—and eventually the idealists will succeed in babbling us into other wars—we shall never again have the time with which to build the implements of war, train men and construct ships." The nature

18. Ibid., pp. 10, 17, 23; memorandum, "The National Defense," Chairman of the General Board to Secretary to the Navy, 7 June 1940, General Board No. 42, Serial 1963, General Board-Secretary of the Navy Files, Naval History Division; Forrestal speech draft, September 1943, file "Miscellaneous I," Box 49, and Forrestal speeches of 2 December 1943 and 11 September 1944, Box 5, all in Forrestal Papers; Knox speech, 14 January 1944, speech file, Box 8, Papers of Frank Knox, Library of Congress; Frank Knox, "Let's Train Our Youth," *Colliers*, 29 April 1944, p. 11.

19. Davis, *Postwar Defense Policy and the U.S. Navy*, pp. 11, 14, 23.

of a future attack against the United States was unpredictable but frightening. "Will it be atomic?" the same officer asked in May 1944. "Will it be electrical? Will it be bacterial? Who knows? But rest assured . . . it will be swift, and it will be sudden and it will be terrible." Given such a vision of future wars, the naval command believed that the capacity for rapid mobilization provided by UMT and the capability to take preventive action against a threatening power were essential for national survival.[20]

Grave as the outlook for future security appeared to them, navy men doubted that their fellow citizens would face up to it. Americans, Forrestal charged in 1943, saw history as "something that occurred on another planet." By nature naive about their country's defense, many Americans believed that they "were in no danger of aggression in this war" and that they "could never be exposed to attack." Because the United States escaped direct attack during World War II, Americans did not appreciate their vulnerability to devastation, Forrestal feared. The odds seemed poor that they would pay for the navy they would need.[21]

Hastily prepared and given little attention by higher authority, the navy's first plans did not develop a reasoned strategic concept. They read like lists of undigested assumptions, assertions, and predictions about the future rather than as a coherent argument about peacetime military needs. But the planners were groping toward an ambitious role for the postwar navy, and their superiors were beginning to articulate that role.

The Army

Like the navy, the army paid only limited attention to force levels in its first phase of planning. An ad hoc Special Army Committee convened in the spring of 1943 did propose a postwar strength of one and one-half million men, including five hundred thousand ground force troops and one million air personnel.[22] But, as advisor to the Special Planning Division, General Palmer concentrated in

20. King, address before the Governors' Conference, 29 May 1944, speech file, Box 27, King Papers; Rear Admiral Thomas L. Gatch, speech before the Columbia University Club of Washington, "After this War," 20 May 1944, file 45-1-10, SecNav.

21. Forrestal address, 10 May 1943, Box 5, Forrestal Papers; Davis, *Postwar Defense Policy and the U.S. Navy*, pp. 30–31, 34–35.

22. Special Army Committee, "Survey of Current Military Program," 15 March 1943, revised 28 April 1943, file 320.2 (1576), OPD.

1943 on drafting a broad statement of policy, the "Outline of the Post-War Military Establishment," and on securing the acceptance of its principles by War Department officials.

Predictably, the cornerstone of Palmer's plans for the postwar army was universal military training, which he had championed for three decades. Finding that UMT still faced opposition from many officers, Palmer set out to convert and commit the army to his cause. By June 1943 "higher authority," presumably General Marshall, approved for planning purposes the assumption that the army would have peacetime UMT. Several weeks later the Joint Chiefs of Staff ratified the army's decision.[23]

Palmer and Marshall believed so intensely in the necessity of UMT that they saw no need for a fresh examination of its strategic value. Devoting most of their efforts to battling the opponents of UMT, they expressed their defense of training largely in response to political challenges. They never authorized a dispassionate appraisal of the system.

Still, they had a strategic rationale for UMT. Palmer worried that the "sudden stress of modern war," the speed with which threats to American security could develop, made it impossible for the United States to expend months or years after the outbreak of a war in training an army. "No nation is prepared for war unless it is able to deploy all or any necessary part of its military man power in time to meet any given emergency." UMT would provide a reservoir of several million trained reservists ready for combat after a few weeks or months of mobilization and refresher courses. Assuming eight hundred thousand trainees a year and a four-year reserve obligation, Palmer hoped for a back-up force of over three million men. By urging abolition of other reserve organizations like the National Guard, a move he recognized as political dynamite, Palmer hoped to streamline the reserve system further and place it under the exclusive control of the federal government.[24]

23. Ibid.; Tompkins to Grunert, Waite, McCullough, and Macon, 18 May 1943, and Palmer to Tompkins, 19 May 1943, both in file 380 (folder 1), SPD; Tompkins to Palmer, 14 June 1943, and Palmer to Tompkins, 15 June 1943, both in file 350.06 (Military Problems June 1943), SPD; Palmer, "Outlines of a Post-War Military Establishment," 29 June 1943, file 370.9, Chief of Staff; Tompkins to General Ray Porter, 15 July 1943, file 320.2, SPD.

24. Palmer, "Outline of Post-War Military Policy," 24 November 1943, file 380 (Postwar Planning, June 24, 1942), SPD; Palmer, "Outlines of a Post-War Military Establishment," 29 June 1943, file 370.9, Chief of Staff.

Speed of mobilization was critical not only to fight wars but to prevent them. "The higher our initial rate of expansion," Palmer reasoned, "the greater will be the deterrent effect of our military preparations upon our prospective enemies." Citing the failure of the policy pursued by the Western democracies in the 1930s, Palmer explained that

> relatively small forces ready for powerful offensive action may liquidate a threatening situation before it grows serious. If the law-abiding nations had been able to take this attitude when Japan first invaded Manchuria, they might have discouraged subsequent adventures in aggression on the part of Italy and Germany.

Hoping that a mass army would deter future aggression, Palmer claimed that, had universal training been adopted in Washington's time, "we would have been prepared for every subsequent war and, in fact, most of them could not have occurred."[25]

If it did not prevent war, UMT would provide the wherewithal to strike against the aggressor before he could gain an overwhelming strategic advantage. Marshall's staff proposed that the future army possess "expeditionary or task forces, great or small, for prompt attack in any part of the world in order to crush the very beginnings of lawless aggression, in cooperation with other nations." Marshall did not object to that definition of the army's mission, although he refused to allow his staff to voice it in public for fear of political repercussions. The new strategic outlook, as Palmer succinctly summed it up, "will mean armed forces formed not for defense but for prompt attack." Like the navy, the army made little effort at this stage in its planning to specify where it would deploy its forces. But it boldly proclaimed that the army's responsibilities would be global.[26]

Palmer argued that by providing maximum manpower at minimum cost, UMT would lessen the financial burden of those responsibilities. In a favorite metaphor, he explained that a small professional force

25. Palmer, "Outlines of a Post-War Military Establishment," 29 June 1943, file 370.9, Chief of Staff; Palmer to Director, SPD, 24 January 1944, file 350.06 (Study 64), SPD; Palmer, "Outline of Post-War Military Policy," submitted 24 November 1942, file 380 (Postwar Planning, June 24, 1942), SPD.
26. Handy to Marshall, 28 October 1943, file 370.9, Chief of Staff; marginal comment in Marshall's handwriting on draft of Palmer's statement for the House Select Committee on Postwar Military Policy, statement titled "Our National Military Policy," n.d. [April 1944], Chronological Files 1943–44, Box 11, Palmer Papers; Palmer to Colonel Perry Brown, 22 October 1943, Chronological Files 1942–43, Box 10, Palmer Papers.

should provide the "steel" skeleton of the modern army: garrisoning overseas bases, carrying out minor police actions, training reserves, readying war plans, and absorbing the first shock of an enemy attack. Reservists would provide the "concrete" of the military structure, the great mass of soldiers needed to fill out the military system in case of all-out war. Although unprepared in 1943 to fix an exact figure for the size of the postwar army, Palmer insisted that UMT be viewed as a substitute for, not an adjunct to, large and expensive professional forces:

> It has been argued that a system of universal military training will involve prohibitive cost. As a matter of fact, its cost will be largely if not entirely offset by great resultant economies in our military budget. The most expensive element in our peacetime military establishment is the regular army. If through a system of universal military training we have a great and well-organized reservoir of trained officers and men in civil life, our peace establishment will be capable of rapid expansion and a relatively small regular army will meet the demands of national security.

The same principle, Palmer believed, applied to naval and air forces.[27]

Consumed with doubts about how much the American people would support the peacetime army, Palmer and Marshall defended UMT most strongly not on strategic but on financial grounds. Marshall searched out every proposal for UMT which crossed his desk to find ways in which the postwar army could operate more efficiently. When General Tompkins suggested that career officers handle most of the training of UMT conscripts, Marshall condemned the proposal as "entirely wrong." Believing that the army's success would hinge on its ability "to train and maintain large numbers without a prohibitive financial burden," the chief of staff insisted that draftees be trained by a "tremendous number of new lieutenants," who would cost the army far less than higher-grade officers. By so doing the army would be "killing two birds with one stone, i.e. training officers and men." The significance of the discussion on this and many similar issues lay less in the details than in the fact that first priority was placed on efficiency and economy rather than strategic mission.[28]

27. Palmer to Director, SPD, 24 January 1944, file 350.06 (Study 64), SPD.
28. Handwritten comments by Marshall on memorandum, Tompkins to Chief of Staff, 18 August 1943, file 370.9, Chief of Staff; Marshall to Tompkins, 3 September 1943, file 370.9 (18 August 1943), Chief of Staff; Tompkins to Marshall, 7 September 1943, file 350.06 (Study 64), SPD.

Beyond an insistence on UMT, the army's initial postwar plan, the "Outline of a Post-War Military Establishment," was vague, despite the extensive staff work which went into it. As approved by the General Staff and on April 15, 1944, by General Marshall, the "Outline" suggested three missions for the postwar ground and air forces: (1) "Supporting such International obligations as the United States may assume"; (2) holding bases to protect "vital sea and air routes" and to "cover vital installations from sustained air attack"; (3) maintaining capability to expand to complete mobilization. To perform those missions the War Department would maintain a small establishment of professional soldiers, though no precise figure was given, and train an estimated seven hundred thousand UMT conscripts annually. Backing up the active-duty personnel would be reservists fulfilling their obligation under universal military training and an "inactive enlisted Reserve."[29]

Like the navy, the army set an ambitious objective for itself. Though receiving no explicit mention in the "Outline," peacekeeping on a global scale was the main task Palmer and Marshall foresaw for the postwar army. But, also like the navy, even as the invasion of France approached the General Staff was not yet ready to explain how the army could carry out that objective and how it could reconcile pursuit of that goal with the limited funds it anticipated.

The Army Air Forces

Appearances were misleading. Palmer and Marshall were old generals plugging an old idea, universal military training. Army Air Forces employed dazzling new technologies which enhanced the appeal of its doctrine of strategic air power. Actually, theories of strategic air power were not new. They emerged a quarter of a century earlier, even earlier insofar as their inspiration came from Mahan's writings, and dominated the Army Air Corps' thinking in the 1920s and 1930s.[30]

Hints of the kind of postwar air force the bomber enthusiasts sought first came from civilian publicists like Alexander de Seversky, the Russian-born ace, aircraft developer, and consultant to the AAF. A strident advocate of strategic bombing, Seversky envisioned an air force much as Mahan saw his battle fleet, as a massive armed force

29. "Outline of a Post-War Military Establishment," 15 April 1944, file 350.06 (Study 64), SPD.
30. Smith, *Air Force Plans*, chap. 3.

which would confront and defeat the enemy in a single decisive battle. In *Victory Through Air Power* (1942), a popular tract which Walt Disney turned into a pioneer propaganda film, Seversky sketched this scenario of future warfare:

> From every point of the compass ... giant bombers, each protected by its convoy of deadly fighter planes, converge upon the United States of America. There are thousands of these dreadnaughts of the skies. Each of them carries at least fifty tons of streamlined explosives and a hailstorm of light incendiary bombs. Wave after wave they come—openly, in broad daylight, magnificently armored and armed, surrounded by protective aircraft and equipped to fight their way through to their appointed targets. Aerial armadas now battle boldly and fiercely, just as great naval armadas used to do in the past, only with a destructive fury infinitely more terrifying.

In a day, "New York, Detroit, Chicago and San Francisco are reduced to rubble heaps."[31] Seversky's writings in that vein, though aimed at the conduct of World War II, carried the obvious implication that the United States should gird itself in the postwar era with an awesome fleet of bombers.

The first glimpse of official AAF hopes came in the spring of 1943 from the Special Army Committee, dominated by AAF and Operations Division officers. Proposing a postwar army of one million five hundred thousand ground personnel, the committee made clear by the deployments it suggested that it expected the air force to play the dominant role in postwar defense. Ground troops would be confined largely to the Western Hemisphere under its plan, but thirty-five hundred aircraft would be assigned to the "European-African" and "Pacific-Asiatic" areas.[32] Air power would provide M-day defense and would police aggressors, with ground forces relegated to garrisoning and protecting bases or performing mop-up and occupation chores.

The Special Army Committee left universal training out of its calculations. In contrast to Palmer, it argued that adoption of UMT would make no difference in the size of the armed forces. The AAF attitude toward UMT, more sharply defined later in the war, was that forces-in-being, not reserves, were necessary for modern defense. Too,

---

31. Alexander P. de Seversky, *Victory Through Air Power*, pp. 7–8; *New York Times*, 19 July 1943.

32. Special Army Committee, "Survey of Current Military Program," 15 March 1943, revised 28 April 1943, file 320.2 (1576), OPD.

the AAF believed that one year was too little time to train skilled air crews. Finally, the committee's coolness toward UMT reflected the AAF's confidence about public support and its rejection of Palmer's fears about the political acceptability of a large professional force. "While public opinion will oppose supporting an excessively large army once the bandit nations have been effectively neutralized," the committee stated, "isolationist pressure will be less than in the prewar period." Palmer and Marshall, who later rejected the figure of 1.5 million men as wildly extravagant, were less optimistic.[33]

A more detailed blueprint of the postwar air force emerged when the AAF's Post War Division drew up the first comprehensive AAF plan, completed on February 14, 1944. Relying on the recommendations of the Special Planning Division, the Special Army Committee, and General Thomas Handy of the Operations Division (OPD), the AAF proposed a permanent air force of 105 air groups and one million active-duty personnel. SPD had encouraged air planners to think boldly by instructing them to regard air power as the nation's primary M-day force. The air staff hardly needed encouragement. It shared with others in the army the conviction that American military power should prevent aggression or punish it before it reached menacing proportions. Strategic air power, the AAF contended, could best carry out that mission because it could strike most swiftly against a threatening enemy. According to the AAF's first postwar plan, "a strong 'M' day Air Force, strategically deployed for prompt action, will be the most effective resistance against a new outbreak of hostilities within range of its bases." In this argument, the speed and mobility of air power were deemed essential. Ground and naval forces, supposedly too vulnerable to attack and too slow to mobilize for instant war, would execute only such secondary functions as protecting bases and guarding sea lanes.[34]

The air planners were convinced that strategic air power would decide future conflicts. "The airplane was not considered just another weapon," according to the historian of AAF plans, "it was the ultimate weapon for universal peacekeeping."[35] By striking at carefully selected jugular points in an enemy's economy or morale, or by

---

33. Ibid. See also Smith, *Air Force Plans*, pp. 85–86.
34. Quotation from 14 June 1944 supplement to 105–group plan, as quoted in Smith, *Air Force Plans*, p. 59. See also Smith, pp. 55, 59–61; Burt to Tompkins, 2 October 1944, file 350.06 (study 102), SPD.
35. Smith, *Air Force Plans*, p. 18.

merely threatening to do so, a bomber force alone could impose America's will on an enemy and provide the muscle for the United States to police the world.

While the AAF was completing its 105-group plan, a Joint Chiefs of Staff study of postwar air bases gave further indication of how the armed services viewed the future role of American air power in international peacekeeping. In 1943 and 1944 an international police force, widely discussed in the United States, seemed a real possibility. Congress shied away from explicit endorsement of such a force, and in public President Roosevelt hid behind vacuous generalities.[36] But in December 1942 the Commander-in-Chief secretly instructed the Joint Chiefs to examine, in preparation for peace negotiations, what air bases a postwar "International Police Force" might need. He added that the chiefs should ignore considerations of national sovereignty.[37]

The Joint Chiefs immediately departed from Roosevelt's instructions. Over the protests of Admiral Leahy and certain JCS staff officers, they broadened FDR's directive to include examination of bases for national defense and commercial aviation as well as for the American component of an international force. Citing the example of Latin American bases during the 1930s, several officers argued that commercial and military aviation were inseparable from each other and from international peacekeeping. National defense had to be the Joint Chiefs' first consideration, another officer reasoned, because "an actual international force may not arrive for six, eight, or ten years." After months of arguing over whether they should plan for national or international air bases, the JCS eventually brushed aside the distinction by asserting that bases prepared for the "primary aim" of national defense might eventually be used by international military forces.[38]

36. Robert A. Divine, *Second Chance: The Triumph of Internationalism in America During World War II*, pp. 42, 144–54; James MacGregor Burns, *Roosevelt: The Soldier of Freedom*, pp. 427–29.

37. Captain John L. McCrea (naval aide to the President) to Leahy, 28 December 1942, in JCS 183, file CCS 360 (12-9-42) Sec. 1, JCS.

38. For the evolution of Roosevelt's request in JCS hands, see King to Secretary of the Navy, 9 February 1943, JCS Memorandum 47; Major General John Deane to General Stanley Embick, 13 February 1943; Report by the Joint Strategic Survey Committee, 6 March 1943, JCS 183/1; extract from the minutes of the JCS 65th meeting, 9 March 1943, all in file CCS 360 (12-9-42) Sec. 1, JCS. Quotations from minutes of the JCS 65th meeting and from Joint Strategic Survey Committee Report 9/3, 25 March 1943, file 360 (12-9-42) Sec. 1, JCS.

The requirements for national security and international peace-keeping appeared complementary to many military leaders because they equated the interests of the United States with those of the rest of the world. An international police force would, they hoped, internationalize and legitimize American power. As an instrument of American policy, an international army would punish or deter aggression. With American strategic bombers as its backbone, it would serve "not as an army to wage war after a situation has gotten out of control, but as a force which will eliminate subversive or dangerous focal points before they can develop to the point where they become a danger to the security of the world." AAF planners even hinted that a world organization might sanction preemptive air attacks in case deterrence appeared to be failing.[39]

Roosevelt, long a proponent of using air power to deter aggression, shared the planners' wish for an international force to sanction American deterrence. Careless about communicating his ideas to the military, vague about the details of his plans, a fuzzy-minded internationalist to some critics, the President was in fact neither naive nor complacent about postwar security. He, too, drew one lesson from recent experience: "that if we do not pull the fangs of the predatory animals of this world, they will multiply and grow in strength—and they will be at our throats once more in a short generation."[40]

To pull those fangs, Roosevelt explained to the JCS in 1943, he wanted the "Four Policemen," consisting of the United States, Britain, China, and the Soviet Union, to stand guard against aggression in behalf of the future international organization. Should a nation threaten world peace, Roosevelt proposed that the four powers deter it from aggression or, if necessary, blockade or bombard it into submission. Invasion would be a last resort. But the four policemen would not share equal power. Russia and China would wield only a nightstick, conventional weapons. At least during the first years of peace, Roosevelt and Churchill agreed, the United States and Britain alone would carry nuclear bombs, with the United States as the dominant partner in the atomic alliance. Furthermore, as Roosevelt and his Advisory Committee on Post-War Foreign Policy envisioned it, the world organization would be even more dependent on American

39. Quotation from notes on a Joint Staff Planners conference of 25 January 1943, as quoted in Smith, *Air Force Plans*, p. 44. See also *Air Force Plans*, p. 49.
40. Quoted in Divine, *Second Chance*, p. 84.

power because it would act primarily through air forces which the United States, as the preeminent aircraft manufacturer, would have to supply. Taking for granted that American interests coincided with those of the rest of the world, Roosevelt, like many military leaders, swept aside the problem of small-power rights and gave little thought to the danger that America's dominant role in an international organization might be seen as coercive by other powers.[41]

The Joint Chiefs drew on Roosevelt's "Four Policemen" plan in writing up JCS 570, their recommendations for postwar air bases. Most likely, they did so on their own initiative, without knowledge of FDR's hopes for a nuclear monopoly, although Roosevelt did communicate directly with them on this matter in November 1943. For planning purposes, the Joint Chiefs assumed that in the postwar era the "major United Nations" would "have maintained their solidarity" and "have established preliminary United Nations' machinery for enforcing the peace—as represented by the Four Powers Pact." The major powers would enforce peace either "on a combined or a regional basis," with the United States' interests confined primarily to "the Western Hemisphere, and the Central Pacific to the Far East." The regional division of responsibilities accorded with suggestions made by Roosevelt in 1942 and with his belief that the American public would not long support the stationing of United States troops in Europe.[42]

Completed in November 1943, JCS 570 proposed bases for three contingencies: (1) "direct defense of the U.S., leased areas, and possessions, including the Philippines"; (2) defense of the Western Hemisphere; (3) the United States' role "as one of the Great Powers enforcing peace, pending a world-wide organization."[43] The phrasing

41. On FDR's views in 1942–43 and statements to the JCS, see U.S. Department of State, *Foreign Relations of the United States: The Conferences at Cairo and Tehran, 1943*, pp. 256, 531–32; Robert Divine, *Roosevelt and World War II*, pp. 56–64; Martin J. Sherwin, *A World Destroyed: The Atomic Bomb and the Grand Alliance*, chaps. 3–4; Martin J. Sherwin, "The Atomic Bomb and the Origins of the Cold War: U.S. Atomic Energy Policy and Diplomacy, 1941–45," *American Historical Review* 78 (October 1973): 945–68. On the Advisory Committee, see Henry Jackson Lowe, "The Planning and Negotiation of U.S. Post-War Security, 1942–1943" (Ph.D. dissertation, University of Virginia, 1971), pp. 94–109.

42. Quotations from map titled "Military Air Base Requirements—Period II," Enclosure "B" to JCS Memorandum to the President, 15 November 1943, file CCS 360 (12-9-42) Sec. 2, JCS. See also Maurice Matloff, *Strategic Planning for Coalition Warfare, 1943–1944*, pp. 338–43; Elliot Roosevelt, ed., *F.D.R., His Personal Letters: 1928–1945*, 2 vols., 2: 1366–67; Divine, *Roosevelt and World War II*, pp. 56–65.

43. JCS map, 15 November 1943, file CCS 360 (12-9-42) Sec. 2, JCS.

was odd in that it implied that the United States could defend itself without maintaining world peace or hemispheric security, a doctrine almost certainly at variance with what the Joint Chiefs intended to suggest.

For "direct defense" of the United States and its possessions, the Joint Chiefs sought bases in several areas: the continental United States, the Caribbean and Central America, Newfoundland, Alaska and the Aleutians, as well as certain Pacific islands extending from the Hawaiian group south to the Society Islands and west to the Philippines. The JCS proposed additional bases in South America, along the west African coast, in the Canaries and the Azores, and in Iceland, Greenland, and Canada to provide for hemisphere defense. To prepare for the third contingency, enforcement of world peace, the United States would require added bases in the southwest Pacific and Borneo, the Japanese islands, the Kuriles and southern Sakhalin Island, and on the east Asian mainland from Siam to north China and Korea.[44]

Curiously, the JCS planners ignored the possibility, soon feasible for long-range aircraft, of an attack against the United States along a polar route, the shortest path to America from many parts of the globe. Civilian scholars during the war urged Americans to think in terms of polar projections and great circle routes.[45] But the JCS staff which made recommendations for bases, a staff consisting primarily of aviators, who should have been sensitive to the changes wrought by the airplane, continued to envision attack across traditional ocean routes. Defense of the nation's east and west coasts held priority. That orientation may have arisen from fears of a resurgent Japan or a tendency to see future conflicts as starting with an attack, like that at Pearl Harbor, against outlying bases. Apprehension over a Russian advance through the Far East and the Pacific may also have troubled some JCS planners.[46]

The Joint Chiefs' recommendations on bases followed the traditional geographic orientation of American military policy toward hemisphere defense and the Pacific. In so doing they reflected FDR's outlook and the Joint Chiefs' own apparent lack of anxiety over possible conflict with Germany, the Soviet Union, or other European

44. Ibid.
45. See Nicholas John Spykman, *The Geography of the Peace.*
46. Smith, *Air Force Plans*, pp. 76–80.

powers. During the war the AAF did not contemplate locating bases in Europe after the occupation period. Even the Atlantic and African bases were late additions to the JCS list, placed there at the insistence of Admiral King, who "felt that to limit the location of bases for national defense puts ammunition in the hands of the isolationists." King's remark illustrated how political considerations often overshadowed strategic needs in the calculations of the planners. Reasoning that additional bases would justify additional forces, they designed their recommendations for bases partly to support claims for higher force levels, and partly to dramatize the American commitment to a more active role in the enforcement of world peace. Yet some officers advised against a more extensive system of bases for fear that they would only become liabilities if Congress refused to pay for an adequate defense of all the military's outposts.[47]

Regional in scope, the plans of the JCS did not appear to match the pretensions to global peacekeeping of the army and navy leadership. But the gap between plans and ambitions may have been illusory. Implementation of the Joint Chiefs' recommendations would have set up a network of bases far exceeding the prewar system in both number and geographic range. From bases in the expanded network, the B-36, with an anticipated range of ten thousand miles and a target date of 1946 for completion, would be capable of striking nearly all the more populated areas of Europe and Asia.[48] A regional configuration of bases did not rule out an attempt to wield power on a global scale. A keen student of air power, Roosevelt surely appreciated the global range of American air power when he made his oft-cited admonitions against counting on a prolonged American military occupation of Europe. With its new bombers, he probably reasoned, the United States could discourage aggression even as it kept its distance.

When freed from the constraints of a formal JCS paper, the Joint Chiefs argued for a global view of American security needs. In November, steaming toward the Tehran Conference on board the

47. Quotation from extract from the minutes of the JCS 71st meeting, 30 March 1943, file CCS 360 (12-9-42) Sec. 1, JCS; See also Smith, *Air Force Plans*, pp. 58, 83; Matloff, *Strategic Planning for Coalition Warfare*, p. 493.

48. Wesley Frank Craven and James Lea Cate, eds., *The Army Air Forces in World War II*, 7 vols., 6: 243–46; Smith, *Air Force Plans*, p. 81.

new battleship *Iowa*, Roosevelt and the four chiefs reviewed the JCS 570 maps and recommendations. General Arnold, anxious that the President quickly approve the JCS plans, prepared a memorandum on the horrors which could befall the United States in the future. Pointing to the arsenal of miracle weapons with which other nations might some day attack the United States, Arnold asserted "that we must meet such attack as far from our own borders as possible to insure against any part of the United States mainland being visited by a sudden devastation beyond any 'Pearl Harbor' experience or our present power of imagination to conceive." Arnold's statement placed no geographical limit on the exercise of American power. He believed the potential threat to American security so grave that "only gross lack of vision or total absence of concern over future security could tolerate avoidable restrictions upon our ability to base and operate military aircraft in and over certain territories under foreign sovereignty."[49]

Roosevelt did not indicate how fully he shared Arnold's anxiety. But, already deeply immersed in postwar issues, the President reaffirmed his wish for a strong peacetime force. When handed the Joint Chiefs' maps by Admiral Leahy, he approved the JCS 570 plan after making some minor additions to the chiefs' list of bases. Later Roosevelt directed Secretary of State Cordell Hull to work with the JCS on diplomatic aspects of securing the desired air bases, as well as ground, naval, and commercial installations.[50] That action, plus the completion of the AAF's 105-group plan in February 1944, concluded the first phase of air force planning. Unlike the army and navy, the aviators had been precise in their requests for forces and bases. But like the other services the AAF was vague about its postwar mission. It viewed its bombers as the principal M-day and peace-keeping force, but in justifying that mission it did not venture beyond alarmist generalities.

49. Arnold to JCS, n.d. [November 1943], file CCS 360 (12-9-42) Sec. 2, JCS.

50. Minutes of meetings between the JCS and the President, 15 November 1943 and 19 November 1943, and FDR to JCS, 23 November 1943, all in file CCS 360 (12-9-42) Sec. 2, JCS. On interdepartmental cooperation in securing air bases, see also John Andrew Miller, "Air Diplomacy: The Chicago Civil Aviation Conference of 1944 in Anglo-American Wartime Relations and Post-war Planning" (Ph.D. dissertation, Yale University, 1971), especially pp. 80–85.

Joining the Issue

In the summer of 1943, victory over the Axis was still distant. Allied bombers were not yet effective against Germany, and the Anglo-American command had postponed for another year the main ground assault against Nazi Europe. Yet the services were already eyeing victory in their own bureaucratic contest. Almost as soon as they initiated planning in 1943, the AAF and the Army General Staff began the first skirmish in their long struggle over postwar military policy. The discord between them arose over the makeup of the postwar army, a political issue which soon exposed deep differences over strategy as well.

At the time, no one questioned the overall figure of 1,500,000 troops proposed for the postwar army by the Special Army Committee, nor the wisdom of a capability to mobilize to 4,500,000 men within one year. But the distribution of those 1,500,000 personnel between ground and air forces immediately came under fire. Tompkins and other staff officers protested the suggested assignment of 1,000,000 men to the AAF.[51] The head of G-3 (Organization and Training) General Ray Porter, challenged the AAF's claim to primacy. "Nothing has been developed to date to indicate that Air Power can either take or hold geographical territory of any appreciable size." Therefore, he argued, the army should garrison its overseas bases with

> small but highly mobile Ground Forces (plus adequate Air Support) and retain the mass of the Air Forces as a striking force in the United States. The mobility of the latter is great enough to permit its speedy concentration in any part of the world provided Ground Forces already there retain control of the bases necessary for Air Force operations. On the other hand, Air Forces without ground support . . . are extremely vulnerable and could be rendered completely ineffectual by the sudden seizure of their airdromes.[52]

Porter stood the air power arguments on their head: since ground forces were less mobile, they had to be positioned in forward bases; air power, far from being self-sufficient, relied on ground troops.

51. White to Chief of Staff, 28 May 1943, file 320.2 (1576), OPD; Project Planning Division, "Progress Report on Demobilization Planning," 30 June 1943, file 370.9, Chief of Staff; Tompkins to Handy, 2 July 1943, file 350.06 (Study 64), SPD.
52. Porter to Tompkins, 18 July 1943, file 350.06 (Study 64), SPD.

Accordingly, G-3 proposed that the peacetime army consist of 892,000 ground forces and only 608,000 air personnel. However even Porter saw ground forces as auxiliary to air power in that their primary mission would be to hold bases for the air force.

Later in the summer of 1943 Tompkins appealed to the Operations Division to settle the dispute over the composition of the 15 million–man army. But OPD appeared to favor the air force position. The postwar army, OPD claimed, must be ready for "immediate" application of force at "any threatened point" and against "any combination of threats." "Because of the rapid rate of development and obsolescence of materiel, the air forces must be maintained at war strength since no adequate war reserve can be built up." The United States, as the "world's greatest air power," could "best furnish the air and airborne components of any International Police Forces." Ground troops could not be an M-day force.[53]

Since OPD's response did not reply to the troublesome points which G-3 had raised, OPD left the issue of ground and air strengths unresolved. In the following months other voices occasionally objected to the predominance which the AAF sought in the postwar army.[54] But the War Department gave little further attention to the question of force levels until the summer of 1944. The issues raised by Porter received no thorough airing.

OPD's sympathy for air power arguments was nonetheless prophetic of subsequent debate over the postwar army, for it showed that those arguments had penetrated far beyond AAF circles. Given the common assumption that the primary utility of UMT lay in manning a large ground army, OPD's position especially brought into question the firmness of the army's commitment to UMT. The extent of defection from the UMT cause among ground force officers was unclear in 1943 because open dissent was uncommon and few officers were involved in drafting the army's plans. The head of G-1 (Personnel), for one, questioned the efficacy of UMT in modern war. Because of the enormous industrial and economic demands exacted by total war, he suggested, many trainees would never see military service in the event of a future conflict. Furthermore, he continued:

53. Hull to Tompkins, 30 August 1943, file 350.06 (Study 64), SPD.
54. White to Tompkins, 25 February 1944, and Delacroix (for the Commanding General, Army Ground Forces) to Chief of Staff (Attn: SPD), 7 March 1944, both in file 350.06 (Study 64), SPD.

> Men who finish their training and return to civil life do not remain static.... They deteriorate physically, they acquire dependents, they acquire higher education and technical knowledge. They develop vocational skills and become engaged in essential occupations from which they should not be withdrawn in time of war. Mobilization of military manpower, therefore, must inevitably be a selective process.

Despite that criticism, the chief of G-1 did not suggest junking UMT. Instead be countered his own arguments against it by noting vaguely that "whatever military training they [trainees] receive will be of value, no matter what their wartime mission becomes."[55]

More extraordinary than G-1's criticisms were the reservations about UMT shared and suppressed by Marshall and other top-ranking officers. In October 1943 General Handy, as assistant chief of staff, recommended that the army adopt "selective military training" because it "would permit the nation to organize an armed force of the strength desired, up to the limit of the manpower available, but would not provide for a larger armed force than the political situation dictated." Marshall called that "a good suggestion."[56]

When Tompkins protested Handy's recommendation, Handy backed off, even though he believed that "purely from the view point of military efficiency, selective military training is better than universal training." Handy explained to Marshall that his decision was

> based on statements of both General Tompkins and General Palmer that universal training is essential to insure acceptance of the [army's postwar] plan by Congress and the public. Also I can see the many difficulties which would arise when some young men were selected for training and others were exempted.

Anticipating that critics would denounce selective service as undemocratic, the General Staff endorsed UMT despite doubts about its military merits. Their curiously casual decision rested on a misreading of what the American people, or at least their representatives, would accept. It rested on deeper convictions as well. Palmer and Marshall believed that the large standing army which selective service might help raise would clash with American traditions, endanger American

55. White to Tompkins, 31 December 1943, file 350.06 (Study 64), SPD.

56. Handy to Marshall, 28 October 1943, with handwritten comments by Marshall, file 370.9, Chief of Staff.

democracy, and levy an intolerable financial burden on the nation. Because it would sharply limit the size of the professional army, UMT would not run that danger, they believed.[57]

Still, Marshall and his assistants privately questioned whether a mass army based on UMT could perform the mission of quickly thwarting aggressors. As Handy wrote:

> Reserves, even though they have received military training, cannot be taken from shops, offices and farms without additional training. To crush the very beginnings of lawless aggression requires a force in being, not a potential one.

Marshall agreed. "Air Power will be the quick remedy," he noted, which was the very point the bomber enthusiasts had seized on. Though a sharp critic of excessive reliance on air power in the years before Pearl Harbor, Marshall regarded air power as the future first line of defense and deterrence. And though skeptical of the AAF's postwar plans, Tompkins agreed that the primary forces-in-being should be air units. "Ground forces would have more time to mobilize, and would have proportionately higher reserve forces," he argued.[58]

Service politics dictated that the War Department's first basic plan, the "Outline of the Post-War Military Establishment," include no statement about the predominance of air forces in the postwar army. But Marshall and his staff accepted many of the air power claims. Though their faith in air power did not prevent them from advocating UMT, it weakened their case for training. Whereas their arguments for air power stressed the critical element of readiness, their case for UMT rested on a belief that the next war would resemble World War II, though quicker and deadlier. The argument for UMT assumed that the United States would have months, though no longer years, to mobilize its forces. It posited that a year's training could impart the complex skills required by modern soldiers and that reservists would retain those skills with little or no retraining. Handed their muskets, the citizen soldiers of the 1950s and 1960s would march

57. Quotation from Handy to Marshall, 31 January 1944, file 350.06 (Study 64), SPD. See also Palmer, *America in Arms*; Palmer, "Outlines of a Post-War Military Establishment," 29 June 1943, file 370.9, Chief of Staff.

58. Handy to Marshall, 28 October 1943, with handwritten comments by Marshall, file 370.9, Chief of Staff; Tompkins to Marshall, 19 January 1944, addendum to memo, file 350.06 (Study 64), SPD. See also Pogue, *Education of a General*, chap. 19; Pogue, *Ordeal and Hope*, pp. 26–32, 76–79.

forth to defend their nation. Or their mere readiness to march would ward off aggression. UMT would give maximun deterrence at minimum cost.

Although it received far less criticism than the army's case for UMT, the air power argument also rested on an unsophisticated strategic analysis. Like other planners, AAF officers developed no scenario of how military force could deter aggression. Infatuated with strategic air power, they ignored less flashy but perhaps more decisive wartime developments in the use of tactical air power. Their single-minded focus on bombardment reflected their ambitions. Since a fleet of heavy bombers would operate largely on its own, strategic air power was the best argument for an independent air force. To acknowledge the case for tactical aviation, which would work closely with ground and naval forces, might strengthen the claims of the army and navy to continued control of air power. The AAF's glorification of strategic air power did not ordinarily constitute conscious deception. So long had the air power enthusiasts been waging their struggle for autonomy that many had internalized their faith in strategic bombing. As with the army's backers of UMT, the sincerity of their convictions hid from them their failure to analyze their arguments.[59]

The Common Ground

Despite their shortcomings and their conflicts, planners of the three services possessed a similar outlook about postwar defense. In the plans each had drawn up by the spring of 1944, they expressed their assumptions in a piecemeal fashion and tailored them to fit their pet goals. But those assumptions transcended their differences.

Top officials agreed, first of all, on the certainty of another major war. "How long before war would resume?" an intelligence officer asked. "Only so long as it would take the most aggressive of the powers to recuperate sufficiently again to attempt the imposition of its will upon others."[60] The point seemed so obvious to military men that they did not even debate it.

The services had a sharp mental model of the kind of nation most

59. Smith, *Air Force Plans*, chaps. 2–3.
60. Colonel John Weckerling, G-2, to Tompkins, 12 February 1944, file "Postwar Army," SPD.

likely to threaten world peace and American security. Repeated reference to the appeasement of the Axis in the 1930s or to "a future Hitler or Mussolini" and the "Hitler or Tojo of 1965" revealed the nature of their apprehensions.[61] The next enemy, like Germany or Japan, probably totalitarian, would be a European or westernized nation, a military colossus bent on world conquest, a master of deception, contemptuous of the rituals and compromises of diplomacy, unleashing lightning attacks on its victims. Accordingly the next war, rather than being a contest for limited aims, would pit good against evil in a death struggle:

> There can be no future war for great powers that is not total war—and "total" in a sense never before experienced. Under the circumstances there is nothing that a foresighted nation can do but make its plans so all-encompassing, so flexible, so adaptable to continually changing conditions that it would enter any new struggle fully prepared to win under the new conditions as they might then exist. A war in the future cannot be measured on a fixed historical yardstock [sic] but only on one projected into the future on the experience of the past.[62]

Projecting the war experience into the future could be dangerous. Planners tended to neglect traditional military responsibilities such as defense of American economic interests and American domination of the Western Hemisphere. Likewise they generally ignored the potential for revolutionary upheavals in colonial nations and the possibility of wars involving lesser powers. Engaged in one holocaust, they concentrated on planning for another.

In 1943 and 1944 the armed services gave only passing consideration to the identity of future adversaries. More than a specific enemy, the nature of war itself now worried them. Aggressors would soon be able to unleash sudden, deadly blows on the American homeland. The advent of planes, submarines, and missiles destroyed isolation both from direct attack and from involvement in wars between other nations. New weapons also diminished the margin of time to prepare for war once it began, military experts noted. Too, at least some planners—and the President himself—recognized that the shield

---

61. Frank Knox, "Let's Train Our Youth," *Colliers*, 29 April 1944, p. 11; John J. McCloy, "Do We Want Permanent Conscription? Yes," *Colliers*, 9 June 1945, p. 114.
62. Weckerling to Tompkins, 12 February 1944, file "Postwar Army," SPD.

from attack once provided the United States by England and other Western European nations was rapidly crumbling as the relative military power of those countries declined.[63]

The consequences for military policy of such changes seemed obvious. "To be effective," warned the army's G-2 Division, "an army must be ready for war at any moment. No time lag can be assumed or tolerated without the greatest risk."[64] Although military advisors differed over the degree of readiness the services should maintain in peacetime, they agreed that a capacity for rapid mobilization was a top priority for the peacetime military establishment. Proposals for a larger peacetime navy, universal military training, and a 105-group air force testified to that conviction.

Although such forces would help the nation fend off future attacks, defense would not be their sole or even primary purpose. Their principal task would be to deter aggression or overwhelm it at its inception. A more aggressive pursuit of national security appeared necessary because, as Forrestal explained, "if we are to keep America safe from the horror and destruction of war we must hit our enemies at great distances from our shores." Edward Mead Earle, one of the few civilian scholars close to the services, elaborated that reasoning. Given "the enormous advantage afforded the aggressor by the techniques of Poland and Pearl Harbor," he argued, "'Defense' no longer has much meaning. Neither has 'peace.' Unless a nation is ready to strike before being struck, it may not be capable of effective defense."[65]

To the military leadership, history taught that armed strength would discourage aggression just as weakness had invited it. The meaning of the 1930s appeared unmistakable. In the face of a well-armed United States, Palmer believed, it was "hardly likely that the Axis powers could have dared to enter upon the adventures of world conquest." In the military view, nations became aggressors not because of their inner dynamics and tensions but because of the

63. Analysis Section, War Department G-2 Division, "The Changing Power Position of Great Britain as a Factor in the Defense Problem of the United States," 30 June 1943, Box 4, Papers of Edward Mead Earle, Princeton University Library; U.S. Department of State, *Foreign Relations of the United States: 1944* (hereafter cited as *FR:1944*), 1:702–03.

64. Weckerling to Tompkins, 12 February 1944, file "Postwar Army," SPD.

65. Forrestal, "Proposed Speech Veterans of Foreign Wars Not Given," September 1943, Box, 49, Forrestal Papers; Edward Mead Earle, "The Factor of Military Technology," outline of comments to be given at a conference of educators and military leaders at Princeton University, September 1944, Box 4, Earle Papers.

impotence of others. According to one admiral, "if all the world understood clearly that our fleet would be used to protect the United States *before, and not after*, a series of Munich conferences, . . . the personal following of any future Hitler would be limited to a few would-be suicides." Confronted with force, aggressors cowered. However fanatical, they acted rationally.[66]

Only on rare occasions did an officer challenge the prevailing dogma of deterrence. Rejecting Palmer's claims that preparedness could prevent war, General Ray Porter contended that the valid argument for preparedness is that "proper preparedness lessens the total cost, human and material, of war." Palmer's "argument that wars can be prevented infers the likelihood of war not coming to our people and acts to undermine the will to fight of our soldiers." Citing morale problems in the recent North African campaign, Porter stated his belief "that the will to fight of Americans needs to be revived."[67] Though narrow in focus, such criticism did point out the danger of extravagant promises for deterrence, promises which suggested that American power could maintain peace without the expenditure of American life and treasure on the battlefield.

But to many defense officials the avoidance of such an expenditure seemed possible. Their confidence emerged in their fondness for equating the challenge of peacekeeping to the difficulties in combating crime and disease. In all three cases, deterrence or swift action guaranteed success. Secretary Knox, describing Axis thinking as "more loathsome to decent men than leprosy," explored the medical analogy at length:

> We do not wait until an epidemic is loosed. United effort is directed against each single individual appearance of the disease.
>
> Exactly thus must the epidemic appearances of predatory conquest be fought, and conquered. Call it fascism, the Axis or the Holy Alliance, the recurring blood-lust which afflicts nations will only be cured when it is caught in its incipient stages.

Another voice warned that the "voodoo charms" of "the pacifists, the 'do-gooders,' the religious freaks, the perfectionists, and all their

---

66. Palmer, "Proposed Legislation for Universal Military Training," n.d. [August 1942], file 380 (Postwar Planning, June 24, 1942), SPD; address by Rear Admiral Thomas L. Gatch, September 24, 1944, file 45-1-10, SecNav.

67. Paraphrase of statement by Brigadier General Ray Porter to officers of the Project Planning Division, 17 July 1943, file 337 (Conferences) (July), SPD.

idealistic ilk" could "not ward off another epidemic of war. We need a real prophylactic." Comparisons to crime-fighting were equally common. The good American policeman, surgical in his precision, would wield his power painlessly. Only the international criminal would suffer.[68]

Such analogies indicated the depth of feeling and the imprecision of thought among military leaders. As the war entered its final year, numerous ambiguities in their postwar proposals remained unresolved. Planners did not distinguish between unilateral and collective exercise of peacekeeping authority. They wavered between a regional and a global view of postwar security needs. They proposed a large ground army while extolling air power. They blurred distinctions between defensive, deterrent, and preemptive military actions. They planned for the future, yet remained mired in the past or preoccupied by the present. The confusion of their thinking and the fervor of their advocacy suggested the ideological nature of the military's programs for the postwar. The services' views on future defense sprang not from a cerebral analysis of strategic needs but rather from an intense emotional and intellectual reaction to the experiences of the thirties and forties. Few of their strategic arguments about technology and deterrence were new. But the case for preparedness was novel when judged by the pervasiveness of its acceptance and the intensity of conviction among its advocates.

The extent to which the American people and their representatives would accept that case continued to cause anxiety among military men. In 1944 the signs from the President were at least hopeful. But the attitude of other Americans toward the military's claims seemed in doubt even as American forces from Normandy to the Philippines were scoring their greatest triumphs. Repeatedly lashing out at the isolationist and pacifistic ideas which supposedly prevailed in the 1920s and 1930s, service spokesmen strove to overcome the naivete about national security which they believed habitual to Americans. A senior army general cautioned against a repetition of "the same sort of psychological disarmament which frittered away our power at the end of the first World War," while King warned the 1944 Governors' Conference against the "policy of inoffensiveness" tried twice by the United States. "With a nation grown so large in a world

68. Knox, speech before the English Speaking Union, Chicago, 6 December 1943, Box 8, Knox Papers; unsigned memorandum, n.d. [February 1944], file 353 (Jan–Feb 44), SPD.

that has shrunk so small," the navy's commander warned, "such a policy cannot succeed." While they still had the chance, Americans had to realize the precariousness of the nation's safety. "There is no such thing as security," Forrestal claimed, "and the word should be stricken from our dictionary. We should put in every school book the maxim that power like wealth must be either used or lost." The persuasiveness of such pleas would receive one of its first tests when the army and navy launched their effort to secure universal military training.[69]

69. Lieutenant General Ben Lear, Commanding General, Army Ground Forces, speech before the Spanish-American War Veterans, Cincinnati, 14 August 1944, file 350.001 (Speeches), SPD; King address before the Governors' Conference, 29 May 1944, Box 27, King Papers; Forrestal, address before the Maryland Historical Society, 10 May 1943, Box 5, Forrestal Papers.

3 THE CAMPAIGN FOR UNIVERSAL MILITARY TRAINING

The military effort to secure universal military training began against a background of discouraging portents. Some military experts questioned the usefulness of a large citizens' reserve in modern warfare, and others the willingness of Americans to support peacetime defense. Most of all, the defeat of UMT in 1919 boded ill for congressional passage of training legislation. Nonetheless, military planners were hopeful of eventual success. Past experience, they believed, revealed not only the need for universal training but the means to secure it. The ordeal of 1919 was less a bad omen than a source of instruction. The military man's perceptions, the "pictures in his head," in Lippmann's phrase,[1] convinced him that he could undo the nation's previous mistakes in rejecting preparedness and the military's own bungling in past campaigns for UMT.

The military leadership knew that disunity had weakened the defense establishment in its pursuit of UMT legislation after World War I. The navy had stood aloof from the effort to secure UMT and the War Department had split over competing postwar schemes. In World War II it appeared that the services might at last close ranks.

For once, the civilian and military heads of the War Department worked as a team. General Marshall's enthusiasm for UMT was matched by that of Secretary Stimson, for over thirty years an advocate of compulsory training. Uniting the army behind them was not easy because some officers, especially in the Army Air Forces, opposed Marshall's plans for a small professional army and a citizen's reserve. By 1943 most officers wanted UMT, however, and publicly at least the aviators remained committed to UMT throughout the war.[2]

The possible defection of the National Guard from the UMT cause

1. Quoted by Robert Dahl in *Congress and Foreign Policy* (New York: Norton, 1964), p. 18.
2. For public endorsements of UMT by the AAF, see General H. H. Arnold, "We Must Not Repeat the Mistakes of the Last War," *U.S. Air Services*, 29 (October 1944): 14; Woodrum Committee, *Hearings, UMT*, pp. 546–55.

was more worrisome than a potential rift within the regular army. Military discipline restricted the freedom of professional officers to speak out against UMT. But as a state institution and, through the National Guard Association, a private lobby, the guard was free of those restrictions. Its thick network of relationships with local communities, state governments, and congressmen, many of whom had served or continued to serve in the guard, magnified its influence. With one foot in the War Department and one foot out, the guard was in a strong position to challenge any army plans it disliked.[3]

As its leaders feared, the guard faced destruction at the hands of General Staff officers, who had long dreamed of a reserve system under federal control. Backed by Marshall and General Thomas Handy, Generals John McAuley Palmer and William Tompkins developed plans for the abolition of the guard, to be replaced by "State Guards" entirely under state control and a federal reserve under Washington's exclusive authority. Whatever the military wisdom of their proposals, their political impracticality was striking. Palmer vainly hoped that the guard would acquiesce in its own extinction. But the guard, which had helped defeat Secretary Garrison's plan for a new federal reserve in 1916 and the army's UMT bills in 1919, now threatened to call on its powerful congressional allies to kill any UMT plan which would demote or destroy it. The General Staff yielded to superior political force. The price of the guard's support for UMT was an assurance that the guard would remain a major combat element of the army. Even that assurance did not end the bitterness between the guard and the regular officer corps, but it did avert a public confrontation.[4]

Cooperation between the army and navy evolved more smoothly. The Joint Chiefs approved UMT as a postwar goal for the services on September 28, 1943.[5] During the next one and a half years, the War and Navy Departments hammered out common policies and political tactics on UMT in order to prevent any embarrassing disagreements between the two services while they campaigned for

3. Martha Derthick, *The National Guard in Politics*, is an excellent account of how the guard's multiple status has enhanced its influence.

4. Ibid., pp. 58–69; Ward, "Movement for Universal Military Training," pp. 19, 56–60; Palmer to Tompkins, 28 June 1943; Tompkins to Marshall, 18 August 1943; Handy to Marshall, 28 October 1943, all in file 370.9, Chief of Staff; Palmer to Brown, 22 October 1943, file 353 (1943), SPD; Tompkins to Handy, 20 April 1945, file 325 (National Guard), SPD.

5. Sparrow, *History of Personnel Demobilization*, p. 47.

training legislation. As with most successful efforts in joint postwar planning, collaboration on UMT proceeded on an informal basis which largely bypassed the official JCS machinery. The Bureau of Naval Personnel and the army's Special Planning Division formulated joint policies which Forrestal, Assistant Secretary of War John J. McCloy, Stimson, and Marshall reviewed. In contrast to 1919, the army and navy would speak with one voice.

The character of the military leadership also accounted for its confidence in securing UMT. Stimson, Forrestal, McCloy and many of their fellow civilian administrators represented the eastern legal and financial elite which dominated American foreign and military policy for much of the 1940s. Their background and the ease with which they got what they wanted from Congress during the war encouraged their confidence that Congress would find their arguments for UMT persuasive. Their cohesion and the inbred quality of their educational, social, and political contacts strengthened their optimism by cutting them off from opponents to UMT. Their ties were strong with pressure groups which were conservative and eastern in orientation, enthusiastic about UMT, and hopeful about its passage. Their contacts with labor and farm groups were few, and their impression of sentiment in colleges and universities was distorted by the closeness of their ties to Ivy League administrators, whose enthusiasm for UMT was atypical among college educators.

Marshall may also have been overconfident. His wartime dealings with Congress had been successful. His reliance on the advice of General Palmer, whose enthusiasm for UMT was lifelong and unshakeable, perhaps distorted his perspective. Certainly Marshall's zeal for UMT, well broadcast to the army, discouraged his staff from expressing doubts to him about the likelihood that Congress would pass a UMT bill.

More than self-deception was involved in the confidence of military leaders, for opinion polls indicated to them a dramatic change in the attitude of Americans toward compulsory training. Fewer than 40 percent of Americans approved compulsory service or training in 1939, but after the invasion of France in 1940 support shot up to 70 percent and remained high throughout the war. Approval of compulsory peacetime training was widespread in nearly all population groups and geographical regions, and especially strong among the young and the better-educated. Other polls attested to the willingness of Americans to repudiate disarmament and isolationism and to support the use of American power to enforce world peace. Carefully watched by Marshall and his staff, those polls raised their hopes that the war had transformed, if only temporarily, American attitudes toward national security.[6]

The support of powerful lobbies was further cause for optimism. The American Legion headed the list of preparedness organizations which pressed for adoption of UMT and worked closely with the services. The United States Chamber of Commerce, in close touch with the Special Planning Division, reported overwhelming sentiment for UMT within its ranks. Staff officers told of encouraging soundings among prewar interventionist groups like the Fight for Freedom Committee, and from the press came not only overwhelming editorial support, including a ringing *Daily Worker* endorsement, but assurances that, as the *New York Times* put it, UMT would face "no serious opposition" on Capitol Hill.[7]

Even educators and labor leaders appeared to be relaxing their traditional hostility to UMT. Given charges that UMT was an old-fashioned means of preparedness, the backing of scientists like Karl T. Compton was especially gratifying. Cheering, too, was the "sympathetic and cooperative" attitude supposedly shown by William Green, Philip Murray, and other labor chiefs who met with Stimson, Forrestal, Marshall, and King on November 10, 1944. Cabinet members told President Roosevelt later that day that labor had undergone a "great change" in its attitude toward military training "owing to the experience of the war." Finally, Congress, if not euphoric about UMT, at least appeared open-minded about it. Powerful representatives like Democrats Clifton Woodrum and

6. The distinction between military service and military training was not always clearly drawn in wartime polls. For poll results, see Ward, "Movement for Universal Military Training," pp. 194–98; Hadley Cantril, *Public Opinion, 1935–1946*, pp. 458–61; Jerome Brunner, *Mandate from the People*, pp. 48–60. For evidence of War Department attention to the polls, see Tompkins to Deputy Chief of Staff, 17 November 1943, file 370.9, Chief of Staff; Ovetta Culp Hobby to Tompkins, 22 November 1944, forwarding at Marshall's request certain poll results, file 353 (Oct–Nov 44), SPD.

7. Quotation from Sidney Shalett in *New York Times*, 12 September 1944. For editorial support, see War Department Bureau of Public Relations, *Universal Military Training, including Post-War Military Establishment* (title varies), Supplemental issue No. 1, bound photoreproductions, copy in the Yale University Library. On organizational support, see Ward, "Movement for Universal Military Training," pp. 60–69, 166–67; Clark to Acting Director, SPD, 6 November 1944, file 353 (Aug–Sept 44), SPD; Howard Petersen to Tompkins, 3 August 1944, file 353 (Aug–Sept 44), SPD.

Andrew May and Republican James Wadsworth were working hard for training legislation.[8]

Most important, the President seemed to be coming around. Through the years FDR had handled the UMT issue with characteristic flexibility. In 1919 he extolled compulsory training as "the surest guarantee of national safety" and a bulwark "against anarchy and Bolshevism, against class hatred, against snobbery." His public enthusiasm for training waned after 1919 but revived with the introduction of selective service legislation in 1940. During the war he tested public opinion on peacetime universal service. Typical were his rambling comments of August 18, 1944, when he discussed the military housing which the war's end would leave vacant. "Well, we will have about five million beds. What are we going to do with them?" he teased the press. "It's an awful problem. That's an awful lot of buildings." He proposed a training program modeled on the Civilian Conservation Corps to teach youth "discipline" and "how to keep clean," a program of social engineering which hardly squared with what the army and navy wanted. Eleanor Roosevelt, whose views were also scrutinized by the military, put even more emphasis on the nonmilitary virtues of citizenship training and national service.[9]

In his January 6, 1945, State of the Union message, drafted with the War Department's assistance, Roosevelt discarded talk of nonmilitary benefits. He urged that "as an essential factor in the maintenance of peace in the future we must have universal military training after this war." With the elections over, his advisors optimistic about the attitude of key New Deal groups like labor, and the

8. For the army staff's impression of sentiment in the educational community, see Tompkins to Petersen, 22 July 1944, file 353 (June–July 44), SPD; Textor to Tompkins, 5 August 1944, and Kent to Shuman, 14 September 1944, both in file 353 (Aug–Sept 44), SPD; Tompkins to Secretary, General Staff, 4 October 1944; Kent to Tompkins, 11 October 1944; Edward W. Smith to Tompkins, 28 October 1944, all in file 353 (Oct–Nov 44), SPD. For contacts between Compton and military officials, see memorandum by Howard Petersen, 13 July 1944, file 353 (1943), SPD; correspondence dating to August and September 1944 in file 353 (March 44), SPD; Compton's correspondence in file 032.2 (House Select Committee on Postwar Military Policy), SPD. On labor, see Walter Millis, ed., *The Forrestal Diaries*, p. 15; Stimson Diary, 10 November 1944. On Congress, see Ward, "Movement for Universal Military Training," chap. 2 passim.

9. Frank Freidel, *Franklin D. Roosevelt: The Ordeal*, (Boston, 1954), pp. 18–19; Rosenman, ed., *The Public Papers and Addresses of Franklin D. Roosevelt*, 13: 228–31; Ward, "Movement for Universal Military Training," pp. 70–80, 85; Stimson Diary, 23 August 1944. On Eleanor Roosevelt's views on national service, see Admiral Edwards to Forrestal, 14 August 1944, file 45–1–10, SecNav.

polls reporting overwhelming public support for training, FDR now endorsed UMT on military grounds.[10]

Roosevelt died before he could elaborate his views on UMT. How far he had committed himself to the military view of universal training remained uncertain, for he never lost his fondness for the Civilian Conservation Corps experience, his political astuteness, or his receptivity to the ideas of his budget director, Harold Smith. Joined by his assistant, Paul Appleby, who communicated his views to FDR through the President's daughter, Smith urged the President to modify the services' proposal for UMT. Like the President, Smith welcomed universal training as a device to combat a depression by siphoning men from the labor market, although FDR branded as "a callous and brazen falsehood" Governor Dewey's campaign charge that his administration wanted conscription to curb unemployment. Smith also endorsed the principle of a citizen's army. But he rejected the service's plans as too narrow in scope, rigid in conception, and sloppy in preparation. UMT, Smith argued, should embrace all but the "hopelessly handicapped" and should allow promising young men to go to college after a few months' training and work off their service obligation at a later time. Contending that the services' plans "err in the direction of asking too little an obligation" from Americans, Smith demanded use of the nation's "total resources" for "national defense." He wanted a "comprehensive postwar program" of education and service for men and women of all ages. In addition, Smith believed, a civilian commission chaired by an elder statesman like Charles Evans Hughes should study the problem of national service. Not only would such a commission have a broader perspective on the issues involved than the army and navy; it might combat the opposition of religious and educational groups to UMT and allay their suspicion that adoption of UMT would jeopardize the success of the world organization agreed upon at the Dumbarton Oaks Conference. Otherwise, Smith cautioned, UMT faced a quick death

10. Quotation from Rosenman, ed., *The Public Papers and Addresses of Franklin D. Roosevelt*, 13: 515. See also, Ward, "Movement for Universal Military Training," pp. 70–80, 85; *New York Times*, 17 August 1944, 9 September 1944, 18 November 1944. For military advice to FDR, see Millis, *Forrestal Diaries*, p. 15; Stimson Diary, 10 November 1944, 31 December 1944, 1 January 1945; McCloy to Stimson, 18 December 1944, file 353 (Dec 44), SPD; Stimson to President, 20 December 1944, file 353 Training (Aug 44–Dec 44), Records of the Office, Administrative Assistant to the Secretary of War (1943–Jan 1946), Records of the Office of the Secretary of War, RG 107, National Archives Building.

because countless Americans would consider it a militaristic proposition.[11]

Roosevelt never entirely rejected Smith's suggestions, but neither Harry Hopkins nor Sam Rosenman warmed to Smith's civilian commission.[12] A March 1945 article by Hopkins may have indicated that Roosevelt stuck closely to the military view of UMT. At least the military, in light of Hopkins's close identification with the President, probably regarded the Hopkins piece as expressing FDR's last word on UMT. Hopkins presented UMT as the necessary deterrent to international villainy:

> Our country is the one that marauders most want to conquer. What a nation to loot! What do they care if they lose two wars, or three, or four—if eventually they win? The final conquest of North America would make a dozen defeats worth while to the pillagers, and if we ever again are so weak that they have a chance to defeat us, World War III will loom on the horizon.

The Dumbarton Oaks Conference, was a first step, but Hopkins noted, "we can't take a chance" that world organization might fail. In Germany and Japan "powerful forces . . . are preparing even now for their new attempt to conquer us." Armed with "robot bombs, armies landed from the air and from submarines, enormous bombing planes, and perhaps gas" and "fifth columns," the future enemy would crush the United States unless she could ward off or anticipate its blows. No military man ever presented the case for UMT more vividly than Hopkins.[13]

11. For the campaign charge and FDR's reply, see Davis R. B. Ross, *Preparing for Ulysses: Politics and Veterans During World War II*, p. 168–69, and Rosenman, ed., *The Public Papers and Addresses of Franklin D. Roosevelt*. 13: 289–90. The views of Smith and Appleby and their contacts with FDR are shown in: Harold Smith, Daily Record, 22 August 1944, 22 December 1944, 30 December 1944, 2 January 1945, 6 January 1945; Smith memoranda of 31 August 1944, 16 November 1944; Smith to Rosenman, 2 January 1945 and 11 January 1945, White House Memoranda, all in Papers of Harold Smith, FDR Library; Paul H. Appleby to Anna Boettiger, 4 November 1944, file "Military Training," Box 194; note, Anna Boettiger to Grace Tully, n.d. [November 1944], Box 194; Appleby to Hopkins, 27 November 1944, Box 137 ("Congress") and Box 194 ("Military Training"), all in Papers of Harry Hopkins, FDR Library; Smith to President, 29 December 1944 (source for Smith quotations), file "Message to Congress, January 6, 1945," and Smith to President, 30 December 1944, both in Box 17, Papers of Samuel I. Rosenman, FDR Library; FDR to Rosenman, 5 January 1945; Rosenman to President, 11 January 1945; FDR to Hopkins, 17 January 1945; Hopkins to FDR, 19 January 1945, all in President's Official Files 109 (1945), Papers of Franklin D. Roosevelt, FDR Library.

12. FDR to Rosenman, 5 January 1945; Rosenman to President, 11 January 1945; Hopkins to FDR, 19 January 1945, all in President's Official Files 109 (1945), FDR Papers; Smith to Rosenman, 11 January 1945, White House Memoranda, Smith Papers.

13. Harry L. Hopkins, "Tomorrow's Army and Your Boy," *The American Magazine*, March 1945, pp. 20, 104.

Roosevelt's State of the Union message, along with his approval of a far-flung system of postwar bases and his apparent decision to maintain an Anglo-American monopoly on the atomic bomb, reflected his conviction that the United States should have powerful military forces after the war. A longtime believer in the diplomatic efficacy of American military power, the President was not going to play postwar diplomacy with a weak hand. In one form or another, he wanted UMT.

FDR's position must have cheered the UMT campaigners and bolstered their confidence that UMT would enjoy broad public support cutting across party and ideological lines. The partisanship and divisiveness of 1919 would be replaced by consensus.

Political Strategy

Military planners believed that by scrutinizing the defeat of UMT in 1919 they could learn the proper course to follow in the 1940s. Palmer's reading of the earlier failure was especially important. Palmer believed that a recrudescence of pacifism and complacency about national security after World War I, as well as political con- fusion in the war's aftermath, had helped to kill UMT. UMT had been "completely lost in the shuffle" in 1919.[14]

In order "to avoid a repetition of this catastrophe," Palmer and Representative James Wadsworth began in 1942 to map the legislative campaign for UMT. Wadsworth, who as a senator twenty-three years earlier had befriended Palmer and spearheaded the congres- sional drive for UMT, argued in the summer of 1942 that UMT "would have a good chance in the next Congress" but if "initiated after the war would almost certainly encounter unfavorable postwar reaction." The first prerequisite for enactment of UMT was to force the issue while the war was still on. Detailed legislation was not urgent, but a congressional commitment to the broad principle of universal training was.[15]

The alternative to speedy passage seemed obvious to the planners. After the war, "the pacifists, the 'do-gooders,' the religious freaks,

14. Palmer, "Notes on the War Plans Division Plan of April 1, 1919," 17 July 1942, file 380 (Postwar Planning, June 24, 1942), SPD; Palmer to Textor, 23 November 1943, file 353 (1943), SPD; Palmer, draft of speech for Representative James Wadsworth, 11 January 1944, file 353 (Jan–Feb 44), SPD.

15. Palmer to Chief of Staff (through Assistant Chief of Staff, G-1), 22 July 1942, Chronologi- cal Files 1942–43, Box 10, Palmer Papers.

the perfectionists, and all their idealistic ilk" would come "to the surface again encrusted with the barnacles of ancient argument." The army and navy had to strike quickly, before there arose "the general lethargy and wishful thinking of this country which invariably sets in after a successful war."[16]

Military spokesmen were wary of openly citing the fickleness of public opinion as a reason for quick action on UMT. They did not want to insult the public or appear insensitive to the charge that precipitate action on UMT might antagonize the nation's wartime allies. Instead they argued that delay in passage of UMT would court military weakness, thwart the popular will, and in case of a military emergency after the defeat of the Axis, unjustly force veterans of World War II back into combat because their younger brothers would be unfit to fight. Enactment of UMT after a few years' peace would arouse more anxiety among other nations than would passage during the war, they contended. Further, if the war ended without a decision on UMT, the services would be forced to shut down their vast training facilities and organization, which could be activated later only with "stupendous" difficulty and cost. However sincerely offered, such arguments obscured the more basic reason for urgency on the military's part, its distrust of public opinion.[17]

The history of popular attitudes toward the military also taught the army and navy that they should play up the civilian backing for compulsory training as well as appeal to the nation's traditions of democracy and civil rule over the military. The services feared that a high-pressure campaign might run them afoul of the Hatch Act, which forbade attempts by government employees to influence legislation before Congress. The wisdom of their caution became

16. Quotations from Colonel William Carpenter (SPD), memorandum, "Universal Military Training," n.d. [February 1944], file 353 (Jan–Feb 44), SPD; McCloy to Dr. William F. Russell (Dean, Columbia Teachers College), 4 December 1944, file 353 (Dec 44), Records of the Assistant Secretary of War (1940–47), SecWar. See also Carpenter to Textor, 15 December 1944, file 353 (Dec 44), SPD.

17. Comments by John J. McCloy, in transcript of Chicago Round Table broadcast (NBC), 26 November 1944, p. 11, file 353 (Oct 43–Nov 44), ASW; memorandum by Anderson, Persons and Smith, 4 December 1944; Weible to Tompkins, 6 December 1944; Carpenter to Textor, 15 December 1944; Textor to Weible, 15 December 1944; Handy to Textor, Persons, McCloy, Weible, Porter, and Henry, 16 December 1944; Textor and Persons to Handy, 18 December 1944, all in file 353 (Dec 44), SPD; "The War and Navy Departments' Views on Universal Military Training," May 1945, pp. 17, 20, file P11-1(30), CNO-Cominch Records; Marshall transcript, "Comments . . . 3 May 1945 . . . ," file Plans and Policy Office UMT Decimal File (1944–48) 020 Chief of Staff, L&LD.

evident in 1947, when a House subcommittee did censure the army for improper use of public funds during a hard-sell crusade for UMT after the war.[18] More important, the army and navy were fearful that an elaborate campaign would provoke the charge of militarism so often leveled at them in the past.

To forestall that charge, the services took several steps. First, they drew on the tactics used for passing selective service in 1940, tactics familiar to Marshall, Palmer, Stimson, and Representative Wadsworth because they were veterans of the earlier effort. In 1940, Roosevelt and his military advisors, afraid that an open request for selective service would antagonize the anti-interventionists, encouraged Grenville Clark's preparedness lobby to push draft legislation on its own initiative. Only after the movement for selective service gained momentum did the administration openly espouse the Burke-Wadsworth bill.[19] Soon after Pearl Harbor, Palmer and Wadsworth agreed to a similar strategy of civilian sponsorship for UMT legislation. Though military endorsement of such legislation could not long be withheld, congressmen like Wadsworth would take the lead in pushing a UMT bill.[20]

Service leaders tried to keep a low profile in soliciting public support. They wrote articles on UMT, appeared occasionally on radio, and made speeches. They also held a series of private meetings with leaders of key pressure groups, among them racial, religious, educational, labor, women's, and veterans' organizations, whose opposition to UMT was especially feared or whose support was deemed critical. But in 1944 and 1945 they concentrated on public appearances before congressional committees in order to preserve the fiction that the services were only responding to civilian demands for information. Confident of popular support, the military eschewed mass merchandising and whenever possible relied on civilians to present the case for UMT.[21]

---

18. For the story of the censure action and the propaganda activities which prompted it, see Ward, "Movement for Universal Military Training," pp. 211–28.

19. For a brief account, see Weigley, *U.S. Army*, pp. 425–27.

20. Palmer to President of the Board on Post-War Planning, 8 August 1942, file 380, SPD.

21. Transcript, "Conference for Service Command Representatives on Universal Military Training, 20 December 1944," file 353 (Dec 44), SPD; transcript, "Conference for Service Command and Supervisory Chaplains on Universal Military Training, 6 April 1945," file 353 (March 45), SPD; General Council Minutes, 1 May 1944.

Similarly, proponents of training stressed how their plans upheld civilian authority and conformed to democratic traditions. General Palmer portrayed UMT as only the modern expression of the militia obligation incumbent on Americans since colonial times and embodied in President Washington's plans for national defense. As a means of raising sufficient manpower to insure preparedness, UMT was the only alternative to a large standing army whose cost would be prohibitive, whose ranks could not be filled without an inequitable draft, and whose power would endanger American democracy. Palmer and Marshall believed that such an army would impose so great a financial burden on the nation that Americans would not dare reject universal training.

Palmer elaborated the political argument for UMT. In a large standing army, he reasoned, power tended to gravitate to a small caste of professional officers isolated from and uncontrolled by democratic institutions. UMT, on the other hand, would exercise a continuous leavening effect on the professional establishment. A professional force might be a ready weapon in the hands of an adventurist president or commander. Under the services' UMT plan, the provision that only Congress could call UMT reservists to active duty would stay the hand of the impetuous leader, who would have at his command only a skeletal professional army. To the contention of some critics that the practice of universal service had fostered militarism in Germany and Japan, Palmer replied that Switzerland and Sweden also relied on universal service. UMT posed no danger in itself, he argued. "It all depends on what the training is for. Universal Training for what is good IS GOOD. Universal training for what is evil IS EVIL."[22]

The services maintained that their scheme was also democratic in that it would impose on all young men an obligation to serve their country. The mingling of well-born and lowly young trainees would be the essence of the democratic experiment. Yet military and political needs dictated certain exemptions from service which

22. Quotation from Palmer to Textor, 23 November 1943, file 353 (1943), SPD. For Palmer's views on the democratic nature of the military's UMT plans, see Palmer, *America in Arms*; U.S. Congress, House Select Committee on Postwar Military Policy, *Hearings, Proposal to Establish a Single Department of the Armed Forces*, 78/2, 1944, pp. 5–13; Woodrum Committee, *Hearings, UMT*, pp. 489–93; War Department Circular 347, in *New York Times*, 3 September 1944.

undermined the claim that UMT would be "truly universal."[23] Marshall insisted on exemptions for boys with religious scruples against military training lest the services "create strong, unreasoning resentment" against UMT.[24] Members of families of foreign diplomatic personnel would be exempt, as would all American women. A large pool of physically, mentally, or morally unfit youngsters would escape service, for the military wanted no part of a program of social, educational, and medical rehabilitation. Of approximately 1.2 million men who would annually enter the training pool, one-third would receive exemptions.[25]

All others, except those who chose to enlist directly in the regular army or navy, would undergo an uninterrupted year of training. Six hundred thousand would go to the army and AAF, and two hundred thousand to the navy. So that privileged young men could not escape duty alongside the less fortunate, enlistment in the National Guard, the reserves, or the Reserve Officers Training Corps, or appointment to a service academy would take effect only after a boy's year of training. Trainees could select the branch of service in which they wished to enrol, within the limits of manpower needs. Their training would fall between the ages of seventeen and twenty. A civilian organization would set the exact date of induction based on time of graduation from high school and the necessity of staggering inductions through the year. Once he completed his training, a young man would face a five-year reserve obligation, but no active duty unless Congress declared a national emergency.

In a further effort to avoid the appearance of militarism, the services confined their arguments for UMT to strictly military considerations. For decades some Americans, by no means just military men, had endorsed UMT as a means to achieve nonmilitary

23. "The War and Navy Departments' Views on Universal Military Training," p. 5, file P11-1(30), CNO-Cominch Records.

24. Marshall to Tompkins, n.d. [October 1944], file 353 (March 44), SPD.

25. The figures here and those which follow varied slightly during the war in the statements used by the military. The most accessible sources for details of the army-navy plan are: "The War and Navy Departments' Views on Universal Military Training," file P11-1(30), CNO-Cominch Records; Woodrum Committee, *Hearings, UMT*, pp. 498–508, 533–46; William F. Tompkins, "Future Manpower Needs of the Armed Forces," *Annals of the American Academy of Political and Social Science* 238 (March 1945): 56–62; John J. McCloy, "The Plan of the Armed Forces for Universal Military Training," *Annals of the American Academy of Political and Social Science* 241 (September 1945): 26–34.

objectives of social regeneration and national unity. Alarmed by the scale of immigration and industrial strife early in the century, political leaders like Franklin D. Roosevelt had seized on UMT as a device to restore cohesion to society and Americanize, as General Pershing put it, "ignorant foreigners" who were "highly susceptible to the anarchistic or bolshevic proposals of numerous agitators."[26] During World War II, the partnership of government, science, and education suggested to some educators the potential of social engineering. Typical was the proposal made by Robert M. Yerkes, a Yale psychologist who believed Americans to be "sadly in need of discipline." Yerkes recommended using UMT to "teach the individual obedience, self-control, self-dependence, social cooperativeness, and also ability to lead and to command." Women, too, should receive training, though because of "the biological and social differentia of male and female" their training would stress "domestic science, homemaking, parenthood, [and] child-rearing." Karl T. Compton and others voiced similar ideas.[27]

Many defense officials opposed the pursuit of any but military objectives. Programs like Yerkes's would only divert the services from their real duties, they argued. Any program to achieve grandiose social goals also would be "exploited by every zealot with a crusade to promote and by every selfish individual and agency with wares to sell." General Porter also pointed out that opponents of UMT would pounce on any claim that UMT would inculcate social or political values "as evidence that the Army is become a gigantic agency of propaganda."[28] The two services should sidestep claims that would subject them to accusations of social regimentation and stick to a policy of defending UMT solely as a program to enhance military security.

The army and navy never fully succeeded in enforcing that policy, partly because they were reluctant to offend those who supported UMT on militaristic grounds. Just as important, the services' own spokesmen, especially civilians like Stimson and Frank Knox who

26. Quoted in Ward, "Movement for Universal Military Training," p. 32.
27. Memorandum by Robert M. Yerkes, forwarded by Palmer to Tompkins in letter of 28 November 1943, file 353 (1943), SPD; Compton to Tompkins, 23 August 1944, file 353 (March 44), SPD; Neal M. Cross and E. A. Cross to Forrestal, 7 October 1944, file A 16-1 (unclassified), Records of the Bureau of Naval Personnel, RG 24, National Archives Building.
28. Porter memorandum, with materials on Compton letter of 23 August 1944, file 353 (March 44), SPD.

were custodians of an older tradition, sometimes violated the policy. Knox believed that UMT would arrest the growth of "mental and nervous disorders" among young Americans. Stimson saw UMT as a means to envigorate America's citified youth and "rub smooth the sharp edges of prejudice, sectionalism, and lack of understanding between groups in different parts of our land."[29] More than the officer corps, the services' civilian leadership was vulnerable to militarism, the employment of military institutions for civilian purposes. The demands of total war made the nature of militarism more difficult to recognize. If war claimed the energies of every citizen, then might not any civilian activity involve "preparation for fighting"? Most service spokesmen recognized the political folly of an affirmative answer to that question.

All in all, the armed services fashioned a training proposal designed to sooth popular sensibilities while maintaining military standards. Young men seventeen to twenty years old would be more pliable in the hands of their military trainers than older men, as the services knew from their wartime experiences; but younger men would also be less inconvenienced in schooling, career, and family responsibilities. A broad liability for service would provide a large manpower pool for the services, but also ward off charges that the military was an elitist, undemocratic organization. The services would use UMT to strengthen national defense, not to revive social unity and moral fiber.

The army and navy decided to resist any compromise of their plans for UMT, especially of their insistence on one continuous year of training. On that matter they caught fire from two sides. Some critics argued that a year's training was too short for the inculcation of the complex skills needed for modern warfare. Others contended that less extensive training, or training broken up over several summers, would suffice. UMT defenders conceded that some soldiers, especially in air units, would need more than a year's training, and they expressed the hope that some men would volunteer for extra instruction. Against the more common charge that a year's training was needlessly long, the army and navy argued that shorter or interrupted training would not impart the skills necessary for mech-

29. Frank Knox, "Let's Train Out Youth," *Colliers*, 29 April 1944, p. 12; Stimson testimony, Woodrum Committee, *Hearings, UMT*, p. 483.

anized warfare. Training stretched out over several summers would necessitate repetition of instruction, require more total time, and extend the period of military liability to an age when a man's usefulness had declined and his civilian obligations had expanded.

The services resisted compromise on their UMT plans despite pressure from Harold Smith, the budget director, and from numerous special interests. Some factions within the military sought exemption from training for appointees to the service academies. The Chamber of Commerce joined military schools and colleges in asking that students at private military institutions be excused from UMT, while the National Guard sought special favors to encourage enlistment in its ranks. Compton and other scientists insisted on exemptions for young men in scientific training. Although educators and college administrators attacked UMT as a violation of the nation's democratic traditions, some also pressed for an undemocratic protection of their own interests. Suffering from diminished enrollments during the war, and convinced that an interruption in a young man's education would sour him on college, they sought various exemptions for college students. Other educators wanted training spread out over several summers.[30]

To succumb to any demands for changes in their plans would, military leaders believed, "open a floodgate" holding back the sea of special-interest proposals. Once a precedent of compromise was set, every interested lobby would clamor for special favors. The subsequent political haggling and logrolling might delay a vote on UMT legislation and, worse, "would do violence to a great principle of democracy," so Marshall believed. Any "doctrine of special privilege . . . for those intellectually and economically protected within our system of higher education" would undermine the political strategy of the services, argued one staff officer. "If a system of compulsory military training seems in the slightest degree unfair, to require from any individual uncommon sacrifice, the ground work is immediately laid for successful attack upon that system."[31]

By autumn 1944, the army and navy hoped that the political

30. *New York Times*, 14 January 1945; Shuman to Tompkins, 17 March 1944; General W. E. Smith to SPD, 1 April 1944, both in file 353 (March 44), SPD; memorandum by Howard C. Petersen, 13 July 1944, file 353 (1943), SPD; Tompkins to Secretary, General Staff, 4 October 1944; Milton G. Baker to Tompkins, 4 November 1944, both in file 353 (Oct–Nov 44), SPD.

31. Marshall to Dr. Lewis Perry, 7 December 1944, file 353 (Oct–Nov 44), SPD; Shuman to Tompkins, 17 March 1944, file 353 (March 44), SPD.

strategy they had developed would ensure congressional approval of universal training. During the previous two years, the demands of the war effort, congressional caution, disagreements among preparedness lobbies, and the 1944 elections had delayed or disrupted their drive. Now they were ready to accelerate the UMT campaign. They had taken the nation's pulse on UMT and allowed themselves to think it strong. To oversee their efforts they had knit together an organization headed by Assistant Secretary McCloy, who coordinated War Department activities with those of the Bureau of Naval Personnel and Forrestal's office in the Navy Department. To avoid "confusion in the public mind," all army statements on UMT were cleared through McCloy's office.[32] Most important, the services had culled from the past the "lessons" that would supposedly guide them to success. Speedy consideration of UMT, as the military saw it, would capitalize on wartime sentiment for preparedness. The soft sell and the emphasis on the congruency of UMT with democratic traditions would allay fears of military aggrandizement. In that event, 1945 would not be 1919 all over again.

An Uncertain Campaign

The UMT drive soon faltered, the victim first of all of bad timing and the unpredictable fortunes of war. In August, just before the drive opened, victory in Europe had seemed at hand, perhaps possible by Christmas. But through the fall German resistance stiffened, then in December erupted in the brief counterattack through the Ardennes forest. By then, Nazi resilience had so chastened the administration that, at the behest of the services, it sought enactment of a national service law. A proposal whose fortunes had ebbed and flowed throughout the war, among its proponents national service legislation gained renewed importance at the end of 1944 because of the Battle of the Bulge, a falloff in draft inductions, and a drift away from war industries by civilians eager to obtain peacetime jobs. A national service law would give the government power to assign all citizens to the jobs it deemed necessary and thus prevent a relaxation on the home front as the war neared its end.

32. General Council Minutes, 27 November 1944; Persons to McCloy, 15 November 1944, file 353 (61), Chief of Staff.

National service was doomed from the start. Businessmen saw in it a dangerous precedent for the coercion of industry. With some justification, labor condemned it as a union-busting device. Fresh Allied victories in Europe soon made it appear unnecessary. By March, service legislation was dead in Congress, but not before it had damaged the UMT cause.[33]

The attempt to get national service forced suspension of the UMT campaign. Stimson and his colleagues wanted to give national service legislation priority over the several UMT bills then pending in Congress. They considered national service more urgent, and they feared, rightly, that the two measures would become confused in the public mind, to the detriment of both. They also did not want talk of postwar measures to deflate war spirit. Therefore they halted their UMT campaign, asked FDR to withhold a message on UMT legislation promised in his January 1945 State of the Union address, and arranged with congressional leaders once again to postpone hearings on universal training.[34]

Delay was not the only injury inflicted on the UMT cause by the futile pursuit of national service. As the army's legislative experts warned, the public tended to confuse UMT and national service. The confusion arose because the two measures were similar in content, supported by the same people, and justified by the same arguments: the services cited the impact of both measures on American and enemy morale as much as they pointed to more tangible military benefits. Labor leaders, long fearful of UMT as an antilabor weapon, were especially prone to equate the two types of legislation. UMT fell heir to the hostility generated by the debate over national service.[35]

Equally disturbing during the last winter of the war was a controversy over the army's policy of sending into combat teenagers with as little as fifteen weeks' training. Critics charged that the War

33. On national service legislation, see Pogue, *Organizer of Victory*, pp. 448–97; Byron Fairchild and Jonathan Grossman, *The Army and Industrial Manpower*, chap. 11; Richard Polenberg, *War and Society: The United States, 1941–1945*, pp. 175–82.

34. Stimson Diary, 2 December 1944, 27 December 1944, 2 January 1945, 9 January 1945, 10 January 1945, 13 January 1945; Patterson to Stimson, 5 January 1945, Box 26, Papers of Robert P. Patterson, Library of Congress; Stimson to President, 12 January 1945, and President to Stimson, 16 January 1945, both in folder "White House Correspondence," Secretary of War's Safe File, SecWar.

35. Ward, "Movement for Universal Military Training," pp. 96–97; Persons to McCloy, 2 March 1945, file 353 (March–April 45), SPD; transcript, "Conference for Service Command and Supervisory Chaplains on Universal Military Training, 6 April 1945," p. 11, file 353 (March 45), SPD.

Department had broken a promise made at the start of the war to give a year's training to any young man under twenty. The army had in fact made no binding commitment on length of training, but the apparent disparity between promise and policy damaged army credibility. Nor was the army practice of sending supposedly helpless boys into combat calculated to reassure public confidence in how the military services might handle peacetime trainees. Finally, the use of fifteen-week trainees jeopardized the army's case for a year's training in peacetime. The War Department pointed out that the boys sent to Germany could fight after a few months' training only because they entered units experienced in combat. In contrast, the army noted, at the start of a future emergency the services would need "whole units composed of trained reserves" and "highly-skilled specialists." Whether the distinction between unit and individual training was convincing to civilians seemed in doubt to army officials. Marshall and General Eisenhower found the dispute over length of training so bitter that they stepped up efforts to publicize the army's victories in the hope of recovering dwindling support for its postwar programs.[36]

Nineteen forty-five also brought mounting evidence, not all of it appreciated at the time, that public support for UMT was not as great as military leaders had hoped. Backing for UMT was widespread, but soft. If most Americans approved peacetime training, few attached a high priority to it, and many regarded it less as a military measure than as a device for building character in young men. In contrast, the opposition to UMT was small in numbers but determined, well organized, and articulate.[37]

Stimson, Forrestal, and their associates had been cheered by their private meetings with religious, educational, and labor leaders, but most of those leaders remained opposed to UMT, or at best

36. Quotations from McCloy to Marshall, 13 June 1945, file 353 (157), Chief of Staff. Pogue, *Organizer of Victory*, pp. 449–502, 552–53, gives a good account of the controversy and the reactions of Marshall and Eisenhower. For congressional and popular criticism of the army, see Cantril, *Public Opinion*, p. 470; Chief of Staff 353 files; and the files of the Adm. Asst. SecWar 353 (Training), for the winter of 1944–45.

37. For analyses of the political outlook for UMT, see Ward, "Movement for Universal Military Training," pp. 166–98; Cantril, *Public Opinion*, pp. 458–61, 469–70, 472; Captain George E. McCracken, "The Army Ground Forces and Universal Military Training", pp. 38–61, useful though it examines a later period in the UMT struggle; Bureau of the Budget, "The Army-Navy Proposal for Universal Military Training: A Preliminary Analysis of the Problem and the Program," November 1944, pp. 2–7, unpublished study, copy in file 353 (March 44), SPD.

neutral. UMT drew support among primary and secondary school educators, but many college officials still feared the effect of UMT on enrollments. Like many educators, leaders of religious groups objected to the allegedly destructive effect UMT might have on international amity and to the regimentation it might impose on American youth. Some religious groups harbored lurid fears of how the military would wrench boys from the strict moral environment of church and family. UMT might expose their sons to the disease and degradation of military bases, where "taverns have proved bases of operations for promiscuous women; sources of exploitation of teen-age, bobby-sox school girls and fertile disseminators of venereal disease." Certain groups may well have viewed UMT as another agent in the disruption of their rural, fundamentalist culture, already under assault because of the sweeping social changes induced by the war. Farm families, enjoying disproportionate representation in Congress, were also cool to the idea of losing their sons' labor for a year. Even the most divergent political interests were sometimes linked in opposition to UMT. Negroes, angry over the "humiliating experience" they suffered at the hands of the military during the war, were sure that UMT would be another instrument of segregation. For their part, white southern politicians condemned it as a scheme to effect integration.[38]

The Budget Bureau warned the armed services about some of the obstacles to passage of a UMT bill. "If the majority is merely lukewarm in its support and the minority becomes sufficiently angry to make a real fight, it can probably stop action." The bureau advised against forcing an early vote on UMT legislation in order to capitalize on war fever:

> It amounts to saying to the public, this has to be done now because two years from now you will be too stupid to permit it. The blunt fact is that this kind of legislative strategy is trickery. It will be recognized by the public as such. If the legislation won't be needed until later, later is the time to enact it.

38. See n. 37. Quotations are from Woodrum Committee, *Hearings, UMT*, p. 294 (remarks by Women's Christian Temperance Union spokesman); "Transcript of Committee Meeting Conference of The Secretary of War and The Secretary of the Navy and Their Staffs With Leading Educators of the Country," 29 December 1944, pp. 24–25 (remarks by the president of Howard University), file 353 (Dec 44), SPD. See also Woodrum Committee, *Hearings, UMT*, pp. 91–107, 111–17, 313–15, 615–17; Truman Gibson to McCloy, 30 January 1945, file 353 UMT (Jan 45–May 31, 1945), ASW.

General Palmer and the SPD staff read the bureau's report, but apparently gave it little heed.[39]

By spring of 1945 the military leadership felt trapped by conflicting political considerations. In March General Persons, chief of the army's Legislative and Liaison Division, advised that it would be "fatal" to have Congress pass on UMT in the near future. In addition to the hostility generated by the winter's controversies, the army was "in for much more criticism over the troublesome subject of communists in the Army." The imminent Allied victory in Europe and the upcoming San Francisco Conference of the United Nations would preoccupy Congress and diminish concern for preparedness. Persons's warnings reached Marshall, who concurred in them. McCloy, Persons, and Admiral Jacobs then met with Congressman Woodrum to arrange still another delay of his committee's hearings on UMT.[40]

Yet if a spring campaign appeared dangerous, the penalty for delay appeared greater. With the war about to end, Persons wrote resentfully in April, Congress was resuming its old ways.

> Until recently Congress has responded to the Army as the desperate householder, whose home is in flames, welcomes the Fire Department; drive over the lawn, chop down the doors, throw the furniture out the window, but save the home. Now, with the flames under control, the Congress, like the householder, is noting for the first time the water damages and thinking that if the Fire Department had acted differently, the lawn would not be torn up, the doors smashed, and the furniture broken.

The "traditional fear" Americans held of "military ascendancy over civilian government" and the desire of Congress to reassert its power spelled trouble for the services.[41]

Attacks on the military seemed to prophesy a return to the 1920s and 1930s, or, as Marshall worried, "to the same misinformed and

39. Quotations from Bureau of the Budget, "The Army-Navy Proposal for Universal Military Training: A Preliminary Analysis of the Problem and the Program," November 1944, pp. 4, 9, file 353 (March 44), SPD. See also SPD Organization Branch to Textor, 8 November 1944, file 353 (March 44), SPD; Palmer to Don K. Price, 23 November 1944, Chronological Files 1943–44, Box 11, Palmer Papers.

40. Persons to McCloy, 12 March 1945, copies in file 353 (March–April 45), SPD, and in file 353 (158), Chief of Staff; General Council Minutes, 19 March 1945.

41. Persons to Marshall, 29 April 1945, quoted in Sparrow, *History of Personnel Demobilization*, p. 111.

nearly disastrous viewpoint [on national security] that prevailed 6 years ago." The chief of staff was uneasy about resentment among soldiers who found themselves shipped to the Pacific after fighting in Europe. He also feared a backlash of public opinion against the military as the war drew to a close. Consequently, he pleaded with his staff to carry out redeployment and demobilization as skillfully and humanely as possible. But he found his own officers slow to recollect the years of retrenchment after World War I, when budgets were "fantastic—if that's the proper word—in their smallness." "I must state to you," he told one group of officers in June, "that I find in the War Department . . . a state of mind that is utterly different from my own. Frankly I can't understand it." War, he sensed, had accustomed officers to think that money was unlimited.[42]

A further setback in the UMT campaign came in April with Rossevelt's death, which forced the services to seek the new President's commitment to UMT. Harry Truman came to his office awed by his responsibilities, ignorant of postwar plans, and essentially unknown to military leaders. As chairman of the Senate War Investigating Committee, Truman had been impressed by Marshall, but the senator had not earned the respect of the military. Stimson, annoyed by Truman's probes of the Manhattan Project, once dismissed him as "a nuisance and a pretty untrustworthy man" who "talks smoothly but acts meanly."[43]

Military leaders soon changed their opinion of Truman. On April 18, 1945, Forrestal and Admiral King sounded out the new President on UMT and found him favorably disposed toward it, an impression confirmed later by Congressman Woodrum. Marshall and Stimson made new approaches to the President in May, and the navy learned that James F. Byrnes, soon to be secretary of state, was enthusiastic about UMT. But a long wait ensued before the new Commander-in-Chief would spell out his views on training. Though Truman would later emerge as a tenacious proponent of UMT,

42. Quotations from unedited transcript of Marshall's comments before the Annual Conference of Supervisory Chaplains, 5 April 1945, file 353 (197), Chief of Staff; transcript, "Army Service Forces Seventh Semi-Annual Service Command Conference, Camp Grant, Illinois, 28, 29 and 30 June 1945," file 337 (Conferences), SPD. See also Marshall, "Comments . . . 3 May 1945 . . . ," file Plans and Policy Office UMT Decimal File (1944–48) 020 Chief of Staff, L&LD.

43. Quotation from Stimson Diary, 13 March 1944. On Truman's attitude toward Marshall, see Weigley, *Towards an American Army*, p. 247.

in his first months in office the urgency of such other business as the war's end in Europe, Russian diplomacy, and atomic policy prevented him from giving close attention to UMT and discouraged his military advisors from pressing him. At a June 1 news conference he confined himself to a vague endorsement of UMT and a statement that his ideas on UMT did not entirely accord with those of the services. The armed services entered the critical Woodrum Committee hearings in June without the President's firm backing.[44]

Just as worrisome was "the hysterical zeal" with which Americans, in the eyes of the military, greeted the San Francisco Conference convened in April to set up the United Nations Organization. The conference, military advisors feared, was eclipsing the UMT campaign and leaving the services vulnerable to the charge of prejudicing the success of the UN. The services "would be at a terrific loss" to explain why Congress should vote on UMT before the United Nations had even determined America's responsibilities in the world organization. Yet further delay on a UMT vote appeared risky to the army and navy. If the conference succeeded—"and though it is a mild success, it will probably be hailed as a great success"— UMT would appear unnecessary. If the outcome of the conference were uncertain, the administration might postpone action on UMT lest it poison future negotiations on the nature of the UN.[45]

The dilemma was not new. For months the services had been stung by criticisms that UMT would violate the ideals for which the war was fought and would alienate the nation's allies. Budget Bureau officials and others had warned of the political potency of such criticisms. As the services knew, they dared not appear to be sabotaging the San Francisco Conference or training their guns on the Soviet Union. Yet the army and navy were reluctant to respond directly to criticisms which involved foreign policy. The ethic of civilian rule, however undermined by the war, taught officers that

44. For military contacts with Truman and Byrnes in the spring of 1945, see Marshall to Tompkins, 1 May 1945, and Marshall to Truman, 5 May 1945, both in file 370.01 (77), Chief of Staff; Weible to McCloy, 11 May 1945, and Robert Cutler, memorandum on talk with McCloy, 11 May 1945, both in file 353 UMT (Jan 45–May 31, 1945), ASW; Stimson to President, 30 May 1945, folder "White House Correspondence," Secretary of War's Safe File, SecWar; Smith, Memorandum on Conference with the President, 5 June 1945, Smith Papers; "Presentation, *Post War Navy*, Thursday, 7 June 1945," folder "Postwar Navy," Box 23, Forrestal Papers.
45. Persons to McCloy, 12 March 1945, file 353 (March–April 45), SPD; Persons to McCloy, 19 April 1945, file 353 UMT (Jan 45–May 31, 1945), ASW.

they were to execute, not formulate, foreign policy. Common sense told them that they would only antagonize their critics if they appeared to usurp the State Department's job.[46]

To resolve the predicament, Stimson in December 1944 implored Secretary of State Stettinius to "join with us" in advocating UMT. The diplomats, Stimson hoped, could respond to critics of the military and lend authority to the services' claims that UMT would strengthen world peace. Not all State Department officials were happy about the military's UMT program. Assistant Secretary of State Archibald MacLeish, for one, condemned McCloy's effort to champion UMT as in conflict with McCloy's role as a delegate to the San Francisco Conference. But Joseph Grew, acting secretary of state during much of 1945, and other senior officials proved to be the willing collaborators whom McCloy, Stimson, and Forrestal sought. The State Department's cooperation, and military efforts to enlist the support of private internationalist organizations, indicated that many policymakers perceived no conflict between preparedness and the "second chance" campaign for a world peacekeeping body.[47]

Perhaps bolstered by the State Department's support, or simply fearful that the danger of further delay outweighed possible embarrassment over the UN issue, the services pressed on with their campaign. Hearings on UMT before the Woodrum Committee were finally set to begin on June 4, even though the San Francisco Conference was still deliberating and Truman's attitude remained obscure. Military leaders held great hopes for the hearings. They would be the highlight of their UMT campaign, the moment to capture public attention. Fresh from the final triumph over Nazi Germany, closing in on the Japanese home islands, the armed forces

46. On reluctance to enter the foreign policy area, see Persons to Hodes, 27 February 1945; Hodes to Tompkins, 3 March 1945, both in file 353 (106), Chief of Staff.

47. Quotation from Secretary of War to Secretary of State, 21 December 1944, file 353 (Training) (Aug 44–Dec 44), Adm. Asst. SecWar. On cooperation between the military and the State Department on UMT and the military response to critics, see: Petersen to Tompkins, 3 August 1944, file 353 (Aug–Sept 44), SPD; memoranda of 4 December 1944, 15 December 1944, 17 December 1944, all in file 353 (Dec 44), SPD; Weible to McCloy, 12 December 1944, file 353 UMT (Dec 1944), ASW; Forrestal to McCloy, 15 January 1945; McCloy to Forrestal, 18 January 1945; Persons to McCloy, 19 April 1945; Grew to Stimson, 15 May 1945, all in file 353 (Jan 45–May 31, 1945), ASW; Persons to Secretary of War, 21 April 1945, and Secretary of War to Secretary of State, 23 April 1945, both in file 353 (Training) (Jan 45), Adm. Asst. SecWar; Persons to Marshall, 5 June 1945, and McCloy to Marshall, 13 June 1945, both in file 353 (157), Chief of Staff; Captain Terrell to Eugene Duffield, 14 June 1945, and list of possible questions which might be asked of the Secretary of Navy and possible answers, n.d. [June 1945], both in file 45–1–10, SacNav.

expected that admiration for their achievements would enhance popular reception of their claims for UMT. Planning had been meticulous, testimony refined and reworked, and arguments honed through months of repetition. The committee was known to be sympathetic to UMT and eager to stage the hearings in a manner flattering to the services' case.[48]

After Grew had offered the State Department's view, Stimson appeared before the committee on June 15. As he started to read his prepared statement, photographers interrupted him, shouting at him to look into their cameras. "No I won't," Stimson snapped. On that testy note he began presentation of the military's case. The secretary assailed the "passivistic [sic] advocates of the voluntary system" and proclaimed the need for compulsory training. But the old man's voice was tired, flat, and fumbling, and the moment devoid of the tension or drama which might capture public imagination. Forrestal, Marshall, King, and others followed Stimson, but the secretary had made an inauspicious start.[49]

War and Navy Department officials soon recognized that the hearings were not the triumph they had expected. True, the Woodrum Committee recommended that Congress enact a UMT bill, the hearings received intensive press coverage, and popular reaction to the services' UMT proposals appeared strongly favorable. But the hearings showed that the leaders of educational, religious, labor, and agricultural interests were "almost solidly against" UMT, as General Porter, the new chief of the Special Planning Division, warned. Even old allies like the American Legion soon proved troublesome. Although the military "flung into the battle every ounce of its prestige," the outlook for congressional action on UMT was darkening. The cornerstone of the services' political strategy had been the approval of their postwar plans before peace came. Instead, the UMT hearings dragged on through much of the summer. Political obstacles and the demands of war frustrated the military's efforts until, General Handy believed, an "'open season' for attacks

48. Ward, "Movement for Universal Military Training," p. 103.
49. "Recordings containing some of the outstanding testimony, such as that by Secretary of War Stimson before the 'Select Committee on Post War Military Policy,' better known as the Woodrum Committee on Compulsory Military Training [sic]. May [sic] and June 1945—Parts 1–13," tape recordings in the Sound Records Unit, RG 165–1, National Archives Building; Ward, "Movement for Universal Military Training," p. 102; Woodrum Committee, *Hearings, UMT*, pp. 478–86.

on the Army" had arrived. Even worse, the sudden end of the war in August found the services still, to their chagrin, in "a position which they should never occupy in the public mind," that of advocating a policy which the President had not yet explicitly approved.[50]

Weaknesses in the case for UMT did not help the military's cause. Illustrative was the failure of the services to back up their claim that without UMT the nation would be forced to maintain a large and expensive professional army. With UMT, they argued, only a "relatively small establishment" would be needed.[51] But they never offered figures on the size of a "small establishment" or on the cost savings possible under a system of universal training. The decision to withhold such figures was made by Marshall and General Handy against the advice of War Department legislative experts. Marshall's postwar planners asserted that, given the impossibility of foreseeing postwar needs, any estimates about the size of peacetime forces would "amount to little more than rank guesses." Yet if that were so, the claim that UMT would lead to enormous cost savings itself rested on "rank guesses." The truth was that the military, lacking convincing figures to back up its claims, avoided any discussion of specifics which might expose the frailty of its position. "While I realize the difficulties which will result from not giving definite or approximate figures," wrote General Tompkins, "may we not create even more difficult conditions by giving them?"[52]

50. Quotations from Porter to Marshall, 4 July 1945, file 353 (157), Chief of Staff; Mary Spargo column, *Washington Post*, 17 June 1945; General Council Minutes, remarks by Handy, 6 August 1945; Carpenter to Deputy Director, SPD, 15 August 1945, file 353 (July–Sept 45), SPD. For the Woodrum Committee's recommendation, see Representative Clifton Woodrum, "Universal Military Training," *House Report 857*, 79/1. For press and radio reaction, see War Department Bureau of Public Relations, *Universal Military Training, including Post-War Military Establishment*, Series 26–29, 30–55. On difficulties with UMT allies, see Woodrum Committee, *Hearings, UMT*, pp. 51–55, 58; Porter to McCloy, 28 June 1945, file 353 UMT, Records of the G-3 Division (1942–1945), RG 165; McCloy to Mark Wiseman, 28 June 1945, file 353 UMT (June 1'45–), ASW.

51. Woodrum Committee, *Hearings, UMT*, p. 481.

52. Persons to Tompkins, 21 April 1945, file Plans and Policy Office Subject File (1944–48) UMT (Folder UMT [2]), L&LD; Tompkins to Acting Chief, Legislative and Liaison Division, 3 May 1945, and draft memorandum to Marshall, n.d. [ca. 3 May 1945], both in file 032.2 (House Select Committee on Postwar Military Policy), SPD. See also McCloy to Marshall, 10 June 1945, file 353 UMT (June 1 '45–), ASW; Tompkins to Marshall, 12 June 1945, and Marshall to McCloy, 12 June 1945, both in file 353 (157), Chief of Staff. Under prodding from the Woodrum Committee, Admiral King produced an estimate that UMT would save the navy perhaps $2.5 billion annually which it would otherwise have had to spend on a standing force, but more detailed figures were not forthcoming from either service; see King to Woodrum, 3 July 1945, file P11-1(30) UMT, CNO-Cominch Records.

During the Woodrum Committee hearings such evasive tactics caused little damage. Sympathetic to the UMT cause and often lacking expertise in military matters, committee members were reluctant to grill UMT spokesmen closely on the military merits of their proposal. Debate in the hearings instead focused on the political issues raised by the proposal. Critics concentrated on the threat UMT allegedly posed to the nation's freedoms, political traditions, and opportunities for securing world peace. Knowing that delay would help their cause, they also accused the military of trying to railroad the nation into UMT while the war still was on. They did not often evaluate UMT as a means of defense. The argument for UMT deserved closer examination than it received in the committee's hearings.

The Case for UMT

By 1945 the arguments for preparedness made by the armed services had assumed a repetitive, predictable, and ideological character. The uniformity of argument was only partly deliberate, for the ideology of preparedness drew on shared emotions, memories, and experiences as much as on a concerted plan for doctrinal unity. The case for universal training, articulated before the Woodrum Committee and other forums, represented a mature expression of the preparedness ideology. The military justified UMT to the public largely in the same terms that it had used in its secret deliberations earlier in the war, a credit more to its honesty than to its political sagacity.

To military men, the "teachings of history" proved the inevitability of war and therefore the need for UMT. The United States, twice threatened by an aggressor seeking "world conquest," required UMT because "a third recurrence" of global war seemed so certain. History also showed the chronic failure of the United States to prepare for war, a mistake which if repeated could inflict on the nation a "bloody and humiliating defeat." The United States enjoyed a new and perhaps last chance to be prepared for war before it began, defense authorities believed.[53] UMT would make the country "forever safe from attack."[54]

53. McCloy to Marshall, 13 June 1945, file 353 (157), Chief of Staff.
54. American Legion statement, as quoted in Frank Knox, "Let's Train Our Youth," *Colliers*, 29 June 1944, p. 12.

But attack from whom? That question, with its annoying implication that there would be no enemies after the defeat of the Axis, agitated the UMT proponents. They believed that, given the fickleness of international relations, no one could predict who the new aggressor might be, only that one would surely arise, as history proved. They condemned as reckless the notion that preparedness could wait until an enemy marched, and refused to single out a particular nation as a potential enemy. Whom was the United States preparing to flight by enacting UMT? "Quite simply," Forrestal once stated, "we are going to fight any international ruffian who attempts to impose his will on the world by force."[55]

The future enemy appeared not only unpredictable, but capable of striking so suddenly that the United States could never again count on the years of time to train her armies enjoyed in the first two world wars. For several decades, advocates of training had cited technological factors as justification for UMT, as they did again in 1940, when the navy's General Board recommended universal military service because of the danger of "attack by probable weapons of the future."[56] A few years later, those weapons had been unleashed. The spectacle of V-1s and V-2s raining down on England and the suspicion that Germany was building rockets for use against the United States made vivid the threat of "an even swifter, more devastating type of blitzkrieg warfare" than in World War II.[57] UMT was necessary because America's unearned security had been "repealed by science," Admiral Jacobs warned.

> Certainly every development of the past five years has shown beyond a shadow of a doubt that we no longer live in an isolated impregnable fortress behind whose walls we shall again have time to select, arm, equip and train the soldiers, sailors and airmen to protect us against attack. Technology has whittled down time and space until we shall have no leeway. The robomb of today is in the same relative state of

55. Woodrum Committee, *Hearings, UMT*, p. 526.

56. Memorandum, "The National Defense," Chairman of the General Board to the Secretary of the Navy, 7 June 1940, General Board No. 42, Serial 1963, General Board-Secretary of the Navy Files, Naval History Division.

57. Quotation from speech by General William Tompkins, 6 October 1944, file 337 (Conferences) (Aug–Sept 44), SPD. For fears that Germany was preparing rockets for use against the United States, see George Fielding Eliot's column, *New York Herald Tribune*, 18 November 1944.

development that the airplane was in 1918. What will it be when the next war opens?[58]

Some military experts advised that "a surprise attack or invasion" against the United States was already "entirely feasible." Without UMT, Admiral Chester Nimitz suggested, the coastal cities of the United States would meet the same fate suffered by Warsaw, Berlin, and Tokyo during the war, though Nimitz did not explain how UMT would enhance air defense.[59]

Military officials like Stimson pointed to "the pitifully small margin" of Allied victory during the war as evidence that the technological imperative made UMT necessary. "Had the robot bomb and the buzz bomb been developed six or eight months earlier," one defender of UMT asked, "who can say what might have happened?" Only the "period of grace" provided by Russian, British, and French resistance had given the United States time to mobilize her manpower, the AAF's chief of air staff claimed. Americans could not count on having for "a third time" the protective shield provided by powerful allies in World Wars I and II. General Marshall, still angry about the "close calls" of 1941 and 1942, told the Woodrum Committee. "Face frankly two things: Either universal military training or the hope—that is all you can possibly have—the hope that you have better than a year for preparation."[60]

Aggravating the time factor, defense officials maintained, would be America's future position as "a tempting prize for aggressor nations." As McCloy explained to a radio audience:

History will record that American manpower and industrial might swung the balance in both World War I and the present conflict. Both times this country was woefully unprepared. Both times our friends

58. Vice Admiral Randall Jacobs, "The Issue Should Be Decided Now," *Annals of the American Academy of Political and Social Science* 241 (September 1945): 72; address by Vice Admiral Randall Jacobs at Muhlenberg College, 25 February 1945, file Plans and Policy Office UMT Decimal File 045 (Admiral Jacobs), L&LD.

59. Denfield to Forrestal, 17 January 1945, file 45-1-10, SecNav; Woodrum Committee, *Hearings, UMT*, p. 529 (Nimitz).

60. Woodrum Committee, *Hearing, UMT*, p. 481 (Stimson testimony), p. 549 (General Ira Eaker, Chief of Air Staff), p. 571 (Marshall); Brigadier General W. H. Wilbur, speech before the Commonwealth Club of San Francisco, 10 August 1945, UMT Files, Box 181, Patterson Papers; Stimson, notes for meeting with labor leaders, 10 November 1944, Stimson Memos, Stimson Papers.

held off the aggressors while we prepared. Next time the aggressor will not make the same mistake, if he is sensible, but will attempt to eliminate the main strength first. War will come suddenly from the air and we will be the first to be attacked.

Military leaders were unanimous in echoing McCloy's warning. American power, it appeared, was as much a burden as a shield. It invited aggression as much as it forestalled it. UMT was necessary because diplomacy, technology, and avarice had conspired to strip America of her traditional insulation from attack.[61]

The technology of modern war appeared to justify UMT as a defensive measure, but it also undermined the very concept of defense. Even if ultimately successful, defensive actions to repel attack might come too late to avoid intolerable destruction of the homeland. The very notion of "defense plans" seemed foolish to Admiral Jacobs, since "nations may wage wars thousands of miles from their own borders, not to repel an attack, as the word 'defense' suggests, but to prevent it."[62] Therefore, the services argued, the United States needed UMT in order to enlarge the nation's capacity to deter or destroy an aggressor before he attacked.

To the UMT campaigners, recent history dramatized the need for deterrence. Under Secretary of State Grew, fond of recalling his conversations before the war with the Japanese, contended that America's moral and military weakness "simply invited contempt" and encouraged Japan to attack. "I don't believe for a moment that Japan would have attacked us," he said, had the United States maintained UMT and other preparedness measures. Similarly Marshall testified that the Japanese were "seriously misled" and "encouraged into this war" by the "statements of our young men in college that 'they were not going to fight,' and that 'they would not participate in any other war even in defense of their country.'" To the Japanese, such statements allegedly constituted "almost an invitation to war," or, as Forrestal put it, "an invitation to Mussolini, Hitler and the Japanese war lords to run the world as they chose."

61. Woodrum Committee, *Hearings, UMT*, p. 547 (Eaker); statement prepared for press release and for McCloy to make in the University of Chicago Round Table Program over NBC, 26 November 1944, statement dated 25 November 1944, file 353 (Oct 43–Nov 44), ASW.
62. Jacobs, "The Issue Should Be Decided Now," p. 72.

A show of American resolution and strength such as that provided by UMT could have prevented World War II, training advocates suggested, and likewise would be a "powerful influence" in discouraging further aggression.[63]

The military rejected criticism that unilateral deterrence would hurt the embryonic United Nations Organization and alarm wartime allies like the Soviet Union. Increasingly concerned about Soviet policy by the spring of 1945, policymakers like Grew and Forrestal may have regarded UMT as a deterrent to Soviet expansion. One official, the president of the National Guard Association, said so publicly.[64] Yet, as a group, preparedness advocates did not consider UMT an anti-Soviet measure. If some observers chose to interpret the military's frequent references to future "aggressors" as code language for advocacy of an anti-Soviet policy, they were leaping to an unwarranted conclusion.[65]

On the other hand, the military had only a superficial explanation of how adoption of UMT might affect international relations. While defense spokesmen emphasized that universal training would strengthen the ability of the United States to contribute troops to an international military force, they did not explain the role reservists might play in such a force. Indeed, by the spring of 1945 the services apparently as yet had undertaken no studies of the place of American troops in an international army.[66] Many proponents of UMT confined themselves to general comments, such as those made by General Palmer in June 1944: "Just as you find it necessary in

63. Woodrum Committee, *Hearings, UMT*, pp. 2–4 (Grew), p. 571 (Marshall), p. 526 (Forrestal); Grew's remarks in "Transcript of the Committee Meeting Conference of The Secretary of War and The Secretary of the Navy and Their Staffs with Leading Educators of the Country, 29 December 1944," pp. 5–8, file 353 (Dec 44), SPD; Harry Hopkins, "Tomorrow's Army and Your Boy," p. 104.

64. Woodrum Committee, *Hearings, UMT*, p. 55.

65. Ibid., p. 572. The committee hearings suggest that Congressman James Mott may have drawn such a conclusion. Military men rarely made reference to the Soviet Union in either their public or private deliberations on UMT. Marshall did make one cryptic comment to the Woodrum Committee when asked if the success of the United States in dealing with nations like the Soviet Union depended on American military strength. Marshall replied: "There are some things that I would not care to say here in open meeting. They would even be amusing if they were not of such tragic import." The committee record does not indicate that the committee went into executive session. Ibid., p. 572.

66. Ibid., p. 2; Grew hinted at the use of reservists in an international force. A speech by Vice Admiral Willson, a JCS staff officer, discussed various ways in which a UN force might be organized; see copy of his speech, 4 April 1945, in Box 25, Forrestal Papers.

Kansas City to use force" to control crime, the "'peace-loving
nations'" should "get together and decide to nip future militarism
and aggression in the bud wherever and whenever it starts."[67]

In the military view, the primary contribution that UMT would
make to international collaboration would be psychological and
symbolic. Quick passage of UMT, Marshall argued, would make
future peace talks more fruitful. The Allies, he said, feared that we
would "withdraw into our shell and at the same time endeavor,
as they put it, to inflict on the world an idealistic policy without,
on our own part, showing any basis for maintaining or backing up
such [a] policy of idealism." Citing his talks with State Department
personnel and officials of other countries, the chief of staff represented
America's allies as desperate for assurances of the determination
of the United States to fight future aggression. Preparedness could
be used to coerce the Soviet Union or other nations, Marshall
acknowledged, but he insisted that UMT, far from antagonizing
the Grand Alliance, would relieve its anxiety over another American
retreat into isolationism. McCloy varied the theme by claiming
that adoption of UMT, by demonstrating American resolve, would
make the smaller nations of Europe "more resistant and independent-
minded toward aggression." Adoption of UMT ran no risk of
alarming peace-loving nations, Marshall asserted, because the
United States possessed a "tremendous asset": "No one charges
us with wanting anything of anybody else's" and "no one is fearful
of our misuse" of military power.[68]

The proponents of UMT made it many things to many people:
a bargaining lever at forthcoming peace negotiations, a way to
strengthen the United Nations, a source of manpower for multilateral
or unilateral police forces, a deterrent to war, even a means to make
possible preemptive attacks, or an essential defensive measure if
it failed in its other purposes. The multiplicity of purposes reflected
both uncertainty about the success of the United Nations Organization and the need for UMT backers to appeal to a broad range of
political factions and ideals. The multiplicity also indicated a weakness in the case for UMT: the services offered so many reasons for

67. Palmer to Peter T. Bohan, 19 June 1944, Chronological Files 1943–44, Box 11, Palmer
Papers.
68. Marshall testimony in Woodrum Committee, Hearings, UMT, pp. 569–74; McCloy to
Dr. William F. Russell, 4 December 1944, file 353 (Dec 44), ASW.

UMT because no one justification had been carefully and convincingly thought out.

The arguments for universal training in addition reflected a more fundamental characteristic of the UMT case. If UMT advocates were hazy about the role reservists might play in future military operations, it was partly because they hoped that universal training would "provide the forces which will prevent war."[69] The principal utility of UMT was not to strengthen military forces but to signal American resolve. Anxious not to appear weak before any future Hitler, policymakers were tempted to value the psychological importance of UMT more than its military usefulness.

That temptation went still further. Adoption of UMT might mold American will at home as well as signal it abroad. Earlier in the war, Secretary Knox had hoped that, in an age when Americans only "put noisy emphasis" on their privileges, UMT would teach boys "duty to the nation, duty to their fellow men, duty to themselves!"[70] Eisenhower, in a statement reluctantly authorized by Marshall and McCloy, acknowledged that reservists might forget the skills taught in their year's service. But he argued that "psychological and moral training" would stick with them and give them "a common understanding of the ideals and reasons for which the United States will fight."[71] An Army Air Forces staff study suggested that political leaders who had a year's training would "more readily vote necessary funds for military purposes." UMT might even instill "in the American people a frame of mind that would induce us to strike first to prevent or shorten the next war when the element of surprise may be all-important."[72] UMT would not only demonstrate American resolution; it would forge it.

If the purpose of UMT was psychological, more to prevent war than to wage it, then defense officials could ignore questions about the actual utility and operation of a universal training system in wartime. Most of the factors cited as necessitating UMT just as readily justified other preparedness measures. The services did not

69. Wilbur Speech, 10 August 1945, UMT Files, Box 181, Patterson Papers.

70. Knox, "Let's Train Our Youth," *Colliers*, 29 April 1944, p. 12.

71. For text of Eisenhower's statement, see *New York Times*, 16 June 1945. See also Eisenhower to Marshall, 2 June 1945, responding to a cable from McCloy; Weible to Marshall, 7 June 1945; and several handwritten notes among McCarthy, Marshall, Handy, and McCloy on Weible's June 7 memorandum, all in file 353 (147), Chief of Staff.

72. Smith, *Air Force Plans*, p. 86.

explain why money was better spent on UMT than on air defense, strategic bombers, submarines, or a host of other options. The case for UMT consisted of general propositions about postwar security rather than a closely reasoned rationale. Could reservists be mobilized rapidly enough to meet the kind of "blitzkrieg" attack envisioned by planners? Could they man an army and navy demanding increasingly sophisticated skills? Could they play an important role in the kind of aerial warfare anticipated by American strategists? Could they provide the ready forces needed for quick police action against an aggressor? Those and other questions, although raised among War Department planners in 1943 and 1944, remained largely unanswered, even unasked, in the public appearances of defense spokesmen. In their private deliberations during the war's final year, defense officials would be challenged to address themselves to those questions.

The military's first postwar plans, hastily devised in 1943 and the first months of 1944, asserted the need for powerful military forces to deter, punish, or repel aggression. Those plans were too sketchy to constitute a final blueprint for the postwar. The armed services still had to agree on the composition of the peacetime force and to ponder whether Congress would finance it. Their big task lay ahead.

Pressures for a more definitive determination of force levels mounted in the spring of 1944. With the assault on *Festung Europa* slated for June, staff officers could foresee an early end to the European war. Already, Allied armies had recaptured North Africa, Sicily, and much of Italy and Russia, while the bomber offensive against the Nazi homeland was gaining momentum. In the Pacific, the painful island-hopping campaigns would soon bring Japan within range of the American B-29 Superfortress. With victory in sight, Congress would soon wish to examine the military's plans, and each service wanted to put in the first claim on the peacetime budget. The Woodrum Committee hearings on unification, begun in May 1944, intensified the services' rivalry. Logistics experts needed an idea of the size of postwar forces to guide their disposal of the materiel amassed during the war. In the War Department, the completion by the Special Planning Division of its plans for the immediate postwar period freed the staff to turn to the problem of permanent forces.

Responding to the renewed pressures for plans, army and navy staffs labored for a year, until May 1945, to construct agreements on peacetime force levels acceptable to all factions in the two military departments. In performing that task they rarely sought or received guidance from each other or from the Joint Chiefs, Congress, the State Department, or the President. That was, perhaps, one reason that they found their chore frustrating and their efforts often unrewarded.

The navy, endowed with greater internal unity, completed its work first, though only after many delays. Naval officers began formulating revised plans in March 1944. Their subsequent efforts were flawed by inconsistencies of argument and the absence of clearly defined political and strategic objectives. The intervention that autumn of Secretary Forrestal, more anxious than ever over postwar security and the navy's struggle with the army, prompted a shakeup in the planning staff and a fresh analysis of the navy's needs. The new effort soon lost momentum, however.[1]

Complicating the planners' task was their deepening concern over the willingness of Congress to pay for the forces they wanted. In 1943, Admiral King's staff had suggested that the navy maintain a force as large as 825,000 men, with an annual cost of $7 billion. Anticipation of congressional parsimony now led the staff to pare those figures. In August 1944 Vice Admiral Frederick Horne argued for a force of 550,000 officers and men (plus 110,000 marines), whose annual cost Horne estimated to be $3 billion. By the spring of 1945 Horne's 660,000-man figure had become fixed in naval planning and from it the navy would not budge for the remainder of the war or long thereafter.[2]

Though fiscal considerations governed the size of the force requested, the navy did have some sense of a strategic mission for the 660,000-man force. The staff planned the force to be in operation until the projected international organization became "fully effective." During that period the task of the navy would be to ward off a world war, a war which, planners suggested, would probably destroy the nation. The assumption, wrote Admiral King, was that "adequate military force, applied in sufficient time against an aggressor nation, is the most effective means of defense and of preventing a world war from developing from its nascent state." Among its primary tasks, the navy had to help "suppress any incipient war by joint action with other powers or, if necessary by independent action." While naval forces would operate primarily in the Pacific and the western Atlantic, they were to be ready to move swiftly "to any part of the world in support of our national policies."[3]

The emphasis in the revised plans on deterrence and a global

1. Davis, *Postwar Defense Policy and the U.S. Navy*, pp. 89–112.

2. Ibid., pp. 72–75, 93–95, 114; Duffield to Forrestal, 31 July 1944, folder "Memorandum for the Secretary of Navy, 1944," Subject File, Box 22, King Papers.

3. King to Forrestal, 3 March 1945, Serial 0604, FF1/A16–3, attached to memorandum from Edwards to Horne, 4 May 1945, file A16-3/EN, CNO-Cominch Records. The King memorandum is discussed in Davis, *Postwar Defense Policy and the U.S. Navy*, pp. 110–12.

policing capability, more explicit than in earlier drafts, reflected the views of the navy's civilian commander as well as King. Forrestal, describing war as "a cancer in world society," believed that "armed force is the surgeon's knife which must be used ... to carve that corrupt tissue from the healthy body of society." The nation's objective, Forrestal never ceased to assert, was not simply defense against attack but policing of aggressors to the "far corners of the earth."[4]

The revised plans left several matters unresolved. While the naval command suggested worldwide responsibilities for the United States, it did not explain how naval power could be effective in the great landmasses of Europe, Africa, and Asia, nor how the navy could police the globe from a regional system of bases. Although Forrestal's fears of the Soviet Union were already intense by the war's last winter, the admirals as yet apparently had no specific enemy in mind. Reflecting the navy's traditional orientation toward the Pacific, they foresaw no important role for the navy in European affairs after the war. Nor had the navy come to grips fully with recent technological changes. Fearful of budgetary restrictions on future shipbuilding, it determined to hold on to all the larger ships accumulated during the war, despite the threat of block obsolescence posed by such a policy. Still dominated by battleship admirals, the naval staff cut back the allotments for aircraft carriers and submarines made in previous plans.[5]

Finally, the navy had no firm concept of mobilization. While still pursuing UMT legislation, the staff seemed uncertain about the value of UMT to the navy, sometimes viewing the training program more as a luxury than an integral part of the postwar fleet. One key officer suggested that the navy "make the basic plan on the assumption there will not be universal training, and then ... see what changes have to be made in it if there is universal training." The concept of trainees as a partial substitute for ready forces, though advocated by the services in public, found little favor with the navy. The admirals had not yet faced up to the possibility that they might have to choose between UMT and a large standing navy, and Forrestal was reluctant to make them do so. "I don't think we ought to try to interpret what

4. Forrestal, address at the American Legion Convention, 20 September 1944, file 45-1-10, SecNav; Forrestal, speech before Navy Industrial Association, 11 September 1944, Speech File, Box 5, Forrestal Papers.
5. Davis, *Postwar Defense Policy and the U.S. Navy*, pp. 107–14.

we think Congress will do," he said during a staff discussion of budgets and force levels. "I think we ought to tell them what we want them to do."[6]

Forrestal's remark epitomized the aggressiveness of his department. The strategic input into the revised plans may have been shallow, but precisely because the navy did not quibble about doctrinal niceties, it had ready by May 1945 a definite figure for force levels—660,000 men, the most it thought it could wring from Congress. By contrast, the War Department, crippled by doctrinal and bureaucratic feuds, found the matter of force levels more vexing.

Army Ambitions

The army's troubles began soon after General William Tompkins, writing on May 31, 1944, ordered the G-3 Division to prepare a plan for postwar force levels. Under SPD's direction, G-3 was to solicit recommendations from the staff divisions and major commands, including Army Air Forces, and draw up an estimate of the size and composition of the postwar army.[7] The orders were simple, but a host of obstacles impeded their execution.

One handicap was confusion among officers over the wisdom of an early start to planning. The Operations Division argued that too little was known about peacetime conditions to make definitive estimates of the army's postwar needs. The War Department should make no disposition of its wartime surpluses on the basis of G-3's plans, OPD suggested. Tompkins and his staff understood how painfully tentative their plans were, but, watching war supplies piling up in the warehouses, they urged quick action to speed disposal of materiel.[8]

Equally troublesome was the failure to establish firm ground rules for the planning. Tompkins, who had no guidance from higher authority, gave little hint of the kind of diplomatic and strategic environment G-3 should assume to exist in the postwar era. He told G-3 to consult the "Outline of the Post-War Army,"[9] and he sketched

6. Minutes of Top Policy Group Meeting 10, 15 January 1945, file Minutes of Top Policy Group Meetings, SecNav.

7. Sparrow, *History of Personnel Demobilization*, p. 59; Tompkins to Assistant Chief of Staff, G-3 (Attn: Chamberlain), 31 May 1944, file 320, G-3.

8. Hull to Assistant Chief of Staff, G-3, 6 July 1944; Somervell to Assistant Chief of Staff, G-3, 10 July 1944; General Ray Porter to G-1, G-4, OPD, SPD, ASF, AGF, AAF, 24 June 1944; Sams (for Assistant Chief of Staff, G-4), to G-3, 14 July 1944, all in file 320, G-3.

9. The outline, described in Chapter 2 above, was still undergoing revision but was no longer the focus of planning.

the army's current plans for universal military training. But Tompkins and the General Staff took no fresh look at the army's future needs. The SPD chief simply gave G-3 the same troop strengths which had circulated in the War Department in 1943: 1,500,000 men from the regular army, including 630,000 trainees under universal service, and 4,500,000 for the army at full mobilization. G-3 was to determine the exact numbers of ground, service, and air forces within an arbitrary ceiling of 1,500,000 men, but the validity of that ceiling went unexamined. Tompkins also instructed G-3 to plan a "balanced force," though he added that air units would comprise a heavy percentage of the 870,000-man professional force.[10]

Some officers insisted that force levels, instead of being limited to some arbitrary figure, should be "built up from the bottom" by a compilation of the personnel needed to man bases envisioned in the JCS 570 series and to carry out projected postwar missions. In planning the deployment of the postwar army, General Handy argued, SPD should consider such broad factors as "the probable relative strengths of the major powers of the world" after the war, and American commitments to enforce world peace. SPD, he wrote, should work with the Joint Chiefs, not unilaterally. Tompkins ignored the suggestion for joint planning, while Handy and OPD recognized that SPD had no time to clarify all the imponderables about the postwar. One OPD official stated bluntly:

> The proposed troop basis cannot reflect accurately the forces necessary to accomplish the missions that will be assigned to the post-war Army. Nevertheless, planning for the post-war Army must begin, and some basis must be established for the planning.

In an atmosphere of uncertainty, no one bothered to reconcile the fuzzy and conflicting assumptions about the postwar world entertained by the army officers.[11]

Pressure to appease powerful interest groups in the War Department further crippled planning. Even before Tompkins's order of

10. Tompkins to Assistant Chief of Staff, G-3 (Attn: Chamberlain), 31 May 1944, file 320, G-3.

11. Quotations from Handy to Tompkins, 12 August 1944, file 370.9 (Top Secret), OPD; Roberts to Assistant Chief of Staff, OPD, 6 July 1944, file 370.9, OPD. See also Meredith (for Commanding General, Army Ground Forces) to Chief of Staff (Attn: G-3), file 320, G-3; Olsen (for Commanding General, Army Ground Forces) to Chief of Staff (Attn: SPD), 23 June 1944, as enclosure to memorandum, Tompkins to G-3, 5 September 1944, file 350.06 (Study 33), OPD.

May 31, 1944, Army Air Forces and Army Ground Forces (AGF) had staked claims to postwar troop strengths which threatened Tompkins's ceiling. The AAF's 105-group plan would require a million men, including trainees. The more modest Army Ground Forces plan provided for 780,000 men, including 380,000 professionals. The combined AAF and AGF requests would alone exceed the 1,500,000 limit, and neither request provided for logistical forces.[12]

To preserve his ceiling, Tompkins on June 15 requested the air planners to draw up a new plan which would trim the peacetime air forces from 1,000,000 to 700,000 personnel. The air planners, already at work on a new plan in anticipation of budgetary restrictions, handed Tompkins a proposal for an air force of 685,000 men, including 75 air groups. But the AAF refused to shelve its more ambitious plan for 105 groups, and Ground and Service Forces commands each insisted on larger allocations of manpower.[13]

Unable to meet the conflicting demands for personnel and still hold to its ceiling, Special Planning abandoned its attempt to limit postwar forces to 1,500,000 men. After further argument, the army commands and staff divisions recommended a postwar army of 1,093,050 professionals, plus 630,217 trainees annually. Their August 19 compromise plan established the air force, with 75 air groups and 430,000 professionals, as the primary M-day force. With 368,000 regulars, the ground army would concentrate its peacetime efforts on training a mass reserve. 280,000 professionals would comprise the logistical force.[14]

But 75 groups still did not satisfy the ambitious aviators. They agreed to SPD's compromise only on condition that its implementation not occur until an international organization, working through the four great powers, was able to maintain peace and regulate

12. Two memoranda, Olsen (for Commanding General, AGF) to SPD, 23 June 1944, file 350.06 (Study 109), SPD.
13. Smith, *Air Force Plans*, pp. 63–64; Burt to Tompkins, 2 October 1944, file 350.06 (Study 102), SPD; G-3, "Provisional Post-War Mobilization Troop Basis," 24 June 1944; G-3 to G-1, G-4, OPD, SPD, ASF, AAF, AGF, 24 June 1944; Somervell to Assistant Chief of Staff, G-3, 10 July 1944; Hull to Assistant Chief of Staff, G-3, 6 July 1944; Meredith (for Commanding General, AGF) to Chief of Staff (Attn: G-3), 13 July 1944; Colonel R. C. Moffat (Chief, Post-War Division, Air Staff, Plans) to G-3, 17 July 1944, all in file 320, G-3.
14. Tompkins to Assistant Chief of Staff, G-3, 15 July 1944, file 320, G-3; Shaw to Tompkins, 18 July 1944, file 350.06 (Study 33), SPD; G-3, "War Department Post-War Troop Basis, 19 August 1944," file Mobilization Plans 1944, G-3.

armaments effectively. Under any other conditions, the AAF insisted, the nation needed 105 air groups. The AAF's conditional acceptance of the 75-group plan was a bargaining tactic rather than an indication of faith in international organization. By claiming that the smaller air force was realistic only under the unlikely condition of world peace, the air staff suggested that under foreseeable circumstances only 105 groups would be adequate.[15] The tactic was typical of those used by the AAF in the mid-1940s to lay claim to a large peacetime force.

The Special Planning Division, having patched together a compromise, did not want to jettison it by challenging the Army Air Forces' conditions for accepting the 75-group figure. SPD obtained the assent of General Joseph McNarney, Marshall's deputy chief of staff, to the AAF's conditions. With McNarney's approval, the August 19 proposal became the official plan for the composition of the postwar army, subject to approval by Marshall and Stimson.[16] SPD had finally arranged an acceptable, if extravagant, compromise.

Through the summer and fall of 1944 SPD also worked on a scheme for the deployment of the 1,093,000 regular troops proposed in the August 19 plan.[17] Army strategists, following prevailing doctrine on the primacy of air power, relied on the broad guidelines laid down in the JCS 570 series. Air units were slated for Iceland, Greenland, Casablanca, Dakar, and numerous Pacific islands. SPD recommended no forces for the European or Asian mainland, and suggested that half of the air units nominally designated for overseas duty be kept within the United States except in emergencies.[18]

A brief squabble erupted over plans for the deployment of the ground army. Army Ground Forces wanted a "strategic reserve" of 150,000 men kept in the United States and ready to meet, in the ominous but unexplained words of one planner, "domestic" or

15. Smith *Air Force Plans*, p. 63; Moffat to G-3, 17 July 1944, file 320, G-3; Burt to Tompkins, 2 October 1944, and Tompkins to Deputy Chief of Staff, 11 October 1944, both in file 350.06 (Study 102), SPD.
16. Tompkins to Deputy Chief of Staff, 11 October 1944, file 350.06 (Study 102), SPD.
17. Only a sketchy picture of SPD's deployment plans is possible because the War Department later destroyed some of the relevant documentation in an incident described later in this chapter. The principal document regarding deployment planning to be destroyed was: "War Department Deployment of the Post-War Army," 1 November 1944.
18. Smith, *Air Force Plans*, pp. 77–78; SPD, "Post-War General Deployments (Tentative)," 5 September 1944, filed as Tab B to memorandum, Tompkins to Assistant Chief of Staff, G-3, 5 September 1944, file 350.06 (Study 33), SPD.

"enemy" threats. But with a characteristically modest view of its capabilities, AGF was

> opposed to scattering its limited Regular Army components over far-flung areas to guard isolated bases. If we have control of the sea, wide-spread defensive bases are unnecessary. If we do not have such control, defensive bases are futile. The history of our own deployment in the Philippines, and of the present Japanese deployment in the Central and Southwest Pacific are examples.

Army Ground Forces did not even contest the hegemony accorded to the AAF in the postwar plans. An AGF spokesman argued that "the initial mission of Army Ground Forces in a future war will be strategically defensive pending mobilization, and that most offensive missions will be restricted to the Air Forces" during the first phases of a war.[19]

Generals Tompkins and Handy rejected the AGF argument. In their view, it failed to "take into account the necessity for ground forces to hold the bases of the air and naval power by which we can control the sea." They insisted on placing ground troops in the Philippines and Alaska "to support the Air Force deployment and to protect the interests and prestige of the United States."[20] So ended another skirmish in a continuing debate over whether air power could operate independently of the other services.

Together, the August 19 force levels and the deployment formula (completed November 1, 1944) comprised SPD's plan for the postwar army. Far more effort went into this 1944 plan than had gone into the 1943 proposals. Yet the new plan was scarcely an improvement. Strategic concepts remained hazy. The planners placed great emphasis on American deterrent power, but deterrence remained an ill-defined concept. They still focused on a clash between great powers and assumed that the next war would be fought like World War II, except for greater use of air power. Their advocacy of "balanced forces" clashed with their faith in the bomber. The political acceptability of the 1944 plan was also questionable. To pacify bureaucratic rivals,

19. Meredith (for Commanding General, AGF) to Chief of Staff (Attn: SPD), 2 September 1944, and Olsen (for Commanding General, AGF) to Chief of Staff (Attn: SPD), 23 June 1944, as enclosure to memorandum, Tompkins to G-3, 5 September 1944, both in file 350.06 (Study 33), SPD; Meredith to Chief of Staff (Attn: SPD), 13 July 1944, file 320, G-3.

20. Tompkins to Assistant Chief of Staff, OPD, 4 August 1944, and Handy to Tompkins, 12 August 1944, both in file 370.9 (Top Secret), OPD.

SPD discarded the ceiling on troop strength it had tried to impose. But the swollen force it proposed would prove expensive.

The War Department knew that the cost of the postwar army was the key to its acceptance by any future president or Congress. Those officers who regarded the prewar years as an era of irresponsible budget-cutting were especially sensitive to the fiscal issue. Budget planning was urgent, especially after the establishment in March 1944 of the House Select Committee on Postwar Military Policy. Throughout 1944, Tompkins and his fellow planners expected the committee to request the army's postwar budget estimates, although the committee, in consultation with the army, postponed its hearings on UMT and budgets until after the 1944 elections.[21]

The objective of budget planning was political. The War Department wanted its cost figures to buttress the army's case for universal training. Tompkins ordered Major General George Richards, director of the Budget Division, to draw up estimates for two types of postwar forces: an active army of 1,093,000 men and 630,000 trainees, as in the August 19 formula; and a force of 2,230,500 without UMT. Under both plans, a year's mobilization was to yield an army of 4,500,000 personnel. The political purpose in drafting cost estimates for two contingencies was to demonstrate that an army based on a system of universal training would be smaller and cheaper than an all-professional force capable of providing the same measure of national security.[22]

In fact, the cost estimates proved nothing of the kind because the two forces would not have provided equal security. The 2,230,500-man army would have constituted the far larger M-day force. Only after a mobilization of one year, the time SPD assumed the army would have to prepare for a future war, would the UMT-based force reach parity with the conventional army. Apparently for two reasons the army nonetheless used both figures in making cost estimates. By using an inflated figure of 2.2 million for a professional force, it

21. For the start of budget planning, see Halverson to Tompkins, 5 May 1944; Textor to Chief, Organization Branch, SPD, and Chief, Fiscal Branch, SPD, 5 May 1944; memorandum for files, Colonel Dunlap C. Clark, 10 May 1944, and supplementary memorandum for files 16 May 1944; Tompkins to Deputy Chief of Staff, 27 May 1944; Tompkins to Deputy Chief of Staff, 2 June 1944; Tompkins to Major General George Richards, 2 June 1944; Clark to Tompkins, 2 August 1944, all in file 350.06 (Study 115), SPD.

22. Tompkins to Richards, 26 August 1944; Richards to Tompkins, 2 September 1944; Irvine to Tompkins, 25 September 1944; Tompkins to Deputy Chief of Staff, 27 September 1944, all in file 350.06 (Study 115), SPD.

strengthened the claim that an army without UMT would impoverish the taxpayer. Second, the staff tolerated an arbitrary comparison because it had never analyzed the size force which the army would need if it failed to secure UMT. Perhaps fearful of appearing to dissent from the decision of Marshall and Stimson to seek UMT, or overconfident about the chances of getting training legislation, the staff avoided contingency planning.

Those weaknesses in army planning did not divert General Richards from making cost estimates, which he completed in November 1944. For the army of 1,093,000 regulars and 630,000 trainees, the War Department would spend $6,835,000,000 annually, Richards advised, while the alternative force of 2,230,500 personnel would cost $8,706,000,000 each year. The difference, not dramatic, was enough to sustain the War Department's case for the financial benefits of UMT.[23]

Not so welcome was Richards's warning that costs under either plan would far outstrip the appropriations which the army could expect to receive. The Budget Division calculated postwar appropriations by projecting prewar spending patterns into the future. Noting, for example, that after recent wars military expenditures usually trebled prewar rates, Richards observed that a tripling of the 1930s rate would yield a billion dollar appropriation. Using this and more optimistic projections, and assuming that the War Department would, as in the past, receive 10 percent of the federal budget and about half of the military appropriations, Richards could hold out hope for just one to two billion dollars in annual army appropriations, far short of what the War Department needed to finance its proposed force of over a million men.[24]

By later standards of economics, Richards's methods of calculating postwar budgets were crude. Like most wartime experts, he grossly underestimated the expansion in the economy and the federal budget which would take place after the war. More striking was the conservatism implicit in his estimates. His reliance on past patterns of federal spending to calculate future army appropriations indicated that he, like most Americans, did not foresee the dramatically changed role military force would play in the American economy and foreign

23. Budget Division study, "Financing the Post War Army," 6 November 1944, file 388, Records of the Budget Division, RG 165.
24. Ibid.

policy or the allocation of 40 to 50 percent of the federal budget to defense. By computing military expenditures as an amount remaining after nonmilitary needs were met, Richards built into his estimates a bias in favor of nonmilitary spending. He assumed, too, that the navy would remain the principal peacetime force, despite the growth of air power during the war. Unchallenged by Tompkins and his staff, Richards's assumptions indicated how much the grip of the past on army planners narrowed their vision of the future. Even for wartime Washington, where prescience was always in short supply, they lacked foresight. However much they wanted a large peacetime army, they could not see how the nation would abandon its traditional "hostility" to military appropriations and deficit spending.

The budget estimates placed the General Staff in a predicament. The cost of an army of 1.1. million men and an elaborate reserve system, nearly $7 billion, would far exceed likely appropriations. As Tompkins's deputy pointed out, either the army had to scale down its plans or it had to lobby for higher defense spending.[25] Though the problem was obvious by September 1944, for two months no one moved to resolve it.

Orders for Economy

The voices of economy and caution in the War Department had been largely mute during the summer and fall of 1944. General Palmer had busied himself with UMT affairs. After the Normandy invasion, a host of crises competed for George Marshall's attention: struggles among American and Allied officers over command assignments and strategic decisions, the prickly matter of DeGaulle's status in liberated France, the row over occupation policy for Germany, and a severe manpower shortage in the army's ranks.[26] At most, Palmer and Marshall had a fleeting sense of the size and cost of the postwar army under consideration by planners.

In August, Palmer apparently became alarmed over the course of SPD planning. He feared that the schemes of some planners to exclude reserve officers from the ranks of the postwar army would alienate Congress, rob the army of leaders who could provide "the main

25. Textor to Tompkins, 5 August 1944, file 350.06 (Study 115), SPD.
26. For Marshall's activities in the June–November 1944 period, see Pogue, *Organizer of Victory*, chaps. 17–24.

political support" for peacetime preparedness, and deprive the armed forces of citizen officers who gave the United States one of its "greatest advantages over the armies of autocracy." He may also have learned of the force levels proposed by SPD. Palmer prevailed upon Marshall to issue a stern statement to the staff of his faith in UMT and his repudiation of a large professional peacetime army. Palmer probably hoped that Marshall's pronouncement of August 24 would rebuke those officers planning a 1.1 million–man army. If so, the planners did not take the hint, and neither Marshall nor Palmer followed up on the chief of staff's statement.[27]

But on November 11 Marshall abruptly shattered the designs of his postwar planners. At the time, he was still preoccupied with the drive into Germany, now faltering because of the weakness of Montgomery's advance through Holland and delays in making use of the port of Antwerp, under attack by the new German V-2s. Despite these operational worries, Marshall met that Saturday with Generals Weible, Smith, and Porter to discuss liaison with the American Legion in the promotion of UMT. When Marshall commented on the need for "practicable and realistic" postwar plans, General Porter, a blunt-speaking officer, ridiculed as "visionary" the force levels and budgets of SPD's plans. Worse than their "impracticality," Porter warned, was another danger: "If the estimates given by General Richards should ever be made public, ... our people would be frightened into a state of violent opposition to all War Department recommendations for the postwar military establishment." Asking for too much could backfire, Porter advised. His disclosures apparently gave Marshall his first careful look at the staff's plans.[28]

Marshall was shocked. The staff's proposals violated all of his political instincts about what Congress and the American public

27. Quotation from Palmer to Tompkins, 11 July 1944, file 350.06 (Study 64, Sec. 2), SPD. See also William Frye, *Marshall, Citizen Soldier*, p. 367; Palmer to Tompkins, 11 July 1944; Tompkins to Palmer, 22 July 1944; Palmer to Chief of Staff (through SPD), 3 August 1944; Tompkins to Chief of Staff, 8 August 1944; Pasco to Marshall, 12 August 1944, with hand-written notes from Marshall to Stimson and Stimson to Marshall, all in file 350.06 (Study 64, Sec. 2), SPD; Palmer to Handy, 13 December 1945, Chronological Files 1942–43, Box 10, Palmer Papers. For Marshall's statement, known as War Department Circular 347, see *New York Times*, 3 September 1944.

28. Porter to Deputy Chief of Staff, 12 November 1944, file 353 (58), Chief of Staff. In addition to hearing Porter's verbal presentation, Marshall probably also examined the plans himself. Marshall may have learned something of the plans even before the November 11 meeting; see Palmer to Marshall, 2 November 1944, folder "1945 January thru February," Chronological Files 1945–46, Box 12, Palmer Papers.

would pay for. Infuriated, he took swift action. On the afternoon of November 11, he ordered the destruction of papers describing the 1.1 million–man army and of certain minutes of the General Council, a top-level committee of officers, which on November 6 had reviewed SPD's postwar proposals. Hundreds of those documents had been printed and circulated around the War Department, but Marshall's subordinates destroyed them speedily. Marshall's order, a rare outburst of temper, testified to his determination to avoid any leaks about the cancelled plans. Too, the order dramatized to the staff just how angry he was about its grandiose schemes.[29]

Marshall directed the Special Planning Division to reexamine the "entire matter of post-war strengths," in effect to begin anew. While specifying no precise figure for the size of the postwar army, the chief of staff made clear his expectation of a drastic cut from the levels set in the August 19 plan. In explaining his order, he pointed to "the debilitation of the Axis powers" after the war. Evidently he foresaw no other enemies threatening the United States once the Axis powers were crushed. He knew, too, that Roosevelt hoped to remove American troops from Europe after a brief occupation period, though he did not explicitly make that point. Ignoring his own unhappy experiences in the 1930s with reliance on war surplus weapons, he suggested that "the huge resources for a long period of years that we shall possess in the form of Army and Navy materiel" justified a big reduction in the projected postwar budget. Finally, Marshall cited the "vastly increased power which will be given us by an annual program of universal military training—something which we have never previously enjoyed."[30]

His faith in UMT was critical to his case against a big professional army. On matters of reserve policy Marshall continued to share the views of Palmer, who approved Marshall's order to SPD to revise its plans. Together, the two insisted that an effective system of

29. On Marshall's orders, see Porter to Deputy Chief of Staff, 12 November 1944, file 353 (58), Chief of Staff; Pasco to Marshall, 11 November 1944, and McCarthy to Marshall, 13 November 1944, both in Memos for the Chief of Staff, Chief of Staff Secretariat Files, Chief of Staff; Marshall to Acting Director, SPD, 13 November 1944, file 350.06 (Study 33), SPD; memoranda of November 13–14 discussing destruction of documents, file 350.06 (Study 33), SPD; routing slips noting disposition of documents, file 370.9 (35, 44), OPD. Of 250 copies of the August 19 "War Department Post-War Troop Basis" originally printed, the author and the National Archives staff could locate only one which excaped destruction. No copies of the "War Department Deployment of the Post-War Army," 1 November 1944, could be found.
    30. Marshall to Acting Director, SPD, 13 November 1944, file 350.06 (Study 33), SPD.

universal training eliminated the need for large standing forces. Planners should reexamine their proposals in light of the premise that no "unit be maintained upon the permanent establishment if an effective unit of the same kind can be mobilized in time from the reserve forces." Marshall's trust in air power undoubtedly allowed him to discount further the need for a large professional ground force.[31]

Marshall's emphasis on UMT also sprang from his continuing fears that political leaders after the war would insist on stringent economy in military operations, an anxiety which likewise informed his determination to seek unification of the services. Aware of the lean years before the war, he remained bewildered that his planning officers, under "the present influence of dealing in the tremendous numbers and unlimited appropriations" of wartime, failed to recognize that politicians would balk at ambitious postwar military plans. His current frustrations over shortages of manpower with which to fight the Axis may have reinforced his fears of public parsimony. If he could not get the forces he believed necessary in the midst of war, then how much more frugal with men and money would the nation be in peacetime? FDR's partiality to the navy might diminish further the army's peacetime appropriations.[32]

In light of those factors, Marshall believed SPD's plans to be "so unrealistic—or rather so improbable of accomplishment however desirable," that their very disclosure would alienate Congress and public opinion and provoke charges of an army plot to aggrandize itself. A small professional establishment backed by UMT would be cheap enough for Congress to accept and strong enough to secure the nation's safety.[33]

Marshall's position typified his caution and his respect for the democratic political process. He rejected a political squeeze play: he might have created a scare about postwar security, submitted to Congress the SPD plan or an even more ambitious scheme, and then settled for a compromise figure. Unlike some of his subordinates and some of his colleagues in the navy, he believed that the military's

31. Quotation from Palmer to Marshall, 16 November 1944, Memos for the Chief of Staff, Chief of Staff Secretariat Files, Chief of Staff. See also Marshall to Tompkins, 22 November 1944, file 000.76 (22 November 1944), Chief of Staff.

32. Pogue, *Organizer of Victory*, pp. 361–64; personal communications from Forrest Pogue. Quotation from Marshall to Acting Director, SPD, 13 November 1944, file 350.06 (Study 33), SPD.

33. Marshall to Acting Director, SPD, 13 November 1944, file 350.06 (Study 33), SPD.

responsibility went beyond preparing a defense program and then placing on Congress the onus of financing it. Political institutions had a legitimate voice in military policy. Attaching no special infallibility to his staff's plans, he could in good conscience scrap them and order his staff to conform to political realities. Compromise would begin even before the army went to Congress. Though he did not always live up to it, his conviction was that the military's task should be to reason with politicians and the public, not to manipulate or coerce them.

For a year, until his retirement as chief of staff in November 1945, the problems of the peacetime military establishment consumed much of Marshall's attention. He exhorted his officers to develop and implement a fair, practical scheme for demobilizing American soldiers. Working closely with Stimson, he redoubled his efforts to win popular approval of UMT. Along with General Palmer, he scrutinized his staff's new proposals. With his orders of November 11, 1944, planning had entered a new, critical stage.

Rebuked by Marshall, Tompkins and his staff, assisted by an ad hoc War Department committee, began work on a new plan for the postwar arm. Marshall's closest assistant, General Handy, kept a watchful eye on the committee's deliberations. Not all of SPD's previous work was at issue. Marshall accepted its proposal for a reserve system which would train 630,000 young men annually and be capable of fielding an army of 4,500,000 men after a year's mobilization. But a cut had to come in the regular army, due to number over a million men under the August 19 plan.[34]

Marshall's instructions guided the committee in its work. According to the chief of staff, the committee should assume that the peace settlement would be "reasonably within our desires," that Axis power would be shattered while the United States would for years have a war surplus of materiel and trained men, and that the army would have the UMT system designed by General Palmer. On its own initiative the committee made the additional assumption that the peacetime establishment would become operative three years after the end of the war.[35]

34. Textor to members of Committee to Re-Survey Post-War Strength, 25 November 1944, file 350.06 (Study 33), SPD.

35. Marshall to Tompkins, 22 November 1944, file 000.76 (22 November 1944), Chief of Staff; Tompkins to members of Re-Survey Committee, 21 November 1944; Textor to committee members, 25 November 1944; Marshall to Acting Director, SPD, 13 November 1944, all in file 350.06 (Study 33), SPD.

Marshall and Handy cited two variables as the critical determinants of the size of the postwar army: the appropriations which the War Department could expect, and the number of men it might hope to obtain through voluntary recruitment (young men serving under the proposed UMT obligation would be liable only for training, not for service). In effect, the chief of staff told the committee to plan as much for what the army could get as for what it needed.[36]

As the staff interpreted Marshall's guidelines, frugality and efficiency were to be prized over peacetime combat fitness, and mobilization potential over instant readiness. "In other words, if an Infantry Regiment of a Field Artillery Battalion was not ready to fight in wartime, it would be a tragedy; but if it is not ready to fight in peacetime, it is not so bad, because the unit is not fighting in peacetime. Of course," the committee added, "air planes must be able to fly in peacetime as well as in wartime," but the rest of the army need not worry about a sudden attack. Should an emergency arise which the smaller regular army could not handle, the nation would meet it "with the citizen Reserves," as had been its "historical practice." Tompkins encouraged the planners to discount readiness still further with his curious argument that since the future "troop commitments" of the army were "unpredictable," it would "not be considered necessary to maintain Active forces for numerous contingencies." In Tompkins's reasoning, uncertainty about the future constituted grounds for decreased rather than increased readiness.[37]

The planning officers, under pressure to design a cheap force, compromised the goal of M-day readiness which had seemed mandated by wartime experience and had been embodied in their earlier plans. The committee avoided complete abandonment of that goal only by assigning the air force a supposed M-day capability. Ground force officers, apparently satisfied that at least they would administer an enormous system for training reserves, willingly capitulated to the air power argument. The committee did pay lip service to the notion of a "balanced force," but only regarding the makeup of the reserve of 4.5 million men. Air units would dominate the ready force, especial-

36. Marshall to Acting Director, SPD, 13 November 1944; Shaw, memorandum for the records re conference Office of Deputy Chief of Staff on 16 November 1944, 17 November 1944; Textor to Assistant Deputy Chief of Staff, 15 November 1944, all in file 350.06 (Study 33), SPD.

37. Shaw, memorandum for records, 17 November 1944; Tompkins to Re-Survey Committee members, 21 November 1944, both in file 350.06 (Study 33), SPD.

ly since most ground troops would be committed to the training of conscripts.[38]

The triumph of air power in doctrine would be a hollow victory for the AAF, however, if Marshall's view of budgetary and recruitment limits reduced each branch of the army to a skeletal force. G-1 estimated that without selective service the armed services could recruit only 500,000 to 600,000 soldiers and officers. If the navy took half of that number, the War Department could count on 275,000 men, an estimate G-1 later raised to 400,000.[39]

More compelling were the limitations established by anticipated appropriations. Revising their budget estimates, Richards and the Budget Division juggled their numbers to come up first with a figure of $2 billion and later $5 billion as "the absolute maximum that could be advocated for national defense in the first years of the post-war economy." If the army commanded 55 percent of the defense budget, War Department appropriations would run to $2.8 billion annually, and far less, the Budget Division conceded, if the threat of war faded from public consciousness.

Even $2.8 billion would not go far. UMT alone would cost $1.5 billion and other reserve activities another $200 million, leaving only $1.1 billion for the regular ground and air force. Even assuming questionable economies in pay, upkeep, and materiel, that amount of money would support only 275,000 regular troops, less than a third of the force contemplated in earlier plans.[40]

Despite the severe cut in forces which would be dictated by a $2.8 billion budget ceiling, Tompkins and the committee held to it. Submitting a revised plan for the postwar army to Marshall and the top command, they recommended a force of 330,000 regulars, less than a third the number of professionals proposed in the August plan. The drastic reductions, shown in the table, indicated the uncritical acceptance by the SPD staff of Marshall's admonitions on economy. Tompkins made the point frankly when he told Marshall

38. Shaw, memorandum for records, 17 November 1944, file 350.06 (Study 33), SPD.

39. Textor to Re-Survey Committee members, 28 November 1944, and Textor to Re-Survey Committee members, 1 December 1944, both in file 350.06 (Study 33), SPD; Kuter to Chief of Air Staff, 16 November 1944, Official Decimal Files SAS 322 Post War, Box 90, Arnold Papers.

40. On cost and budget estimates, see Smith, *Air Force Plans*, pp. 66–67; Textor to Re-Survey Committee members, 28 November 1944; Murray to Chief, Special Projects Office, AAF, 10 January 1945; Tompkins to Chief of Staff, dated 27 December 1944 and sent 25 January 1945, all in file 350.06 (Study 33), SPD.

that in framing the new plan he had been "concerned solely with the practical considerations of *men* and *money*." Strategy and security had at most been secondary considerations.[41]

Army Postwar Plans before and after Marshall's Intervention

	August 1944 Plan			February 1945 Plan		
	Regulars	*Trainees*	*Totals*	*Regulars*	*Trainees*[a]	*Totals*
AAF	406,745 (42.1%)	200,000	606,745	120,000 (43.5%)	2000,000	320,000
AGF	302,998 (31.4%)	320,200	633,188	100,000 (36.5%)	320,000	420,000
ASF	256,494 (26.5%)	110,017	366,511	55,000 (20.0%)	110,000	165,000
Trainers	111,813		111,813	55,000		110,000[b]
Totals	1,093,050[c]	630,317	1,723,267[c]	330,000	630,000	1,015,000[b]

a. These figures tentative as of February 1945.

b. Includes 55,000 reserve officers serving on active duty as trainers, cost chargeable to UMT program.

c. Includes approximately 16,000 in overhead personnel.

Source: Tompkins to Assistant Chief of Staff, G-3, 15 July 1944, file 320, G-3; G-3, "War Department Post-War Troop Basis, 19 August 1944," file Mobilization Plans 1944; Shaw to Tompkins, 18 July 1944, and Tompkins to Chief of Staff, dated 27 December 1944 and sent 25 January 1945, both in file 350.06 (Study 33), SPD; memorandum by Donovan, 25 April 1945, file 370.01 (Top Secret), Records of Headquarters Army Ground Forces, RG 337, National Archives Building.

Palmer approved the new plan in December, and in February Handy, Marshall, and their assistants did likewise.[42] All figures were subject to revision in light of the changing international and domestic environment, and the percentages of forces assigned to ground, air, and service units remained open for discussion. But at last the army had developed a plan which Marshall thought the nation would pay for.

Revolt of the AAF

SPD and ground force officers accepted the new plan without protest, but the air staff was less meek. The new plan provided the AAF with

41. Tompkins to Chief of Staff, 27 December 1944 and sent 25 January 1945, file 350.06 (Study 33), SPD (Tompkins's italics).

42. Palmer to Deputy Chief of Staff (through Acting Director, SPD), 18 December 1944; Hodes to Handy, 10 February 1945; Handy to Marshall, 16 February 1945, all in file 370.01 (65), Chief of Staff.

16 air groups. It had received 75 groups under the August 19 proposal and had, in its own plans, been designing a 105-group force employing a million men. Because the new plan would thwart air force ambitions, the air staff moved to defeat it.

Air planners criticized their SPD counterparts for elevating political and budgetary considerations above defense needs. The duty of the armed services was to inform the nation of the minimum requirements for its security, the AAF argued. Congress might decide to cut force levels below minimum needs, but the military should not reduce its request in anticipation of congressional frugality. General Arnold's deputy commander informed SPD that the AAF headquarters would accept no plan "based on any assumed limitations of men and money short of total national resources" if those limitations weakened national defense. In short, Army Air Forces, at least as a bargaining tactic, staked an almost unlimited claim to the national purse.[43]

Less worried about congressional pennypinching than Marshall and Palmer, the brash aviators were confident that the AAF's wartime achievements would sweep aside any obstacles to their program. The past, they claimed, should guide neither political nor military strategy. Prior experience was indicative neither

> of future requirements for the military establishment nor of the future temper of the people in respect to the proportionate amount of the nation's total resources which can and must be continuously devoted to the maintenance of that establishment.

The "estimates of economists based on our pre-war experience" should be ignored in planning budgets. The AAF planners hoped that peacetime defense budgets would run to at least $7.8 billion annually, not $5 billion as predicted by the Budget Division.[44]

War Department plans were particularly exasperating to the fliers because the army so passively accepted existing patterns of defense spending. Angry that the Budget Division ceded to the navy about half of defense appropriations, the AAF rejected "a split, however generous, of the Army's traditional short end of the peacetime defense

43. Quotation from Lieutenant General Barney M. Giles (Chief of Air Staff) to Chief of Staff (through SPD), 22 January 1945, file 350.06 (Study 33), SPD. See also Smith, *Air Force Plans*, p. 68.

44. Quotations from Smith, *Air Force Plans*, p. 68. See also Smith, *Air Force Plans*, pp. 68–70; RCM [Colonel R. C. Moffat] to Chief of Staff (Attn: SPD), draft memorandum, 14 January 1945, Official Decimal Files SAS 320.2 Post-War Army, Box 68, Arnold Papers. Although only a draft memorandum, a copy of the Moffat memorandum reached SPD; see file 350.06 (Study 33), SPD.

appropriations." The AAF rejected, too, the army's timid vision of total defense expenditures:

> If the Army and Army Air Force propose for themselves a policy of retrenchment and economy, they may find themselves standing alone in a country determined to keep the system working. The principles of disarmament are today publicly discredited. The Navy, headed by one of our most competent financiers [Forrestal], who is thoroughly familiar with fiscal policy, will align their objectives with those of the nation and, if the Army policy is not astute, will assume the responsibility for national defense.

The AAF feared that if Marshall's attitude prevailed only the navy would profit from the public's new willingness to fund peacetime defense, a prospect offensive on both political and strategic grounds. Since naval forces could no longer guard "against sudden and serious attack from abroad," they no longer deserved first place in the military establishment.[45]

In their attempt to downplay the importance of naval forces, the air planners tendered a new strategic argument. "The size of the standing Navy and Air Forces must be related to those of potential enemies," they argued. Since only England would "emerge as a first-class Naval power" after the war, whereas both Britain and Russia would "emerge as strong in Air power," air units commanded first claim to American resources. That statement was one of the first in which planners cited specific potential enemies. In January 1945, however, the air staff did not pursue its suggestion that the Soviet Union might be the nation's next adversary.[46] More important than the reference to the USSR was the narrow manner in which the AAF (and often the other services) defined its utility. In the staff's reasoning, air power could be used only against air power and navies only against navies. Enemies were identified by capability rather than intent.

The other strategic arguments in the AAF's dissent from Marshall's policy were familiar air power doctrine. A powerful air force was necessary to provide deterrence and defense against possible enemies.

---

45. Smith *Air Force Plans*, pp. 69, 70; Giles to Chief of Staff, 22 January 1945, file 350.06 (Study 33), SPD.

46. Smith, *Air Force Plans*, p. 69.

Since air power, "augmented as [it] may be by buzz-bombs and other new airborne weapons," would be the principal vehicle for launching an attack on the United States, air power had to be the primary M-day defense force. Furthermore, the AAF argued:

> A static air defense alone will not do. Like a Chinese wall or a Maginot line, it would drain our resources and fail us in the test. Rather, the sources of enemy air power, the bases from which it would spring, must be held ever subject to threat of interdiction by the striking power of the defending Air Force. Our victory or defeat in the next war may well hinge upon whether our Air Force is overthrown in the early phases as were the air forces of Poland and France in the present war.

Time would be critical, the planners noted. The only effective air fleet would be an M-day force: air power was too complicated a weapon to be mobilized quickly after the start of hostilities, and future enemy strikes would occur too swiftly to permit gradual mobilization. Either airplanes were ready at the start of an attack or they were useless. The air force also had to be large enough to support an aviation industry capable of continuously reequipping the military establishment with new craft. To the air staff, it was obvious that a 120,000-man, 16-group air force could not perform all those functions.[47]

The air staff's protests against the plan formulated by the special committee did not budge Marshall or Tompkins. Citing once again the political and budgetary restraints sure to rule in peacetime, Tompkins skirted the AAF claim that the new plan would jeopardize national security. If air strengths proved inadequate, he told Marshall, they could be reviewed at a future date.[48]

General Arnold now personally entered the fight. He complained to Marshall and Stimson about an order from the chief of staff to delete from the AAF's annual report a warning about the need for "world-wide bases" after the war. "I do not think I am an alarmist," he told his superiors in February, but the

47. Quotations from RCM [Moffat] to Chief of Staff (Attn: SPD), draft memorandum, 14 January 1945, Official Decimal Files SAS 320.2 Post-War Army, Box 68, Arnold Papers. See also Smith, *Air Force Plans*, pp. 68–69; Davison to Tompkins, 22 December 1944, file 350.06 (Study 33), SPD.

48. Addendum to memorandum, Tompkins to Marshall, dated 27 December 1944 and sent 25 January 1945, file 350.06 (Study 33), SPD.

potentialities for production of weapons capable of sudden and over-powering attack are such . . . that the air power on which we must rely for protection against them must have available to it and under our control a system of air bases extending far beyond our domestic shores and not limited to our present insular possessions.[49]

On March 30, in a memorandum drafted by his staff, Arnold ridiculed the plan for sixteen air groups as constituting "virtual disarmament in air strength." National security had to come before political considerations, he wrote, but this "miniature Air Force . . . would be acceptable only under world conditions the attainment of which appears . . . to be highly improbable." The air force would not even be able to man the bases proposed under JCS 570, already approved by the President. "Surely it will not be the War Department Policy that the Navy is to provide the peacetime M-day air force," Arnold added pointedly.[50]

Whereas Marshall doubted the willingness of Americans to support postwar defense, Arnold cited popular reaction to international agreements at Yalta and elsewhere as evidence of "a new and sturdy resolve on the part of the American people after this war to really *do* something toward enforcement of international law and order." In a compelling summary of the air power argument, he hinted that the public would side with the AAF if the War Department tried to oppose the airmen's ambitions:

> They [the American people] will remember that air power is subject to revolutionary developments and changes; and that the possibility of a sudden, unpredictable and paralyzing blow from the air must always be taken into consideration. Next time, the United States may well be the first target of the aggressor. If he is allowed to mount and launch a surprise attack, it is unlikely that there will be opportunity for our gradual mobilization, or any chance to rely for our early protection on the efforts of other nations. Our elaborate mobilization plans could be buried and lost in rubble, and our trained reserves might never see a battle.

49. Arnold to the Secretary of War and the Chief of Staff, 25 February 1945, file 321 (AAF), Chief of Staff. At the time this memorandum was dated, Arnold was convalescing from a heart condition, and may not have given the memorandum his personal attention. However the unusually personal phrasing of the memorandum indicates that he probably did approve it. The phrase "world-wide bases" was used in Pasco to Marshall, 14 February 1945, Memos for the Chief of Staff, Chief of Staff Secretariat Files, Chief of Staff.
50. Arnold to Chief of Staff, 30 March 1945, file 350.06 (Study 33), SPD. Portions of this memorandum are published and discussed in Smith, *Air Force Plans*, pp. 88–90.

The American people recognized that "the only certain protection against such aggression is to meet and overcome it before it can be launched or take full effect." They would therefore be willing, Arnold implied, to support not only a strong air defense but the use of air power to deter or even preempt an enemy attack.[51]

Finally, Arnold uncovered the doubts about UMT which for months many of his staff had entertained. The staff was suspicious that one year of training would be insufficient for teaching the complex skills of an air crewman. Arnold's major objections to UMT were political and strategic. Marshall insisted that with a large pool of reserves the nation would need only a small M-day force. In contrast, Arnold asserted that universal training would require a professional air force larger than otherwise necessary. In order to train reservists the AAF would need a cadre of 50,000 additional men, while the time element in war made it impossible for him to risk a cut in M-day forces. He took Marshall's argument in behalf of UMT, the need for a ready force to deter aggression, and turned it against universal training:

> If it [UMT] can only be maintained at the expense of so great a portion of the peacetime regular establishment that the available M-Day force will be unable to prevent our quick overthrow before the nation can be mobilized, then universal military training will defeat its purpose.

The AAF welcomed UMT only so long as it constituted an adjunct to a large standing air force. If the War Department could not support both UMT and the 75-group or 105-group air force that Arnold dreamed of, he wanted to discard UMT. His attitude, along with Marshall's insistence on economy in the postwar army, made a crisis over UMT and the 330,000-man force certain.[52] As the war in Europe reached its climax, so too did the struggles within the army over its future shape.

Those struggles soon yielded to deadlock, in part because the planners, even with the intervention of the high-powered Operations

51. Ibid. Arnold's statement suggesting deterrence and preemptive action had appeared almost verbatim earlier in his published report to Secretary Stimson: "We must recognize that the only certain protection against such aggression is the ability to meet and overcome it before the aggressor can strike the first blow." See General Henry Harley Arnold, *Second Report of the Commanding General of the Army Air Forces, February 27, 1945, to the Secretary of War Reports*, in *War Reports*, p. 414.

52. Quotation from Arnold to Chief of Staff, 30 March 1945, file 350.06 (Study 33), SPD. See also Smith, *Air Force Plans*, pp. 86–92; Kuter to Arnold, 17 January 1945, Official Decimal Files SAS 320.2 Post-War Army, Box 88, Arnold Papers.

Division, reached no genuine agreement on which world conditions would permit reduction of the army to 330,000 men. Arnold had stated his willingness to accept a force of that size "if there should ultimately supervene an ideal international situation." Tompkins hinted that he might accept such a precondition.[53] But a truce between the two generals based on Arnold's precondition was meaningless. Everyone could endorse a small army if world peace and disarmament triumphed. The tough decision involved the type of force adequate in less utopian circumstances.

Brigadier General George A. Lincoln, one of the keenest minds in OPD, pointed out the real obstacle to effective planning: the failure of the Special Planning Division to develop systematic assumptions about world conditions in the periods for which it was planning. The army needed "new planning techniques" with which to study "*new weapons, capabilities, and attitudes of potential enemies, potential speed of military expansion,*" and other variables of postwar defense. Too, there existed an "impelling need for broad and enduring guidance" on planning from higher authority and for efforts on a "Joint level." Tompkins was wary about sharing War Department plans with the navy, however, and neither he nor OPD heeded Lincoln's plea for sophisticated predictive techniques.[54]

The imprecision of strategic assumptions complicated the efforts of Marshall and his staff to counter the AAF's claims and resolve the twin issues of UMT and force levels. Not new, those issues were argued no more cogently in 1945 than earlier, and no more sensibly in private than they were in public. The General Staff did not, for example, effectively rebut the AAF's contention that push-button aerial warfare would make M-day readiness all-important and render large reserves of ground forces helpless. UMT defenders, citing historical trends, argued that while mechanization diminished the size of combat forces, it required increased support troops which UMT might train. But UMT proponents did not explain how reservists, most of whom would need refresher training before going to war, could be readied for action in time to meet a sudden attack. The army might have made an effective argument that UMT would prove useful if an initial aerial clash proved indecisive in a future war.

53. Tompkins to Deputy Chief of Staff, 7 April 1945, file 350.06 (Study 33), SPD.
54. Two memoranda, Lincoln to Assistant Chief of Staff and to General Hull, 15 April 1945, file 320 (80), OPD (Lincoln's italics).

As Tompkins once pointed out, "if for any reason the first aggressive move fails . . . war inevitably degenerates into an even more bitter trial of the ultimate strengths of the nations involved." But Marshall's staff never rigorously analyzed how a mass reserve of ground forces might be useful in that contingency, or in situations short of world war, such as counterrevolutionary activity, police actions, and occupation duties.[55]

The General Staff was no more successful in its defense of UMT on grounds of political and fiscal necessity. The economizers argued that, given a Congress unwilling to fund a large standing army, UMT was the best way of providing the nation a measure of security at minimum cost. Marshall emphasized repeatedly during the spring of 1945 that he was "opposed to a large Regular Army."

> You can't possibly pay for one. You can't get enough money in taxes to support it. You can't hire a regular army. You cannot get the men. I know that from my own experience—both as to the men and to the appropriations made by Congress. The national budget is a matter of vital importance to both political parties and the minute you get on a peace establishment, the last thing they want to hear about is a military problem.

Mindful of the fate of the National Defense Act of 1920, Marshall explained that he would be "very much depressed" if Congress passed a law for an expensive army because he knew "it would be emasculated within a year and a half." Without UMT, he declared, "you have kissed goodby" to effective defense.[56]

General Handy, whom Marshall delegated to deal with Arnold on the force levels issue, developed that point further. Handy believed that Arnold was mistaken in thinking that the War Department had a choice to make between a large professional army without UMT and a small force based on universal training. Rather, the choice lay between a small force backed up by UMT and a small army with no effective reserve system at all. An army dependent on UMT might not be the ideal M-day force, Handy conceded, but it would serve national security better than if the War Department had no effective

55. General George C. Marshall, *Biennial Report of the Chief of Staff of the United States Army, July 1, 1943, to June 30, 1945, to the Secretary of War,* in *War Reports,* pp. 292–93; Tompkins, "Future Manpower Needs of the Armed Forces," pp. 56–57.

56. Marshall, "Comments . . . 3 May 1945 . . . ," transcript, file Plans and Policy Office UMT Decimal File (1944–48) 020 Chief of Staff, L&LD.

reserve system and "depended entirely upon such a regular establishment as the Congress might see fit to provide."[57]

But if funds were limited, were they best spent on UMT or on bolstering the M-day air force? In April 1945, G-3 calculated that with the $2.8 billion which the army would supposedly have to spend after the war, the War Department could pay for 330,000 regular troops and 630,000 trainees, or for 700,000 regular soldiers if it abandoned UMT. That is, UMT would drain $1.5 billion and 370,000 men from the ready force.[58] The staff did not, however, systematically analyze the alternatives open to them and assess whether the $1.5 billion was best spent on air power, UMT, or other preparedness measures. The General Staff simply assumed that the nation would have time to mobilize its trained reserves, though the army staff never really contested the AAF's assertion to the contrary.

Worse, Marshall's men gave the appearance of sacrificing national security to domestic politics. In a memorandum prepared with Marshall's help, General Handy acknowledged that security had priority over political considerations but argued that there was "little hope of maintaining a standing Army throughout the peacetime years large enough to provide the degree of national security this country should have." What Congress would pay for, not national security, had to be "the most realistic consideration," and Congress would certainly be miserly.[59] There was wisdom in Handy's comments. Certainly Arnold's attempt to lay unlimited claim to the national treasury was irresponsible. But Handy's argument could have been used to justify air power as much as UMT. The UMT program could be persuasive only if sold on sound strategic as well as fiscal grounds. By stressing the latter, Marshall's staff allowed the AAF to cast the issue as one of security versus economy, when in fact the dispute was over competing means to achieve security with limited funds.

The position of the UMT defenders was also weak because they shared the same strategic outlook as the AAF. All factions continued to believe that the destructiveness of modern weaponry and the dangers of appeasement made deterrence the first priority of American

57. Handy to Arnold, 5 May 1945, file 350.06 (Study 33), SPD.

58. Edwards to Tompkins, 29 April 1945, file 350.06 (Study 33), SPD.

59. Handy to Arnold, 5 May 1945, file 350.06 (Study 33), SPD. For Marshall's role in drafting this memorandum, see the handwritten request by Marshall for Handy's comment on Arnold's memorandum of March 30, and Handy's memorandum to Marshall, 1 May 1945, file 370.01 (65), Chief of Staff.

policy. Tompkins, justifying UMT before a secret session of the House Military Affairs Committee, warned that the next war would "hit us with sudden fury," while a colleague spoke of "the possibility of a one hundredfold 'Pearl Harbor.'" Even as Marshall was trying to rein in the big spenders in the army, he called on one of them, General Arnold, to assist him in alerting the American people to the dangers which lay ahead:

> For your private information, I am planning in my next Biennial Report due 30 June 1945 to present the strongest possible case for our postwar needs. I can think of no more conclusive argument in support of this plan than a revelation in simple graphic language of the potentiality of the robot bomb, the various kinds of V-weapons, the jet-propelled plane, and other scientific developments not now known to the public. To be effective, this must be realistic and yet shocking in its impact.[60]

Playing into the hands of their opponents, the UMT advocates did not grasp that their arguments for peacetime readiness could be used just as effectively to justify air power. If the nation's safety was so precarious, critics like Arnold asked, then how could Marshall submit to the political limitations imposed by a naive or misinformed public? If enemies might strike with robot bombs allowing only minutes of warning, then how could he shackle air power, rely on a reserve that might take months to mobilize, or accept SPD's assumption of "at least a year's warning of the imminence of war" in which to mobilize?[61] Marshall's response to critics was that UMT struck a fair balance between security needs and political considerations. To the air staff, as well as to many in the navy, the nation's safety could not be compromised. The only acceptable policy was one which guaranteed national security.

Given the confusion over strategic assumptions, debate on the relative merits of UMT or a 75-group air force proved barren. Marshall's stand against the air force demands failed to check the pressure for a larger professional force. Figures ranging from 388,000 to

---

60. Testimony of Tompkins before the House Military Affairs Committee executive session, 4 May 1945, and testimony of Brigadier General E. A. Evans, 7 May 1945, file 032.2 (House Military Affairs Committee), SPD; Marshall to Arnold [written by Colonel H. M. Pasco], 18 May 1945, file 319.1 (7), Chief of Staff.

61. Quotation from Tompkins to Assistant Chiefs of Staff of G-1, G-2, G-4, and OPD, 14 May 1945, file 370.9 (14 May 1945) (Top Secret), OPD.

1,500,000 men for the postwar army circulated among army officers in April and May. Force level planning soon degenerated into a morass of competing schemes.[62]

The proliferation of figures above the approved 330,000 ceiling occurred partly because SPD lost its grip on the planning apparatus as other agencies, especially the Operations Division, began to take an interest in postwar matters. More important was a growing uneasiness in the War Department over competition for men and money from the navy. By April, the admirals were completing their plans for a postwar navy of 660,000 men. While Tompkins and his staff may not have known of that figure, they certainly believed that the army would place itself in a poor bargaining position if it asked for much less than the navy. On May 7 an army officer suggested to a secret House committee meeting that the army would need 500,000 men after the war, though the War Department quickly repudiated that figure when it leaked to the press.[63] Mounting pressure from congressmen for estimates of the size of the postwar army may have heightened the sense of an impending battle among the services over the division of resources, while the need for alternative plans in case Congress rejected UMT was finally becoming apparent.[64]

Pressures within the War Department also encouraged the rash of new proposals. Confronted with competing claims for men and money, the planning bureaucracy, with its structural and temperamental bias toward avoiding rather than resolving conflict, raised the estimated force levels. At the same time, more and more officers

62. Irvine to Tompkins, 14 March 1945; M. S. J. to Chief, Strategy and Policy Group, OPD, 20 April 1945, both in file ABC 040 (2 November 1943) Sec. 5-1/2-B, OPD; Tompkins to Assistant Chiefs of Staff of G-1, G-2, G-4, and OPD, 21 April 1945, file 370.9 (21 April 1945) (Top Secret), OPD; Tompkins to Assistant Chiefs of Staff of G-1, G-2, G-4 and OPD, 14 May 1945, file 370.9 (14 May 1945) (Top Secret), OPD; Edwards to Director, SPD, 28 April 1945, file 350.06 (Study 33), SPD; SPD to Marshall, draft memorandum, n.d. [ca. 3 May 1945]; Niegarth to Tompkins, 2 May 1945, both in file 032.2 (House Select Committee), SPD; "Comments of Major Commands re Troop Basis 'A,'" unsigned handwritten notations, n.d. [May 1945], file Subject File Top Secret Sec. 71 (Permanent Postwar Army), Records of the G-1 (Personnel) Division, RG 165.

63. For the secret testimony and the story of the leak to the press, see New York Times, 9 May 1945, and the collection of news stories on the incident in file News Summaries (1944–1948) Universal Military Training May–August 1945, Chief of Information, Public Information Division, Records of the Chief of Staff of the United States Army, RG 319, National Archives Building.

64. E. W. S. to Persons, 10 April 1945, file 032.2 (House Select Committee), SPD; Tompkins to Assistant Chiefs of Staff of G-1, G-2, G-4, and OPD, 21 April 1945, file 370.9 (21 April 1945) (Top Secret), OPD; Edwards to Tompkins, 28 April 1945, file 350.06 (Study 33), SPD.

questioned the adequacy of a 330,000-man force. Arnold's theoretical arguments, rather than international factors, probably prompted the reevaluation. OPD, long sympathetic to the AAF's claims, challenged the 330,000 figure, and even Handy, despite his stand against Arnold, seemed to grant the need for a larger force.[65]

Beset by conflicting demands and interests, the army's planning machinery stalled just when its forces in Europe triumphed. By June, Marshall's ceiling on postwar force levels had collapsed, and planning for the size of the army had practically ceased. At the same time, the urgent task of redeploying American forces to the Pacific further obstructed effective planning, while the expectation of twelve to eighteen months' more combat in the Pacific invited procrastination. Bureaucratic politics and the demands of global war had thwarted Marshall's determination to complete a postwar program by war's end. Only the navy met the deadline. While the services shared a common ideology, they could formulate no common plan for force levels. In another matter, however, that of scientific preparedness, they were reaching agreement more easily.

65. Memorandum by Donovan, 20 April 1945, file 370.01 (Top Secret), Army Ground Forces; memorandum for the record, 23 April 1945, file 370.9 (21 April 1945) (Top Secret), OPD; M. S. J. to Chief, Strategy and Policy Group, OPD, 20 April 1945, file ABC 040 (2 November 1943) Sec. 5-1/2-B, OPD; Hull to Deputy Chief of Staff, 14 April 1945, file 350.06 (Study 33), SPD.

5 SOLDIERS AND SCIENTISTS

As American forces sliced through Germany in the closing days of World War II, army ordnance experts discovered that Nazi scientists had been working on a devastating new rocket. The A-10 rocket, with a range of thirty-five hundred miles and the capability to reach New York City, was scheduled for use against the United States by early 1946. In the wake of such findings, the Allied victory over Hitler appeared to have come at the eleventh hour. "Our margin of time was not great," a team of officers reported, "and it is certain that more extensive attacks were dangerously near." Had Germany stalled the Allied advance a little longer, the Americans speculated, her miracle weapons might have reversed the war's outcome. That realization suggested a clear lesson to American planners: the United States would now have to harness science in peacetime "to insure a continuation of [its] national existence."[1] Mindful of that and other lessons of the war, soldiers and scientists resolved to make their wartime collaboration a permanent partnership. Their success in doing so was one of the most enduring legacies of the war.

Only a few years earlier the prospects for such a partnership appeared dim. Once fruitful in the nineteenth century, institutionalized cooperation between civilian science and the military was moribund prior to World War II except in the field of aircraft development, in which the National Advisory Committee for Aeronautics made important theoretical and practical advances. The limited weapons research pursued was largely decentralized among many army and navy technical bureaus (Ordnance, Aeronautics, and Signal Corps, among others), which in peacetime rarely acquired the services of top-notch scientists. The services invested little in weapons research, and got little from it.[2]

1. Quotations from The General Board, United States Forces, European Theater, "V-2 Rocket Attacks and Defense," Study No. 42 in the Reports of the General Board, n.d. [1945–46], copy in Office of the Chief of Military History, Washington, D.C. See also James McGovern, *Crossbow and Overcast* (New York, 1964).
2. Clarence G. Lasby, "Science and the Military," in David D. Van Tassel and Michael G. Hall, eds., *Science and Society in the U.S.*, pp. 255–59.

Responsibility for the dearth of weapons development was hard to assign. During World War II, scientists and military men, in addition to faulting each other, blamed politicians and the public for failing to finance adequate research. The accusation was only partly true. In the 1920s and 1930s, Congress never cut the research and development budgets submitted by the executive, and occasionally even increased those budgets. The armed services or the Budget Bureau, perhaps unduly sensitive to pacifist opinion and to opponents of government spending, did sometimes trim requests in anticipation of congressional disapproval. Contrary to later allegations, however, pacifist protests and revisionist agitation over the American role in World War I had little effect on funding for research. Army and navy budgets for research and development, which ranged between $4 and $7.7 million during the interwar period, reached the low figure in 1930, well before the Nye Committee gathered, and peaked in 1935, at the height of committee activities so often cited as a bar to preparedness. The priority assigned to military research was low throughout the period, but, especially during the depression, budgetary considerations did more to squeeze research funding than did antimilitarism.[3]

The services themselves were partially responsible for the lack of funding. The huge surplus of weapons from World War I encouraged complacency in the military as well as in Congress about promoting new weapons. Further, many officers, schooled in nineteenth-century techniques of warfare, simply failed to recognize the importance of peacetime research. As an official army historian later admitted, they "knew tactics and strategy far better than they knew supply." Confronted with limited budgets, defense officials chose to sacrifice investment in new weapons for maintenance of manpower and officer strength. Congress and the Budget Bureau, lacking enough expertise about military matters to assign priorities in military budgets, did not challenge the services' decision.[4]

---

3. For factors affecting the level of military research spending before World War II, see Watson, *Chief of Staff*, chap. 2; Huzar, *The Purse and the Sword*, pp. 133–56; Miller, "The United States Army During the 1930s," pp. 13–16, 27–38, chaps. 3–4; Furer, Tompkins and Compton to Charles Wilson, 3 August 1944, Frank Jewett File 50.1324D, National Academy of Sciences Archives, Washington, D.C.; "Report of the Conference on Research between representatives of the War Department, Science Advisory Board and National Research Council, January 2, 1934," in Science Advisory Board Files, NAS. Detailed figures for army research spending are in Richards to Tompkins, memorandum, "Appropriations for Research and Development, War Department Military Establishment, For Fiscal Years 1921–1945," 24 January 1944, file 350.06 (Study 114), SPD.

4. See n. 3. Quotation from Watson, *Chief of Staff*, p. 55.

Civilian science, especially pure research, was scarcely better off. To be sure, applied science had entered the mainstream of American culture and politics even before the Progressive era. Agronomists and statisticians, geologists and engineers, foresters and doctors demonstrated their utility in promoting the nation's expansion, rationalizing its government, and managing its environment. They also developed constituencies which profited from and supported their claims to government aid. But pure science, the pursuit of knowledge for its own sake rather than for practical application, had no constituency. Scientists tried to generate support by arguing that pure research, though pursued because of intellectual curiosity, yielded practical applications. Without replenishment from basic research, the scientists contended, the American economy would stagnate and the nation's security would suffer.[5]

The scientists' "trickle-down" arguments about the benefits of basic research were plausible but ultimately unprovable. The arguments, one writer has noted, bore a kinship to classical economics, which "assumes public benefit to be the unintended by-product of individual self-interest; the scientist, by satisfying his own curiosity about nature, gives society what it wants—the means for further technological and economic progress." Scientists maintained that government could not control their creative work without crippling it, any more than government could interfere with the delicate workings of the free market. Yet because science did have utilitarian results, government should support it.[6]

Before World War II, such claims did not help scientists gain federal assistance. World War I had been too short, and American scientific endeavors too unsuccessful, for scientists to make a dramatic case for the fruits of pure research. By the 1920s pure science, exemplified by Einstein's work, had become so esoteric that its practical application and even its credibility seemed remote. Scientists' scruples about government support further undermined their efforts to secure federal aid. Suspicious that dependence on government funds might contaminate their intellectual and political integrity, they would

5. Ronald C. Tobey, *The American Ideology of National Science, 1919–1930*; Don K. Price, *Government and Science*, chap. 1; Daniel S. Greenberg, *The Politics of Pure Science*, chap. 3; Lasby, "Science and the Military."

6. Quotation from Michael D. Reagan, *Science and the Federal Patron*, pp. 40–41. See also Greenberg, *Politics of Pure Science*, pp. 29–34.

accept federal money only if channeled through their own institutions, such as the National Academy of Sciences. The men of science cherished their isolation from government and society even as they sought to overcome it.[7]

Consequently, proponents of basic research failed in several attempts to overcome their poverty. Frustrated in efforts to convert the academy into a base for federal support and coordination of science, scientists turned in the 1920s to private industry and philanthropy to raise an endowment for basic research. Despite the backing of men like Elihu Root and Herbert Hoover, the endowment scheme failed. In the summer of 1933 scientists did secure an executive order establishing a Science Advisory Board. Upset by retrenchment in government support of science during the depression, they hoped that the board would help them secure assistance under the impending National Industrial Recovery Act. Their hopes proved unfounded. Quarrels among scientists undermined the campaign for aid. The exclusion of the biological, medical, and social sciences from the board offended a large section of the academic community, while leaders of the National Academy of Sciences were indignant that Roosevelt's executive order excluded the academy from selection and operation of the board. Physicist Karl Compton, the board's chairman, pressed for a "Recovery Program of Science Progress," under which the government would appropriate $16 million for the academy to distribute. But the National Resources Board, a bastion of the social sciences, promptly blocked that request.[8]

In 1934, members of the Science Advisory Board sought to rekindle military interest in research. Robert Millikan, dean of American physicists, warned military officials that "research is a peace-time thing and ...moves too slowly to be done after you get into trouble." Frank Jewett, president of Bell Telephone Laboratories, offered the National Academy of Sciences' National Research Council as an agency of military-science collaboration. Most officers responded with only polite interest. Like many of their colleagues before World War

---

7. Tobey, *The American Ideology of National Science*, pp. 20–23, chaps. 4–5; Greenberg, *Politics of Pure Science*, pp. 60–61.

8. Tobey, *The American Ideology of National Science*, pp. 33–61, 200–05; Lewis E. Auerbach, "Scientists in the New Deal: A Pre-War Episode in the Relations Between Science and Government in the United States," *Minerva* 3 (Summer 1965): 457–82; Carroll W. Pursell, Jr., "The Anatomy of a Failure: The Science Advisory Board," *Proceedings of the American Philosophical Society* 109 (December 1965): 342–51.

II, they appeared complacent about the military's preparedness and confused about what civilian science could do for defense.[9]

With the failure of the Science Advisory Board, the position of pure science in American politics and society reached its nadir. In the depression, scientists felt useless or, even worse, blamed for the economic crisis. Compton later bitterly recalled:

> We were told by some that unrestrained enterprise and technological progress had overbuilt production way beyond our capacity to consume the goods produced. We technologists wondered if we had any right to be alive, let alone to do our job, as we heard and read the theories of those who believed that higher standards of living are assured by curbing production, not stimulating it; by making production more expensive rather than cheaper; by distributing wealth by laws without much thought of how this wealth can be created.[10]

Like businessmen, scientists experienced a painful sense of rejection during the 1930s.

The Axis menace gave them a new purpose. Scientists rallied early to the antifascist cause. Their frequent contacts with European scientists and the flight to the United States of such luminaries as Einstein and Enrico Fermi sensitized American scientists to the perils of fascism, especially to the possibility that Germany might build an atomic bomb. "Remember that we in this laboratory are the only persons in the world who can possibly prepare this weapon before the Nazis," Arthur Holly Compton remarked to a colleague early in the war.[11] To counter the potential German threat, nuclear scientists decided in 1939 to approach the Roosevelt administration about building an atomic bomb.

At the same time, leaders of science urged mobilization of civilian talent in other areas of weapons development. Jewett, Karl Compton, Vannevar Bush (president of the Carnegie Institution), and Harvard president James Conant all believed that the services' technical bureaus were unreceptive to the contributions of civilian researchers. As Bush recalled, they shared an anxiety that the United States could not escape involvement in the war and that "the military system . . . would never fully produce the new instrumentalities which we would

9. Science Advisory Board, "Report of the Conference . . . January 2, 1934," Science Advisory Board Files, NAS. Quotation from pp. 14–15 of the report.

10. Karl Compton, "Technological and Scientific Resources," *Annals of the American Academy of Political and Social Science* 218 (November 1941): 66, from a speech delivered 16 July 1941.

11. Marjorie Johnston, ed., *The Cosmos of Arthur Holly Compton* (New York, 1967), p. 44.

certainly need, and which were possible because of the state of science as it then stood." In 1940 they persuaded President Roosevelt to establish a civilian agency for military research, the National Defense Research Committee, followed in 1941 by the Office of Scientific Research and Development (OSRD). The armed services played an advisory role in OSRD, but civilians like Bush, who was director of the new organization, ran the crash program in military research. Two other agencies also came to perform important service. Specializing in aircraft was the National Advisory Committee for Aeronautics, established in 1915 and governed by a joint board of civilian scientists and military representatives. The patrician National Academy of Sciences, a private organization chartered by Congress, rendered technical advice to military and civilian agencies.[12]

By 1943 the superiority of civilian science over military efforts was accepted by both officers and scientists. Civilian agencies like OSRD, rather than the technical bureaus of the services, achieved most of the scientific breakthroughs during the war. The army did take over the atomic bomb project in 1942, but only after scientists had completed basic research, and then only to perform development and production tasks beyond the capacity of OSRD. To OSRD went primary credit for the development of the incendiary bomb, the artillery rocket, the proximity fuse, and, in partnership with the British, radar. In use by 1943, those weapons dramatized the revolutionary impact of science on warfare. The proximity fuse, for example, detonated shells by proximity to their target rather than time or distance from launch. It so enhanced the deadliness of Allied anti-aircraft and artillery fire that for months the Allies refused to use it over land for fear the enemy would capture a dud. Its success hinged on the development and mass production of a tiny radio whose glass tubes had to withstand an initial blast generating twenty thousand times the force of gravity when the shell was fired. The radio would then determine target proximity and trigger the explosion of the shell. By their important role in developing weapons like the proximity fuse, pure scientists now possessed a convincing case for the utility of their work.[13]

12. Quotation from Vannevar Bush, *Pieces of the Action*, p. 34. See also Bush, *Pieces of the Action*, pp. 30–45; Greenberg, *Politics of Pure Science*, chap. 4; Richard G. Hewlett and Oscar E. Anderson, Jr., *The New World, 1939/1946*, chap. 2.

13. James Phinney Baxter, *Scientists Against Time*, surveys OSRD's achievements. See also Bush, *Pieces of the Action*, pp. 106–14; Hewlett and Anderson, *The New World*, chap. 3.

Rebounding from the poverty and abuse of the 1930s, scientists welcomed the funds earned for them by their wartime inventiveness. Besides strengthening the military arsenal, their work helped fulfill their "peace-time objectives." Karl Compton, an OSRD official and president of the Massachusetts Institute of Technology, informed MIT in 1941 that much wartime research

> is actually an intensification of investigations already under way and is so fundamental that we would have welcomed at any time the opportunity to undertake it with the effectiveness that subventions from government and industry now make possible. While contributing directly to wartime needs, it is yielding new developments, new techniques and new understanding which will have important peacetime applications and which presage a new prosperity for science and engineering after the war.[14]

Compton and other proponents of pure science saw the chance to turn a temporary windfall into permanent federal support. By 1943 the lure was enormous. OSRD alone spent $115 million in fiscal 1944, while the army and navy spent $513 million, plus another $860 million for the Manhattan Project. Much of the money went to the nation's campuses. A few years earlier, in 1939, the total military budget for research and development had been a puny $13 million. [15]

There were less tangible rewards as well. Scientists who had long labored in quiet obscurity must have found their sudden importance exhilarating. Millions of Americans were told that this was a chemist's or a physicist's war. Bush and others attracted lavish attention from the glossy popular press. One scientist later recalled how

> suddenly physicists were exhibited as lions at Washington tea parties, were invited to conventions of social scientists, where their opinions on society were respectfully listened to by lifelong experts in the field, attended conventions of religious orders and discoursed on theology,

14. Karl Compton, "Some Educational Effects and Implications of the Defense Program," *Science* 94 (17 October 1941): 368–69.

15. National Science Foundation, *Federal Funds for Research Development, and Other Activities*, vol. 17 (Washington, 1968), p. 215; U.S. Congress, House Select Committee on Postwar Military Policy, *Hearings, Surplus Material—Research and Development*, 78/1, 1944 (hereafter cited as Woodrum Committee, *R&D Hearings*), pp. 228–29. Since no precise agreement exists on what constitutes "research and development," figures for science spending vary among sources. The 1939 figures do not include expenditures by the National Advisory Committee for Aeronautics.

were asked to endorse plans for world government, and to give simplified lectures on the nucleus to Congressional committees.[16]

The time seemed ripe to press the scientists' claims for public support.

Compton, Bush, and their kind were not necessarily representative of all scientists. Though possessing impressive credentials as researchers, they had long ago subordinated laboratory work to administration. As "science politicians" (Bush's label for this group), they were an elite, generally politically conservative, whose interests may not have been identical to those of active researchers. But holding as they did the commanding positions in the politics of science— usually several positions, simultaneously, in and out of government —they were the primary spokesmen for their profession. As such, they led the drive to institutionalize the war-born partnership with the military.

The Common Goal

The incentive for scientists to seek public support had long existed. New in 1943 was the identity of interest now perceived by soldier and scientist. At stake now, it appeared to both partners, were not the fortunes of one interest group, but the fate of both, and of the nation. The war seemed to prove that national security would hinge on scientific readiness more than any other element of military power. The partners invoked the ideology of preparedness to advance their claims for peacetime research.

Scientists often articulated the ideology more aggressively than their military colleagues. Even before postwar planning began, they argued that Allied weakness and naivete had caused the war. As one scientist observed:

> The weariness of the struggle and the distaste for carnage and destruction, coupled with a naive faith that men had learned finally the lesson of war's futility, gave rise to the era of small appropriations to the military, to disarmament conferences and to the League of Nations and similar efforts to organize the world for settlement of international controversies by reasonable methods rather than by recourse to mass murder.

16. Quoted in Greenberg, *Politics of Pure Science*, p. 95.

Bush made the point more simply in 1944. "If we had been on our toes in war technology ten years ago, we would probably not have had this damn war."[17]

By that logic, weapons research could also deter a future war, a claim argued with particular vigor by the Compton brothers. Karl Compton left little to the imagination as he sketched the threats postwar America would face:

> If we are not to become easy and inviting prey to the next well-prepared aggressor, we must be alert to be ourselves prepared to meet what may come. What this may be, who can tell? Pilotless aircraft? Automatically guided missiles? Disease germs? Super-long-range bombardments with super explosiveness? Devices not even envisaged? What can we do to keep such horrors from being unleashed, or to protect ourselves against them if they are?

Compton had a ready answer. By supporting weapons research, the United States "should be able, with only reasonable attention and effort, to keep itself in a position too impregnable to give any encouragement to any would-be aggressor." There was "no danger of America's becoming war-minded or seeking conquest," Compton claimed. Indeed, "the strong pacifist sentiment of the 1920's and 1930's" showed that the problem was just the opposite. "The Nazis, Fascists and Japs," Compton explained, "were encouraged, not deterred, by the pledges of our youth never to bear arms, or by our refusal to strengthen the defenses of Guam or to mount modern guns on Corregidor."[18]

Arthur Holly Compton had earlier voiced similar ideas. Less concerned with historical patterns, the Nobel Prize physicist stressed the beneficence and power of science. Technology was restructuring both physical and human relationships in the United States. "Only those features of society can survive which adapt men to life under the conditions of growing science and technology." And just as science reshaped the United States in its own image, America would reshape the world in her image:

17. Frank Jewett, "The Mobilization of Science in National Defense," *Science* 95 (6 March 1942): 236; "Yankee Scientist," *Time*, 3 April 1944, p. 57.

18. Karl Compton address, "National Security and Scientific Research," 19 April 1945, published as pamphlet by the Technology Press, Massachusetts Institute of Technology, n.d. [1945]. copy in file 609, Papers of Vannevar Bush, Library of Congress. Excerpts in *New York Times*, 20 April 1945.

> People in other parts of the world look with dread to the time when
> their lives will be altered by technology. ... We do not dread science
> and technology; it is natural to us as part of our lives. Of necessity
> the world must look to America as the pioneer in finding how to live
> a satisfying life in a society based on science.

Buoyed by faith in both his discipline and his country, Compton
believed that the "alert government should be able to prevent serious
wars" and thwart any nation which sought "mastery of the world."
While acknowledging the value of a "world police force," Compton
argued that "peace in the new world ... can not be ensured unless the
dominant power [apparently the United States] keeps up a vigorous
and continued growth of science." Compton assumed that the United
States could maintain a technological superiority that no other nation
could duplicate or defy. Like many scientists, he was both fearful of
the nation's weakness and smug about its superiority.[19]

In the last two years of the war, military and industrial leaders
echoed the Comptons' contentions. The world need not worry about
American power, argued General Electric's Charles Wilson in
defending military research. "We can possess the mightiest and
deadliest armament in the world without becoming aggressors in
our hearts, because we do not have the intoxicating lust for blood
and power which periodically transforms the German military
caste." Navy Secretary Forrestal justified weapons research as a
device to strengthen an American "police force" capable of patrolling
the world. More commonly, defense officials contended that the
United States could deter aggression merely through the possession
rather than the use of awesome military power. Under Secretary
of War Robert Patterson defended peacetime research as providing
"a strength that will foreclose the possibility of others attacking us."
The alternative, he cautioned, was "a repetition of the twenties or
thirties," when the United States lacked the strength to keep the
peace.[20]

To critics who questioned the impact of an American program of

19. Arthur Holly Compton, "What Science Requires of the New World," *Science* 99 (14
January 1944): 23–28.

20. Charles Wilson, "For the Common Defense: A Plea for a Continuing Program of Industrial Preparedness," *Army Ordnance* 26 (March–April 1944): 285–88; James Forrestal, speech
before Navy Industrial Association, excerpts in *New York Times*, 12 September 1944; Woodrum
Committee, *R&D Hearings*, p. 126.

scientific preparedness on United Nations harmony, defenders of
weapons research made the predictable replies. American strength,
they contended, would only give the United Nations the credibility
it needed to enforce world peace. They foresaw no conflict between
American goals and the purposes of the United Nations. Scientific
preparedness was "not inconsistent in any way with the development
of a peaceful family of nations cooperating to the fullest," Bush
explained to Congress in May 1945. "Such a program is essential,
moreover, unless we wish this Nation to be in perpetual peril from
a sudden, ruthless, and devastating aggression which would completely extinguish our liberties."[21] Pointing to the record of the
previous thirty years as sufficient evidence of the certainty of future
aggression, preparedness advocates denied that their program was
aimed at any one nation.

Military and scientific leaders were uncertain whether weapons
research could prevent wars or simply strengthen the nation's capability to fight them. Their confusion was rooted in their reading of
recent history. Persuaded that the timidity of democratic nations
had encouraged fascist aggression, planners believed that preparedness could avert such aggression in the future. Yet the experience of
two world wars generated such pessimism that no one was willing to
place his bets on deterrence alone. References to the "next war"
peppered discussions of postwar military research by preparedness
spokesmen, hopeful that, in the words of one admiral, Americans were
"now ready to face the fact that the war to end all wars has not yet
been fought."[22] The postwar provided the opportunity not only to
prevent war but to be prepared for war should it recur. If preparedness
failed to deter war, it would still supply the strength to police or defeat
aggressors.

In promoting weapons research, preparedness spokesmen also
emphasized the technological imperative. War moved too swiftly to
permit scientific research to wait until after the first shot was fired.
Technological invention was shrinking space and collapsing time so
abruptly that it imperiled conventional notions of preparedness. As
Bush put it, Pearl Harbor was

---

21. U.S. Congress, House Committee on Military Affairs, *Hearings on H.R. 2946 (Research
and Development)*, 79/1, 1945, p. 3.
22. Admiral Julius Furer, "Post-War Military Research," *Science* 100 (24 November 1944):
461.

only a mild warning of what might happen in the future. The new German bombs and rocket bombs, our own B-29, and the many electronic devices now in use which were unknown 5 years ago, are merely the forerunners of weapons which might possess overwhelming power, the ability to strike suddenly, without warning, and without adequate means of protection or retaliation. I do not mean that some methods of protection or retaliation could not be developed. I only mean that we might not be given sufficient time within which to develop those means, once hostilities had begun, before disaster overtook us.

It was "imperative," Bush said in public testimony, "that after this war we begin at once to prepare intelligently for the type of modern war" which might soon occur. Privately, Bush had cause for even greater alarm, for he understood the likelihood of atomic and hydrogen weapons. "Every center of the population in the world in the future is at the mercy of the enemy that strikes first," he wrote Stimson in discussing international control of atomic energy.[23]

To underscore the nation's peril, Bush reminded congressmen of "the exceedingly close margin by which we and our allies clung to survival in the dark days of 1940, 1941, and 1942." "Twice we have just gotten by because we were given time to prepare while others fought." Psychologically, perhaps no theme was more powerful in the campaign for postwar research than recollection of how narrow had been the United States' margin of survival. "We had a period of grace" in both wars, Admiral Julius Furer commented in March 1945, "but we should not count on a third dispensation of that kind." That language suggested an undeserved stroke of luck, even a divine intervention, which saved the United States from the sins of military weakness.[24]

General Arnold, head of Army Air Forces, pointed to another reason for scientific preparedness. Because the United States had been "the determining factor in the defense of civilization," it would be the first target of any future aggression. The nation's economic strength, once so decisive in warfare, would no longer be as critical, for the United States would not have the time to turn its civilian

23. Woodrum Committee, *R&D Hearings*, p. 238; Bush and Conant to Stimson, 30 September 1944, Harrison-Bundy File No. 77, Manhattan Engineer District, Records of the Office of the Chief of Engineers, RG 77, National Archives Building.
24. House Military Affairs Committee, *H.R. 2946 Hearings*, p. 4; Vannevar Bush, "Science and Security," *Sea Power*, July 1945, p. 35; Admiral Julius Furer, "Scientific Research and Modern Warfare," *U.S. Naval Institute Proceedings* 71 (March 1945):269.

industries to mass production of weapons. Technological sophisti-
cation in peacetime would replace volume of production in wartime
as the key index of power. Quality, not quantity, of weapons would
determine national strength.[25]

The very swiftness of weapons development further aggravated
the danger posed by sluggish preparedness. Formerly, the achievement
of a wide technological lead over enemies was difficult because most
inventions were refinements of old weapons rather than wholly new
devices. Now science's knowledge exploded exponentially. The time
scale for weapons development had so shrunk that any tardiness in
devising instruments of war could put a nation at a fatal technological
disadvantage. The weary could never rest after producing a new
weapon, for, as Patterson pointed out in 1944, "there has never been
a time since the invention of gunpowder when obsolescence was as
swift as at the present time."[26]

Fearful of obsolescence, Patterson and other defense experts
questioned traditional practices of stockpiling surplus wartime
armaments. The under secretary cautioned Congress that surpluses
would be "an incubus hanging over us" that would "surely create
stagnation and decay." Retention of wartime leftovers would encourage a false complacency about national preparedness which would
stifle research in and production of new weapons. Yet talk of the
destruction of wartime armaments troubled military men suspicious
that they would receive starvation funding after the war. As one
congressman advised, perhaps the services should accumulate all
they could during the war, for they would not get new weapons in
peacetime. "Of course," Patterson said in summing up the dilemma,
"it is better to have an obsolete weapon than to have none... But
that is not the solution."[27]

The solution to the twin threats of obsolescence and sudden annihilation was "to go into production . . . as fast as the new developments
come along," Patterson argued, rather than waiting for the onset of
war. Perhaps for reasons of political expediency, however, Patterson
made no explicit call for a high level of industrial mobilization in
peacetime. Even as he warned of a devastating attack from aggressors

25. Quotation from Arnold, *Second Report*, in *War Reports*, p. 415. See also Furer, "Scientific
Research and Modern Warfare," p. 269.
26. Woodrum Committee, *R&D Hearings*, p. 124.
27. Ibid., pp. 68–70, 125, 133.

striking "even faster than in the past and with tenfold fury," he failed to come to grips with the implications of such an attack. Still less forward-looking was the army's Special Planning Division, charged with formulating mobilization policy. Postulating only a repetition of World War II, it assumed that the nation would have a year's warning of the onset of war and that a future war would last five years. The entrenched position of older officers in the military compounded the problem. In the navy, for example, battleship admirals devoted to traditional weaponry refused to scrap their dreadnaughts for the sake of newer weapons. Their power waned during the war, but slowly.[28]

Although the services were slow to modernize industrial mobilization policy, the more sophisticated propagandists of scientific preparedness were not. They viewed weapons research as part of an integrated program of peacetime mobilization. Edward L. Bowles, scientific advisor to Secretary Stimson, called for a "continuing working partnership" among industry, educational institutions, and the military. "We must not wait for the exigencies of war to drive us to forge these elements into some sort of machine," he warned. The concept of integrating and mobilizing those elements in peacetime "must transcend being merely doctrine; it must become a state of mind, so firmly imbedded in our souls as to become an invincible philosophy."[29]

Bowles's exhortation typified the ideological fervor exhibited by scientists and many of their military colleagues in their quest for a new program of peacetime weapons research. Driven by both self-interest and anxiety about the nation's security, they developed an unshakeable commitment to a peacetime alliance. Many of the scientists' arguments about the utility of research, especially pure research, were hardly new, but the climate in which they advanced their claims had changed. The diplomacy of the 1930s seemed to prove the value of sophisticated technology in deterring war. Spectacular achievements like radar and rockets dramatized the value of science. Now popular heroes, scientists backed their assertions with

28. Ibid., pp. 124–25, 131–32; Special Planning Division, "Report on the Status of Demobilization and Postwar Planning, April 15, 1945," pp. 11, 49, file 310, SPD; Davis, *Postwar Defense Policy and the U.S. Navy.*

29. Edward L. Bowles, speech, "Integration for National Security," 31 March 1945, filed by speech title in Edward L. Bowles Files, Records, Office of the Special Assistant to the Secretary of War, SecWar.

unprecedented prestige. The political experience gained during the war encouraged them to shed their political inhibitions and state their claims more aggressively. Most important, they enjoyed the partnership of the military elite, now abruptly aware of its dependence on science and technology.

Plans for Partnership

Soldiers and scientists easily reached agreement on the need for peacetime research which would arm the nation's military machine. Finding an institutional mechanism to effect that objective, and selling it to Congress and the President, proved to be far more tedious and frustrating tasks.

The very first postwar plans bore witness to one of the greatest obstacles to partnership: the resentment within the officer corps over the sudden glamor scientists had achieved. OSRD, charged one naval planner in 1942, "has effectually terrorized and intimidated the Army and Navy and have [*sic*] almost completely alienated the sympathy of the best young officers in the Army and Navy." Scientists, ignorant of practical military needs, produced "nothing of note ... except a fuse."[30] Officers in the military's technical bureaus complained about the ambitions and arrogance of civilian scientists, and viewed with dismay the popular approbation heaped on civilian organizations like OSRD.[31] Dissatisfaction extended to the top ranks in the navy, though less so in the army. Admiral Julius Furer, the navy's coordinator of research and development, found that both Admiral King and Secretary Forrestal distrusted scientists and misunderstood the scientific method. "The Admirals," Furer complained to his diary, "are afraid that they can't control high-spirited talent of this kind. I tell them I have had no difficulty in getting them [scientists] to play ball as a team."[32]

30. Unsigned memorandum, probably Admiral Harold Bowen, "Office of Scientific Research and Development and National Defense Research Committee," n.d. [December 1942?], file "OSRD, Organization of, etc.," Box 6, Papers of Harold Bowen, Princeton University Library.

31. Constance M. Green, Harry C. Thomson, and Peter C. Roots, *The Ordnance Department: Planning Munitions for War*, pp. 230–31; "The History of United States Naval Research and Development in World War II," prepared by the University of Pittsburgh Historical Staff at the Office of Naval Research, n.d. [1950–51], vol. 1, pp. 107–27, unpublished official history, copy in Naval History Division.

32. Diary of Admiral Julius Furer, 9 April 1943 and 9 October 1944, Box 1, Papers of Julius A. Furer, Library of Congress.

For their part, scientists chafed under the supposed ignorance, conservatism, and obsession with security of the military leadership. The tensions in the Manhattan District, though most notorious, were not unique. Vannevar Bush engaged in a running feud with the navy, especially with Admiral King. Lunching with Furer at the Cosmos Club, the OSRD director dissected the navy's strategy for the landings at Tarawa in November 1943 and condemned the navy for having wasted hundreds of American lives. Furer said that Bush gave him "the impression as he has many times before that he is very much put out over the fact that he is not called in by King to discuss the grand strategy of the Navy." Even Furer, an admirer of Bush, found the outburst "childish and peevish." But he had little luck in calming either Bush's resentment at his exclusion from the military elite or the admirals' fears of the ascendant scientists.[33]

Bush had more substantive complaints. He maintained that before World War II the military high command had failed to appreciate or promote weapons development. Even during the war, he observed, neither the army nor the navy worked out effective centralized supervision of weapons development: the army's New Developments Division and Admiral Furer, the navy's coordinator of research and development, could cajole but not compel. Furthermore, the high command failed to integrate new weapons into strategy. Responsibility for the development and introduction of new weapons rested with low-level authorities, who could not grasp the significance of a new device or were powerless to effect its utilization. Strategy remained wedded to existing weapons, whereas in the future weapons would dictate strategy. Therefore, Bush believed, scientists had to participate in the making of strategy.[34]

Bush also insisted that the armed services abandon cherished practices of training and promoting their officers. The habit of regarding combat duty as the sole criterion for advancement robbed the military of officers experienced in and appreciative of weapons research. Conversely, all officers should receive enough technical training to value weapons research even though they might not

33. Furer Diary, 14 January 1944. See also Bush, *Pieces of the Action,* pp. 87–91, 306.
34. For Bush's ideas on reforming military research, see Vannevar Bush, "Report to the President on Activities of the Office of Scientific Research and Development," 29 August 1944, pp. 62–77, copy in Harvey Bundy Subject File (S 20 to Surgeon General), SecWar; Woodrum Committee, *R&D Hearings,* pp. 237–50; Bush, "Science and Security," *Sea Power,* July 1945, p. 35.

specialize in it. The assignment of military research to the technical bureaus which designed and purchased weapons was fatal, Bush warned, because procurement units were by nature bent on refining the production of existing weapons, not devising new ones. They judged results by standards hostile to creative research:

> Since research is speculative, a research scientist must be paid—or promoted—whether or not he succeeds in solving the assigned problem. In the case of procurement, on the other hand, one must furnish a particular product to meet stated specifications and one is, therefore, only paid—or promoted—for a product which satisfies those specifications.

Soldiers had to accept scientists on their own terms, as "equals and independent in authority, prestige, and in funds." The researcher "is, after all, exploring the unknown. He cannot be subject to strict controls." Only when research was divorced from military supervision and had direct access to the high command of the services would it come into its own.[35]

Other issues troubled the wartime alliance. Scientists protested the conscription of technical personnel whom OSRD desired to employ, and charged the army and navy with failure to use the skills of scientific personnel drafted into the services.[36] Bush's decision in the summer of 1944 to begin planning for demobilization of OSRD angered the military. Officers like Furer viewed Bush's decision as precipitate, calculated to produce unrest and a relaxation of effort among scientists. Forrestal and his aide Lewis Strauss interpreted it more harshly, as a sign that scientists were trying to desert the war effort early in order to grab peacetime jobs. In vain did Bush explain that the unrest was "already there and quite intense" among scientists, and that he only sought to calm their restlessness by devising a workable and equitable phaseout of their jobs.[37]

Given the record of mistrust between soldiers and scientists, both parties assumed that scientists would flee government employment as soon as victory permitted. They would never suffer the pay scales,

---

35. Woodrum Committee, *R&D Hearings*, pp. 244, 248–49.
36. Baxter, *Scientists Against Time*, pp. 127–34.
37. Quotation from Bush to Furer, 30 September 1944, file 300 (1943–44), Records of the New Developments Division, RG 165. See also Borden to Bush, 15 September 1944, file 350.06 (Study 114, Sec. 2), SPD; Furer Diary, 2 October 1944, 12 October 1944, 30 October 1944.

civil service rules, security restrictions, and patent regulations involved in peacetime government employment, much less supervision by nonscientists or involvement in partisan and bureaucratic politics. Scientists were amenable to military research after the war, but only in university and corporate laboratories free of government scrutiny. The war also provided ideological justification for their demands for autonomy, since, as scientists proclaimed, it apparently proved that science thrived under the democratic controls of the United States and suffered at the hands of Axis regimentation.[38]

Planners therefore faced the challenge of devising an institution which would grant the scientists the autonomy they demanded, while permitting sufficient military involvement in their work to allow each party to know the other's needs. Navy planners began working on the problem as early as the spring of 1942, but their proposals and those made by James Conant in OSRD in 1943 made little headway. Admiral Furer persuaded Secretary Frank Knox that concrete planning at that time would be "premature." [39] In November 1943, however, another suggestion from OSRD caught the navy's fancy. Its authors, Luke Hopkins and Charles Garland, were Baltimore banking executives serving in administrative positions at OSRD's Applied Physics Laboratory, operated by the John Hopkins University. Alarmed over the "sad state of preparedness" of the nation in peacetime, they circulated a plan for a "National Institute for Ordnance Research." Although they did not play a major role in subsequent planning, the two contributed a proposal whose fundamentals proved remarkably lasting in the coming months. Garland and Hopkins suggested that military research be administered by a self-perpetuating board of trustees representing both the services and civilian science. The board, which would be independent of direct military or presidential authority, would contract for research with

38. For typical expressions of the need for scientists' autonomy, see Furer memorandum, 15 December 1943, folder "Post-War Research—D," Problems File 1941–1945, Records of the Coordinator of Research and Development, Executive Office of the Secretary of the Navy, RG 80, Washington National Records Center; "Report of Meeting of Committee on Post-War Research, June 22, 1944," file 350.06 (Study 114), SPD; testimony of Frank Jewett in Woodrum Committee, *R&D Hearings*, pp. 285–86.

39. For early navy planning, see Furer Diary, 12 October 1943, 25 October 1943; Furer memorandum, "Post War Scientific Research for the Navy," n.d. [October 1943]; Furer, memorandum for files, 27 October 1943; James Conant, "Proposal for the Creation of a Joint Army-Navy Technical Service and Its Relation to Termination of NDRC," n.d. [summer 1943], all in folder "Post-War Research—D," Problems File 1941–1945, Coordinator's Records.

private industrial and university laboratories rather than use government facilities. Further, the board would encourage basic research and leave weapons development to the services. The objective was to maximize the scientists' independence while securing their contribution to national defense.[40]

The services welcomed the Hopkins-Garland plan despite its provision for scientists' autonomy from military control. Long a champion of OSRD, Admiral Furer had already developed ideas similar to those offered by the two bankers, and in January 1944 he discussed their blueprint with the army's Special Planning Division. Thereafter the pace of planning accelerated. Garland and Hopkins met with Assistant Secretary of War John J. McCloy, Under Secretaries Patterson and Forrestal, and General Joseph McNarney (Marshall's deputy chief of staff), as well as with Bush, Conant, and Jewett. Extended discussions within and among the army, navy, and OSRD produced an acceptance of the fundamentals of the Hopkins-Garland plan. Military and scientific leaders also agreed to expand its scope from ordnance to all aspects of war-related research, and to give the entire matter of postwar research more detailed study. McCloy's enthusiasm over the plan was typical: "I cannot endorse this idea too heartily and feel that a permanent committee, having supervision of research, is absolutely necessary for the maintenance of interest in this field."[41]

Mindful of the need for quick action, Admiral Furer and General William Tompkins, director of SPD, after overcoming Bush's doubts that further planning was premature, worked out with him the next steps for organizing postwar research. They agreed to summon a conference on postwar military research to determine the views of prominent scientists and officers and the broad outlines of postwar

40. Luke Hopkins and Charles S. Garland, "Suggested Plan for Furtherance of Research and Development for Army and Navy Ordnance," draft dated 16 November 1943, file 350.06 (Study 114), SPD. An earlier draft of this plan had received little attention. On Garland-Hopkins, see Baxter, *Scientists Against Time*, p. 230; *Who's Who in Commerce and Industry* (Chicago, 1944), vol. 4, pp. 376, 491.

41. McCloy to McNarney, 27 January 1944, file 350.06 (Study 114), SPD. On Furer's earlier views, see his memorandum, "Post War Scientific Research for the Navy," n.d. [October 1943] and his memorandum, 15 December 1943, both in folder "Post-War Research—D," Problems File 1941–45, Coordinator's Records. On early discussions of the Hopkins-Garland Plan, see Furer Diary, 4 January 1944, 18 January 1944, file 334 (Report of Air Coordinating Committee), SPD; McNarney to McCloy, 24 January 1944; Bush to Hopkins, 3 February 1944; Tompkins to Marshall, 14 February 1944; McCloy to Tompkins, 28 February 1944; Hopkins and Garland to Tompkins, 24 February 1944, all in file 350.06 (Study 114), SPD.

needs. A small working committee would then translate those general views into detailed plans or legislation.[42]

At the April 1944 conference, academy president Frank Jewett took the lead in translating the general consensus into concrete proposals. Jewett had had a long career in research, industry, and the politics of science. A pioneer in electronics and former head of Bell Telephone Laboratories, he was now a vice-president of American Telephone and Telegraph and a member of the National Defense Research Committee as well as head of the academy.[43] The primary challenge for him and the other conference participants remained the accommodation of the scientists' demands for independence and their moral scruples against weapons research. James R. Newman, later a key advisor to the atomic scientists' movement, once explained the fine distinctions of scientists' morality:

> There is a strong element of morality and personal ethics which appears to the average scientist. He will work quite readily on a synthetic product of an electro-magnetic devise [*sic*], or on a new type of atom disintegrater [*sic*] even if, subsequently, the results of his research … turn out as useful military weapons. But, if he is told to work in an ordnance laboratory or arsenal, he will feel that he is devoting his entire life to the making of lethal weapons and, except in war, he will reject the suggestion.[44]

Jewett's solution to this problem was that the military circumvent the scientists' sensibilities by appealing to their interest in scientific problems rather than in war work. Scientists would then apply their "best efforts," even though they might not support "going all-out for long-range military preparation."[45] Many scientists did not possess sensibilities which required such subterfuge, and others would not have been fooled by it. But it made sense to make research as intellectually challenging to scientists as possible.

42. Furer Diary, 24 February 1944, 28 February 1944, 9 March 1944, 11 March 1944, 16 March 1944, 8 April 1944, 12 April 1944; Bush to Hopkins, 3 February 1944, file 350.06 (Study 114), SPD; correspondence from and to Tompkins, February–April 1944, file 350.06 (Study 114), SPD.

43. Jacques Cattell, ed., *American Men of Science* (Lancaster, Pa., 1949), p. 1263; Tobey, *The American Ideology of National Science*, pp. 202, 207, 214.

44. Newman to Robert Patterson, 9 October 1944, file "Scientific Research and Development," Box 173, Patterson Papers.

45. "Proceedings of Conference to Consider Needs for Post-War Research and Development for the Army and Navy," 26 April 1944, p. 14, unpublished transcript, Frank Jewett File 50.1324D, NAS.

Jewett also proposed that the research organization suggested by Garland and Hopkins operate under the sponsorship of the National Academy of Sciences. Among the numerous advantages of Jewett's "Academy Plan," as it later became known, was that supposedly it could be established without legislation. Jewett contended that since Congress had chartered the academy, only an executive order was needed to set up the new board under it. Jewett and others made it clear why such a stratagem was necessary: legislation would run afoul of the scientists' gadfly, Senator Harley Kilgore, chairman of the Senate Subcommittee on War Mobilization. "You may find yourselves with a type of law and a type of organization which does exactly the opposite of what you desire," Jewett warned. Kilgore's advocacy of tight federal controls over patents and government science spending, and his insistence that scientists share control of federal programs with other interested parties, were anathema to scientists, who saw in the senator's proposals an invasion of their intellectual and political independence. Jewett's warning to sidestep Kilgore was not forgotten in the coming months.[46]

After the April conference, Tompkins, Furer, and Bush organized the working committee to give detailed consideration to postwar research. Bush, pleading the press of other business and the appearance of impropriety should he plan the successor to his own OSRD organization, declined to sit on the committee. The thirteen-man Committee on Post-War Research, formally appointed by Stimson and Forrestal, represented a broad spectrum of political and scientific interests and reaffirmed the military's commitment to civilian participation in planning. Furer and Tompkins headed four-man delegations from the navy and army. Jewett, Karl Compton, and Jerome Hunsaker joined Merle Tuve, a leader in OSRD's proximity-fuse project, to form a distinguished scientific contingent. Bush suggested some prominent academicians to chair the committee, but Tompkins and Secretary Forrestal wanted Charles E. Wilson, the industrialist and vice-chairman of the War Production Board. Aside from Wilson, known as a vigorous exponent of military-industrial-scientific collaboration in peacetime, few business leaders participated in planning the postwar research agency, though several defense

46. Ibid., pp. 14–15, 17, 23. See also Daniel J. Kevles, "The Debate Over Postwar Research Policy, 1942–1945: A Political Interpretation of *Science—The Endless Frontier*," manuscript provided the author by Daniel J. Kevles, *Isis*, in press.

contractors later served in the agency set up in 1945. The committee's focus on basic research appealed more to academic scientists.[47]

The Wilson Committee, as it was generally called, met five times during the summer of 1944, its deliberations dominated by Furer, Tompkins, and the four scientists. Watching the European war climax and knowing of Bush's determination to disband OSRD, the members quickly concurred on the urgency of setting up a successor agency. They agreed that the new organization should not be dominated by the services, and that it should concentrate on basic research. They also decided that, in order to free scientists from the government restrictions they found so annoying, the agency should empoly existing facilities and contract with private laboratories rather than build up its own facilities. Contracting with nongovernment laboratories, common during World War II, had little precedent in previous peacetime military research.[48]

In another demonstration of its concern for the autonomy of scientists, the committee decided that the new agency should be run by a board rather than a single director. Both civilian and military representatives agreed that in peacetime scientists would boycott any agency established on the authoritarian model of wartime agencies like OSRD and dominated by one individual. The proposed Research Board for National Security would consist of forty members. The president of the National Academy would appoint ten army and ten navy members nominated by the service secretaries, and twenty civilian scientists of his own choosing. By later agreement, Jewett, the academy president, also secured the right to name the chairman of the five-man executive committee, which was to administer the board's affairs. The academy would also assume auditing and bookkeeping responsibilities. Jewett and other scientists believed that these arrangements would protect researchers from the evils of political patronage, favoritism, and corruption. The provision that half of the board members would be military representatives insured integration of scientific resources with military needs. But civilian

47. See Bush to Tompkins, 27 April 1944; Bush to Tompkins, 4 May 1944; Tompkins to Bush, 9 May 1944; Tompkins to Marshall, 23 May 1944; Bush to Tompkins, 7 June 1944, all in file 350.06 (Study 114), SPD; Furer Diary, 23 May 1944. For Wilson's views, see Polenberg, *War and Society*, pp. 236–37, and Wilson, "For the Common Defense."

48. "Report of Meeting of Committee on Post-War Research, June 22, 1944," file 350.06 (Study 114), SPD; Merle Tuve, "Notes for Second Meeting of Committee on Planning for Army and Navy Research," 6 July 1944, Jewett File 50.1324D, NAS.

scientists would dominate the executive committee by a margin of three to two. Not dependent on government jobs for their livelihood, scientists would presumably be immune to the pressures that political appointees would endure. With power vested in a committee, no irresponsible individual could corrupt the board. Finally, research projects would be assigned by scientists sitting on panels attached to the board, not by officers or government employees, who, through ignorance of science or susceptibility to political influence, might select foolish projects or incompetent researchers.[49]

The prominent role accorded the National Academy of Sciences under Jewett's plan sparked a sometimes bitter debate in the Wilson Committee, but Jewett's formula retained its appeal as the only proposal which would not, in the committee's eyes at least, require legislation. Compton and others, sounding out prominent congressmen like Harry Byrd, were warned that a Congress eager to recapture the power lost in depression and war might object to the establishment of another agency by executive authority. But the distrust of Senator Kilgore was too passionate and the need for a successor to OSRD seemingly too urgent for the committee to risk securing congressional approval. The committee feared that if legislation failed to pass quickly, OSRD would demobilize with no agency to pick up its work, and scientists would then lose interest in military research. The academy arrangement had a further advantage to men suspicious of politicians. As Jewett reminded Compton, a board set up by executive action "can be abandoned at any time conditions change or a better scheme is devised," while agencies set up by Congress "are long-lived beasties... it is almost impossible to kill or alter one that has been brought into existence." Admiral Furer shared that outlook.[50]

49. See n. 48; "Report of the Committee on Post-War Research to the Secretary of War and Secretary of the Navy, September 14, 1944," printed in House Military Affairs Committee, *H.R. 2946 Hearings*, pp. 64–69; Jewett to Stimson and Forrestal, 26 November 1944, file 350.06 (Study 114), SPD.

50. Jewett to Compton, 17 August 1944, Jewett File 50.1324D, NAS. On Furer's views, see Furer to Assistant Secretary of the Navy, 26 February 1945, folder "Research Board for National Security—D," Problems File 1941–1945, Coordinator's Records. For communication with Congress, see Furer, Tompkins, and Compton to Charles Wilson, 3 August 1944; Jewett to Compton, 17 August 1944, both in Jewett File 50.1324D, NAS; Compton to Harry Byrd, 11 August 1944, and 12 August 1944, file 350.06 (Study 114), SPD. For the committee's sense of urgency, and for the distrust of Kilgore and the committee toward each other, see Lyman Chalkley to Furer, 1 May 1944, folder "Post-War Research—D," Problems File 1941–1945, Coordinator's Records; Kilgore to Forrestal, 26 June 1944, folder "Post War Problems," Problems File 1941–1945, Coordinator's Records; Bush to Tompkins, 7 June 1944, and Rising to Tompkins, 21 June 1944, both in file 350.06 (Study 114), SPD.

A similar distrust of the legislative process guided the deliberations of planners on the best methods of funding postwar research, a troublesome issue because of the questions it stirred about responsibility for past weakness in scientific preparedness. The military and scientific elites frequently blamed the American people and their representatives for that weakness and feared that innocence about national security was an ingrained national trait bound to reappear. The chief of the navy's Ordnance Bureau told delegates to the April 1944 conference: "If the early Twenties are any criterion, we may look for another witch-hunt . . . that will seek 'Merchants of death'" and curb "active interest in ordnance research." Even Bush made the same point. "The fundamental difficulty" before World War II, he explained to the Woodrum Committee, "lay in the attitude of the American people toward preparedness for war," an attitude which made it "impossible" for the services to stay prepared. In a seeming contradiction, however, Bush, having blamed the American people for the nation's weakness, exonerated the people's representatives, who, he acknowledged, had "regularly voted the research appropriations requested by the services.[51]

Though confused, embittered, and often inaccurate, the recollections and fears of scientists and their military colleagues moved them to consider several extraordinary proposals for a research-and-development "endowment" or "trust" fund. Under those proposals, Congress would set aside a fixed percentage of the annual federal budget for military research, or establish a trust fund, the interest or income from which would finance the operations of the Research Board for a specified period of time. Such schemes were to place scientific preparedness beyond the whims of popular and legislative opinion, free scientists to follow their creative impulses, and guarantee that basic research, regarded as a unique and indeterminate process, would be managed by experts immune from political pressures. Because the board would concentrate on basic research, viewed as inexpensive though critical to weapons development, the fund envisioned was never large, at most $25 million in annual income. As one Wilson Committee member commented, larger funds might become "a conspicuous target for criticism" and "the continuity of funds

---

51. "Proceedings of Conference . . .," 26 April 1944, pp. 4–5; Woodrum Committee, *R&D Hearings*, p. 239.

for research is far more important than the magnitude of the funds."⁵²
From the start some planners, especially officers like Furer and
Tompkins, scoffed at the idea as politically impractical, but it was
not tabled until congressmen and War Department legislative experts
made it clear that Capitol Hill would regard an endowment as a
"dangerous national precedent."⁵³

Faced with the necessity of annual appropriations, the Wilson
Committee still had two alternatives. The Research Board might
seek its funds directly from Congress. Or, as Jewett and others suggested, the armed services might themselves seek the appropriations
and transfer them to the academy, which, as an organization chartered
by Congress, supposedly could receive and disburse federal funds.
The services were uncertain about which course to take. A board
unable to lobby for its own funds and at the mercy of the military
might not secure adequate financing, the military recognized. "An
aggressive independent agency," on the other hand, might, as the
army saw it, "secure a disproportionately large portion of this money,
thereby reducing Army and Navy funds and objectives." An independent agency might also prove insensitive to military needs. Especially
among the technical bureaus, some fear of the board as a competitor
for funds existed.⁵⁴ Scientists like Compton and Jewett also preferred
funding through military appropriations. Always fearful of direct
involvement in politics, they did not want scientists on the board
placed in the position of soliciting money. Jewett also observed that
direct funding, by relieving the military of its responsibility to support
research, might leave scientists vulnerable to recriminations and
"open the door wide to a block of alibis in time of emergency."

52. Quotation from Merle Tuve, "Notes for the First Meeting of Committee on Planning
for Army and Navy Research," Jewett File 50.1324D, NAS. On the endowment and trust fund
schemes, see also: Garland-Hopkins Plan, 11 June 1943, file 1267, Bush Papers; Garland-
Hopkins Plan, 16 November 1943, file 350.06 (Study 114), SPD; Furer Diary, 5 January 1944,
6 July 1944; Compton to Harry Byrd, 12 August 1944, file 350.06 (Study 114), SPD; fourth
and fifth drafts of the Research Board plan, Jewett File 50.1324D, NAS. Scientists backing a
proposed National Science Foundation made similar suggestions for a trust fund; see Kevles,
"The Debate over Postwar Research Policy, 1942–1945."
53. Furer, Compton, and Tompkins to Wilson, 3 August 1944, Jewett File 50.1324D, NAS.
See also Richards to Director, Legislative and Liaison Division, 26 August 1944, file 388,
Budget Division.
54. Quotations from Richards to Tompkins, 20 July 1944, file 33, Budget Division. See also
General William Borden, "A Plan for Coordinating Peacetime Research and Development,"
file 350.06 (Study 114, Sec. 2), SPD; Hensel to Forrestal, 31 May 1945, file 70–2–18, SecNav;
Green, Thomson, and Roots, *The Ordnance Department*, pp. 230–31.

Military members of the Wilson Committee shared Jewett's fears about divided responsibility.[55]

Other officials disliked the proposal to channel funds through military appropriations and to the academy. Certain scientists, especially younger ones sensitive to the academy's inactivity before the war and its caution in conferring membership, branded the academy too intellectually conservative and politically inept to sustain an aggressive research program. Forrestal, influenced by Lewis Strauss, held similar doubts. The academy, the navy secretary once commented, "didn't do a damn thing between [the] wars that was serviceable or practical to the business of war."[56] Others were loath to trust the military with the task of securing the board's funds lest the services again belittle research as they had before the war. "As we get away from a war, there is a tendency to reduce appropriations," warned one congressman when the Woodrum Committee reviewed the matter in November 1944. "The first items hit are military items," and the services "inevitably" slash their research expenditures before cutting back on training or operations. Unmoved by the assurances of Patterson and Furer that the military now gave research first priority, the committee wanted the board to go after its own funds rather than remain beholden to admirals and generals.[57]

In the end, practical politics resolved the funding issue for the Wilson Committee. The urgency of creating the board and of circumventing Congress by use of the academy arrangement ruled out direct funding of the board, which would have required time-consuming legislation authorizing appropriations to the new agency. As recommended by the committee in September, the board was to be financed by funds marked as separate items in the War and Navy Departments' annual appropriations. The board would not directly request its

55. Quotation from Woodrum Committee, *R&D Hearings*, p. 291. See also *R&D Hearings*, pp. 160–61, 174–77, 275; Robert Millikan to Jewett, 28 August 1944, Jewett File 50.1324D, NAS; Jewett to Charles Wilson, 3 July 1944, and "Report of Meeting of the Committee on Post-War Research, September 14, 1944," both in file 350.06 (Study 114), SPD.

56. Quotation from Minutes of Top Policy Group Meeting 9, 8 January 1945, file Minutes of Top Policy Group Meetings, SecNav. See also Merle Tuve, "Notes for the First Meeting of Committee on Planning for Army and Navy Research," Jewett File 50.1324D, NAS; Daniel J. Kevles, "Scientists, the Military, and the Control of Postwar Defense Research: The Case of the Research Board for National Security, 1944–46," *Technology and Culture* 16 (January 1975): 26, 29–30.

57. Quotations from Woodrum Committee, *R&D Hearings*, p. 140. See also *R&D Hearings*, pp. 130, 139–43, 150–51, 160–72, 174–77, 179–85, 199, 300–01, and U.S. Congress, *House Report 505* (Report of Representative Clifton Woodrum, 2 May 1945), 79/1, 1945.

own funds, though it might appear in support of army and navy requests.

The committee also recommended later legislation to establish the board on a more permanent basis, independent of the academy and receiving funds directly from Congress. The committee's vote on this recommendation came by a narrow seven-to-six margin. Many members, especially Jewett, hoped to make the academy plan permanent, as did some officers fearful that scientists in an independent agency would be unresponsive to military needs. Acting on the committee's more urgent recommendation, Stimson and Forrestal on November 9, 1944, made the official request of Jewett to establish the Research Board for National Security under the academy's auspices. Hearings before the Woodrum Committee followed a few weeks later, but since that committee had no power to initiate legislation, its deliberations had no immediate impact on the fate of the board.[58]

The establishment of the board by the services was an anomalous act for them. While the army and navy fought over the unification issue and many other aspects of postwar planning, they worked with each other and with scientists whom they had often regarded as rivals to cement a partnership for defense research. Planning for postwar research had also violated customary military procedures. The army and navy sidestepped the highly formalized official planning channels. They threw open their deliberations to civilians and substituted informal discussion for the usual position papers, concurrences, and reviews. General Tompkins, chief of army Special Planning, personally supervised army preparations for the Research Board, even though SPD customarily delegated detailed planning to other agencies.

The military's traditional indifference to science ironically had facilitated planning. Research and development had as yet gained no high station in the military hierarchies. The services' technical bureaus, at odds with each other and losing power to other agencies during the

58. "Report of the Meeting of the Committee on Post-War Research, September 14, 1944," file 350.06 (Study 114), SPD; Jewett to Charles Wilson, 12 September 1944, Jewett File 50.1324D, NAS; "Report of the Committee on Post-War Research to the Secretary of War and Secretary of the Navy, September 14, 1944," printed in House Military Affairs Committee, *H.R. 2946 Hearings*, pp. 64–69; Woodrum Committee, *R&D Hearings*, p. 290; J.L. Sundquist, memorandum for files, 13 December 1944, Series 39.32, file E8-20/44.1, Records of the Bureau of the Budget, RG 51, National Archives Building.

war, could not effectively oppose the movement to share power with scientists. The absence of strong vested interests in research may have lessened the agitation within the services for promotion of research, but it also insured that planning for science did not get bogged down in the intricate balancing of interests which characterized so much military planning. As a result, aggressive advocates of civilian science like Furer and Tompkins dominated policymaking, encouraged civilian participation in it, and moved it along with uncommon speed and flexibility. Less than a year elapsed from January 1944, when the army and navy began discussions on the research question, until the establishment of the board in November. Other postwar plans, initiated far earlier, still remained unfinished at war's end.

Such departures from orthodoxy reflected the significance the military leadership now attached to research and development. Unlike some other "lessons" of the war, such as the need for unification of the services, the crucial role played by science in modern war was incontestable, and the War and Navy Departments as yet perceived few rival interests in matters of weapons research. They were even willing to share power with an outside group, civilian scientists, if only to secure their assistance.

The board's establishment by no means solved all problems of postwar research. For one thing, the board's sponsors did not address themselves to the problem of atomic energy after the war. Consideration of that problem was still embryonic. In 1944, Arthur Holly Compton and the scientists working at the University of Chicago began urging and delineating a program of postwar research. Finding themselves idled as the most pressing work on the bomb shifted elsewhere, and citing postwar national security as one important justification for their program, the Chicago group itched to get started immediately on new research endeavors. In the same year, OSRD began drafting preliminary plans for a peacetime commission on atomic energy. Neither the OSRD nor the Chicago initiative made headway, the latter only rankling Washington officials, who saw in it more self-interest than good sense. The preoccupation of most scientists with the bomb, tight security regulations, Stimson's caution, Roosevelt's secrecy and penchant for delaying resolution of issues—all those factors, plus the impossibility of disentangling domestic research from the thorny issue of international control of nuclear energy, conspired to block progress on the organization of peacetime nuclear research. Not until the summer of 1945 did the issue receive sustained attention. As a consequence, until then the Research Board for National Security, itself considering programs in nuclear energy, stood alone as an institutional forum for exploring postwar military research. Certainly atomic energy, as peril or promise, was on the minds of nuclear scientists. But they could do little to plan for it.[59]

The board's establishment also failed to mollify critics of traditional military practices. Bush, in particular, remained dissatisfied. He supported the board and the autonomy it granted scientists, but he questioned the academy's fitness for supervising research. Still alarmed by Senator Kilgore's proposals for an organization responsive to nonscientists' interests, Bush was working on his own plans for a more broadly based, permanent federal agency to conduct civilian and military research. He also still believed that the organization of a civilian-military agency was secondary to the necessity for sweeping changes within the services themselves.[60] At the same time, in the atmosphere of continuing recriminations among scientists and soldiers, some defense officials still worried that scientists remained too naive about national security to recognize the importance of peacetime research. In public the defender of scientists, Forrestal privately ridiculed them, questioned their fitness to run the new board, and insisted that "people in business . . . are the people you have to rely on" to promote the nation's defense. "Like the rest of us," he said, scientists "will be back in bed as soon as the war is over."[61]

Nonetheless, military attitudes were changing, and defense officials, focusing increasingly on their own failures, effected a transformation in their attitudes which Bush did not fully grasp. The observations of Navy Captain Carroll Tyler indicated the new spirit of self-criticism. Tyler wrote that military officials had a childlike notion of how scientists worked, what they could contribute, and the threat they offered to the officer's status. They still regarded scientists as "long hairs,"

59. Hewlett and Anderson, *The New World*, pp. 322–46, 408–11.

60. For Bush's views, see "Report to the President . . . ," 29 August 1944, pp. 62–77, Harvey Bundy Subject File (S 20 to Surgeon General), SecWar; Bush to Furer, 30 September 1944, file 300, NDD; Bush to Isaiah Bowman, 6 February 1944, file 315, Bush Papers; Woodrum Committee, *R&D Hearings*, pp. 237–51; House Military Affairs Committee, *H.R. 2946 Hearings*, pp. 6–7; Kevles, "The Debate Over Postwar Research Policy, 1942–1945."

61. Minutes of Top Policy Group Meeting 9, 8 January 1945, file Minutes of Top Policy Group Meetings, SecNav.

impractical people who " 'lock the cat and put out the door,' " even
as they saw them as "people who can go into their mysterious laboratories, stir around among test tubes and rheostats, and if they feel
like it, come out with a death ray." Scientists, Tyler felt, had good
reason to distrust the services since "the military mind is not only
highly conservative but definitely reactionary."[62]

With that awareness as a starting point, some military men went
further. Admiral Furer, for one, understood as well as Bush what
was necessary. A graduate of the same class of 1901 that produced
Admiral King, Furer never achieved the rank of his more famous
classmates, perhaps because he concentrated on technical service.
But he doggedly promoted reform of naval research. Like Bush,
whom he knew well, Furer stressed the dismal state of weapons
research before the war and faulted the military. Because the military
rewarded ability to administer large groups rather than technical
capacity, the civilian scientist was "treated rather as a hired hand
than as a partner in the enterprise." Furer was as eager as Bush to
grant scientists freedom and status. "One cannot assign somebody
to make a discovery," he observed. He proposed changes in the
training and promotion of officers, the creation of a new post of
assistant secretary for research, and a more powerful Joint Chiefs
of Staff committee to assure coordination between the services in
research matters. Claiming that advances in weapons ultimately
resulted from fundamental research, he urged the navy to fund basic
research even though no predictable benefits for the navy could be
assured. Like Bush, he also believed that scientists should play a
role in determining strategy and policy at the highest level.[63]

At the War Department, General William Borden, Furer's counter-
part, and Dr. Edward L. Bowles pressed for similar reforms. Equally
striking was the support for reform given by the chiefs of the various
army and navy technical bureaus. Though less zealous for change
than Furer or Borden, they supported some reforms in hopes of

62. Tyler, "The Relationship Between the Military Services and Science in the National
Security Program," undated memorandum forwarded to the Secretary of the Navy on 23
April 1945, in folder "Naval Research—Post War," Problems File 1941–1945, Coordinator's
Records.

63. Quotations from Furer et al., "Science and the Armed Services," pp. 2, 10, draft of
paper intended for the Secretary of the Navy, 25 August 1945, Article File, Box 10, Furer
Papers. See also, Furer, "Post-War Military Research," *Science* 100 (24 November 1944):
461–64; Furer, "Scientific Research and Modern Warfare," *U.S. Naval Institute Proceedings*
71 (March 1945): 259–63.

forestalling more drastic ones. Of special importance was their recognition of the value of fundamental research conducted by civilians. The Research Board for National Security would make basic discoveries and maintain the interest of civilian science in weapons, while the bureaus would play their traditional role of refining those discoveries and supervising manufacture of practical applications.[64]

The services' commanders also gave prominence to research. While neither Marshall nor King took a personal interest in weapons development, both emphasized research in their final reports. General Arnold viewed weapons innovation more urgently, as "the first essential of the air power necessary for our national security." The military press carried the message about research to the ranks in a flurry of articles which dramatized the role of weapons research in winning the war and exhorted soldiers to abandon their traditional aloofness from the scientific and academic communities. Perhaps Patterson best summed up the change in attitude. "We will make our plans to suit our weapons," he proclaimed in October 1944, "rather than our weapons to suit our plans."[65]

The New Alliance

Enthusiasm for the new board was intense as the last winter of the war began. Though the board's permanency was in doubt, the precedent it would set for peacetime military-scientific collaboration was unmistakable. The board "was to be a pioneering experiment," Jewett later wrote. "In a different sector and on a grand scale it was like sending Lewis and Clark to explore the northwest country or Major

64. Borden, "A Plan for Coordinating Peacetime Research and Development," file 350.06 (Study 114), SPD; E.L. Bowles to Borden, 8 October 1944, file 300, NDD; Bowles, speech, "Integration for National Security," 30 March 1945, Bowles Files, SecWar; "Proceedings of Conference . . . ," 26 April 1944, Jewett File 50.1324D, NAS; Admiral W. H. P. Blandy, address before the Maryland Historical Society, 10 May 1943, copy in file "Miscellaneous I," Box 49, Forrestal Papers; Chief, Bureau of Aeronautics, U.S. Navy, to Chief of Office of Research and Inventions, 10 July 1945, folder "Research Board for National Security Vol. 2," Problems File 1941–1945, Coordinator's Records; Rear Admiral G. F. Hussey, "The Indispensable Material," *Sea Power*, July 1945, pp. 39–41.

65. Marshall, *Biennial Report, 1943–1945*, in *War Reports*, pp. 254–63, 292–93, 299; Admiral Ernest J. King, *Third Official Report, December 8, 1945, to the Secretary of the Navy*, in *War Reports*, pp. 715–22; Arnold, *Second Report*, in *War Reports*, p. 415; Robert Patterson, "Industrial Research and National Defense," speech at the Standard Oil Forum on Industrial Research, 5 October 1944, published as pamphlet by Standard Oil Development Company, n.p., n.d.

Powell to traverse the Grand Canyon of the Colorado for the first time."[66]

The self-proclaimed pioneers at first made rapid progress. Jewett, Furer, and General Tompkins worked together to organize the board. Operating under the secretaries' letter of November 9, 1944, they secured approval for Karl Compton to be chairman of the board's executive committee, which consisted of Compton, Furer, Tompkins, Jerome Hunsaker of the National Advisory Committee for Aeronautics, and Roger Adams, a chemist. Jewett, the services, and the committee in turn gathered an impressive contingent of academic and industrial scientists to serve on the board, including Lee A. Du Bridge, Ernest O. Lawrence, Linus Pauling, and I. I. Rabi. Soon the board was soliciting research projects and preparing for the takeover of certain long-range studies which OSRD would not be able to complete. It prepared for projects in a broad range of fields: missiles and jet propulsion, nuclear physics, chemical and biological warfare, and psychological testing and warfare. It also entertained proposals to gather intelligence on foreign scientific efforts, to maintain a registry of scientific personnel for possible mobilization in future emergencies, and to coordinate the board's activities with industry. In addition, Compton sensed a broader opportunity. He hoped to use "this new organization as effectively as possible to educate the public in the value of preparedness." The sensational weapons of the war would provide "an excellent starting point" for dramatizing the importance of science to preparedness.[67]

Some scientists saw few moral limits to the use of their skills. One, criticizing opposition to research in biological warfare, contended: "The danger in our plans for preparedness for a third war is, as happened after World War I, that we prepare ourselves thoroughly to fight the last war over again. What we must do primarily is look forward to new means of warfare. Whether the policy makers at the top decide to use them or not, we at our level must have them prepared." Not all scientists so baldly ignored the consequences of their work, nor embraced preparedness so uncritically. Some, like

66. Jewett to Harvey Bundy, 8 May 1945, folder "Contract," RBNS Files, NAS.
67. Compton to Major General Levin H. Campbell, Jr., 6 February 1945, RBNS File, Project File for 1945, NDD. For organization and planning of the board, see the Research Board for National Security Files, NAS, and Compton to Bush, 1 March 1945, file 609, Bush Papers.

James Conant, did alert their colleagues to dangers posed by the emerging status of science, lest people forget that "science, alone, untempered by other knowledge, can lead not to freedom but to slavery." Like Conant, the prominent astronomer Harlow Shapley worried about the "evil influences" of military research contracts with universities, especially the damage to the quality of teaching and the possibilities for "scientific pork barrels." But even they voiced no criticism of military research itself. Apparently no scientist questioned the establishment of the board (made public in February 1945) or agonized over the weapons it might help create.[68]

A gala dinner on March 10, 1945, formally inaugurated the board. On the eve of victory in Europe, the elite of the scientific and military professions—Bush and Conant, Forrestal and Patterson, King and Harvey Bundy—joined the board in supping on "green turtle soup, pompano with almond dressing, breast of guinea hen," and other wartime delicacies. Pleas for peacetime preparedness and expressions of delight with the board's founding characterized the obligatory speechmaking.[69]

Only three weeks later President Roosevelt abruptly suspended the board's activities. In letters to Stimson and Forrestal, he forbade the transfer of funds from the army and navy to the board. The Research Board, awaiting completion of a contract between the academy and the War and Navy Departments, had to that date survived on funds provided by the Carnegie Institution. Since no legislation authorizing appropriations for the board had yet reached Congress, Roosevelt's March 31 letter deprived the board of its only source of federal funds. The President also directed Bush to continue OSRD research projects which were to have been taken over by the Research Board. In the ensuing weeks, the board continued to plan projects in anticipation of a reversal of the presidential order, and the Interim Committee on atomic energy considered use of the board for research. But the Board could not initiate or fund any scientific work.[70]

    68. Robert F. Griggs to Ross G. Harrison, 3 March 1945, folder "General," RBNS Files, NAS; James Conant, "Science and Society in the Post-War World," *Vital Speeches of the Day*, 15 April 1943, p. 394; Harlow Shapley to Jewett, 15 July 1944, Jewett File 50.1324D, NAS.
    69. Folder "Dinner," RBNS Files, NAS.
    70. Roosevelt to Stimson and Forrestal, 31 March 1945, original in RBNS File, NDD; Jewett to Lewis Strauss, 23 February 1945, Jewett File 50.8, NAS; Roosevelt to Bush, 31 March 1945, file 330-B, President's Official File, FDR Papers; notes of the Interim Committee meeting, 31 May 1945, p. 16, Harrison-Bundy File No. 100, Manhattan Engineer District Records.

Responsibility for terminating the board rested not with FDR, who probably gave the matter little attention, but with Harold Smith, the influential director of the Budget Bureau, who prevailed upon the President to sign the letter cutting off the funds.[71] Several concerns prompted Smith's animus against the board. He was jealous that FDR had earlier assigned Bush the task of studying the nation's postwar research needs. He also nursed an often churlish dislike of scientists. "There has been more leaf-raking and boon-doggling on some of these research projects than there ever was in the WPA," he complained to Roosevelt.[72]

More substantively, Smith wanted tight governmental control of federal science policy and wished to avoid any repetition of the chaotic proliferation of agencies which characterized New Deal efforts in other areas. The scientists' attempt to escape congressional and executive supervision of their activities especially disturbed him. He doubted the legality of congressional appropriations to the academy, a private organization. The academy, he advised Roosevelt, "is very jealous of its non-government status, and under its control the Research Board for National Security would not be responsible to any part of the Government." He believed that "the proposal to finance the Board by transfers from the War and Navy Departments would not only relieve the Board from accounting for its funds to the General Accounting Office, but would also shift and divide the responsibility for justifying its program each year before the Bureau of the Budget and Congress."[73]

Though an abrasive man prone to exaggeration and caricature of his opponents' intention, Smith was correct in contending that a fundamental issue of democracy was at stake in the scientists' attempts to control their own affairs. In June, writing to Furer, he rejected

> the assumption that researchers are as temperamental as a bunch of musicians, and consequently we must violate most of the tenets of democracy and good organization to adjust for their lack of emotional balance. I do not agree that they are that kind of person, in the first place, and in the second place, I can think of better ways of adjusting for emotional unbalance.

71. On 12 April 1945 FDR wrote a short note to McCloy regarding the Research Board which implied ignorance of his March 31 letter to the secretaries; original in RBNS File, NDD.

72. Quotation from Smith, Memorandum of Conference with the President, 23 March 1945, Smith Papers. See also Smith to Roosevelt, 30 March 1945, file 330-B, President's Official Files, FDR Papers; Furer Diary, 10 April 1945, 7 May 1945.

73. Smith to Roosevelt, 30 March 1945, file 330-B, President's Official Files, FDR Papers. See also Smith to Conant, 30 March 1945, Smith Papers.

"The real difficulty," he thought, was that physical scientists "do not know even the first thing about the basic philosophy of democracy. ... However, most of them have learned to accept governmental funds with ease, and I think they can adapt themselves to government organization with equal ease."[74]

Admiral Furer, already angry that Smith had supposedly reneged on an agreement made in 1944 to accept academy sponsorship of the board, believed the letter to be the "peevish expression of a small man who has a grudge against someone, —the someone in this case is undoubtedly Vannevar Bush."[75] The admiral's comment showed how defenders of the board reduced a vital issue to a matter of one man's irascibility. Their misunderstanding of the issue was more striking in light of the skepticism about the academy arrangement already shown by the Woodrum Committee and the House Military Affairs Committee and in light of Senator Kilgore's efforts to create a centralized science organization strictly accountable to Congress and the President.

The misunderstanding arose in part because scientists so stoutly believed in their own political innocence, impartiality, and selflessness, references to which suffused their rhetoric. They could see only the threat which might arise from what outsiders could do to science: the dangers of patronage, of supervision of scientists by political or military hacks, of the award of contracts by political pressure rather than scientific expertise. They could not recognize the appearance of impropriety among their own kind. No one complained when Karl Compton, already a key figure in OSRD and president of the largest university contractor during the war, became chairman of the Research Board as well. Few scientists questioned the peer system under which they played dual roles as dispensers and recipients of federal dollars. Even Bush, who was more sensitive than many of his colleagues to political questions, scoffed at the notion that the Research Board might include "men who have ulterior interests that might warp their judgments."[76]

Scientists manifested a similar attitude when the army and navy

74. Smith to Furer, 14 June 1945, folder "General," RBNS Files, NAS.
75. Furer to Hunsaker, 21 June 1945, folder "General," RBNS Files, NAS; Furer Diary, 22 June 1945. On at least one occasion the previous summer Smith did meet with Furer and Tompkins; Smith, Daily Record, 21 July 1944, Smith Papers.
76. House Military Affairs committee, *H.R. 2946 Hearings*, p. 16.

insisted on certain auditing procedures and patent rights in Research Board contracts with private laboratories. Universities and other organizations threatened to refuse Research Board work lest they be subject to "endless audits by various government agencies." If scientists had to put up with "all the rigidities and petty red tape they have found so irksome," Jewett pointedly told Congressman Woodrum, they would simply boycott the board. "We are not here concerned with two parties with conflicting interests dealing at arms length," Jewett wrote Harvey Bundy. He expressed his dismay that the War Department would insist on contractual arrangements "such as one might enter into with an organization suspected of sharp practice." The dismay was genuine, and typical of the scientists' inability to acknowledge that they, like other interest groups, had an ax to grind in their relationships with government.[77]

Compromise on the issues was impossible amid the bitterness and misunderstanding engendered by Smith's actions. Admiral Furer joined Harvey Bundy, Patterson, and Generals Borden and Tompkins in elaborate attempts to reach agreement with the Budget Bureau. These efforts failed. Each compromise suggested by the parties involved met with someone's disfavor. In particular, Jewett refused to allow any diminution of academy authority over the board. The War Department, angered by Smith's refusal to meet with Stimson, toyed with the idea of taking the issue over Smith's head to the President, but after FDR's death Stimson seemed too unsure of his influence with the new President to raise the matter with him. Bush's intervention with Truman proved fruitless.[78]

To complicate matters further, the ranks of the board's supporters divided. Naval officers fell to quarreling over the matter in the spring of 1945. Furer remained sympathetic to the academy plan, at least

77. Allis to Borden, 21 April 1945, RBNS File, NDD; Jewett to Woodrum, 17 April 1945, Jewett File 50.82, NAS; Jewett to Bundy, 8 May 1945, folder "Contract with Military—Negotiations," RBNS Files, NAS. On disputes over contractual arrangements, see also Bowen to Strauss, 25 April 1945, file "Research Board for National Security," Box 6, Bowen Papers.

78. Furer Diary, 17 May 1945, and attached memorandum, Furer to Struve Hensel, 17 May 1945; Tompkins to Bundy, 17 May 1945, file 350.06 (Study 114), SPD; draft of letter from the service secretaries to the President, dated 13 April 1945, drawn up by Harvey Bundy, RBNS File, NDD; Bundy to Stimson, 16 May 1945 and 5 June 1945, folder "Memos," Bundy Files, SecWar; Holoran, memorandum for files, 23 June 1945, file 350.06 (Study 114), SPD; Stimson Diary, 12 April 1945, 30 April 1945; Shapley to Barker, 13 April 1945, Series 39.32, file E8-20/44d, Bureau of the Budget. On Bush's intervention, see Bush to Truman, 12 June 1945, folder "General," RBNS Files, NAS; Bush to Fred Vinson, 14 June 1945, RBNS File, NDD; Furer Diary, 22 June 1945.

as a temporary expedient. But Forrestal, Strauss, and Assistant Secretary Struve Hensel, who had long disliked academy sponsorship of the board, deserted the academy plan entirely in May, to Harold Smith's delight. Probably at Forrestal's instigation, Furer was retired that same month from his post as the navy's coordinator of research and development.[79]

Finally, the army and navy split on the Research Board matter. The War Department joined prominent scientists like Jewett and Bush in support of legislation, first drawn up even before Smith raised his objections, which continued academy sponsorship of the board but provided that appropriations go directly to it rather than through War and Navy Department budgets. That legislation passed the House by voice vote on June 19. The navy backed Senator Harry Byrd's bill setting up the Research Board as an agency entirely independent of the academy. Neither bill was approved by the full Congress. Desperate to save the board, Forrestal and Strauss finally eased their opposition to academy sponsorship, but to no avail. The legislative route to resolving the board's difficulties proved a dead end, all the more so in the fall of 1945 when new legislation for a National Science Foundation and for atomic energy overshadowed the question of the board's future. After several months of haggling, the services allowed the Research Board to expire quietly (in February 1946). Despite aggressive planning, the military found that in science policy, as in so many other areas, it was ending the war without a clear course to pursue.[80]

The military's vigorous support of the board underscored its fears that scientists would desert war research. The board's demise threatened to make scientists feel they had been double-crossed, it appeared. Stimson was worried. "The scientists who we have gotten to organize this Board are angry and disgusted with the government," he said, "and it will be difficult to get their aid again on these vital matters

79. Furer Diary, 18 May 1945, 29 May 1945; Smith, Daily Record, 26 May 1945, 8 June 1945, Smith Papers; Hensel to Forrestal, 31 May 1945, file 70-2-18, SecNav.

80. U.S. Congress, *House Report 505,* 79/1, 1945; Furer Diary, 26 February 1945; Furer to Assistant Secretary of the Navy, 22 Feburary 1944, and Compton to Woodrum, 11 April 1945, both in Jewett File 50.82, NAS; *H.R. 2946 Hearings,* pp. 3–7 (Bush), 42–72 (Jewett), 64 (Army); *Congressional Record,* 79/1, 1945, vol. 91, pp. 6305–17; U.S. Congress, Senate Committee on Naval Affairs, *Hearings, Establishing a Research Board for National Security,* 79/1, 1945, pp. 4–5 (Navy); Kevles, "Scientists, the Military, and the Control of Postwar Defense Research," pp. 39–44. Bush and Kilgore each sponsored bills for a National Science Foundation. Both bills contained provisions for a Research Board for National Security within a broader federal science organization; see U.S. Congress, Senate Committee on Military Affairs (Subcommittee of the Committee), *Hearings on Science Legislation,* 79/1, 1945, pp. 5, 231.

affecting new weapons." The director of the army's Special Planning Division expected that the "repudiation of the Academy" would create "disgust in the minds of civilian scientists as to government procedure and 'red tape' and ... lead many of them to withdrawing from their desire to assist the government in the post-war period." Forrestal, Bundy, and Furer shared the same forebodings. Their concern in turn reflected a fear that Congress and the scientific community would lapse back into prewar attitudes of pacifism or isolationism at the first opportunity. The military regarded the board's defeat not simply as the product of political disagreement but as a test of future support for preparedness, a test which hardly augured well.[81]

Yet neither the President, Congress, nor the scientific community had in fact repudiated preparedness. Even in its failure the board established the pattern for the peacetime mobilization of science, just as the controversy over the board presaged later debate on science policy. As Karl Compton recognized at the height of the Research Board controversy, there appeared to be "no difference of opinion whatsoever in any quarter with regard to the desirability and importance of postwar research of a fundamental far-reaching character on problems of national security." The organization of military research was in question, but not its wisdom. This was true both for Harold Smith and for the congressmen—largely anti–New Dealers more willing than liberals to probe the board's set-up—who criticized the board as another Rooseveltian evasion of congressional authority and accountability.[82]

Most important, despite the board's termination, the majority of scientists held to their commitment to defense research. As a participant in the board episode later remarked, "The scientists as a class always seemed to be quarreling with military officers as a class, even while they were developing one of the most effective partnerships in history." The relationship between the partners was complicated. "Something between seduction and rape occurred," Daniel Greenberg

81. Stimson Diary, 12 April 1945; Tompkins to Bundy, 5 June 1945, file 350.06 (Study 114), SPD. See also Bundy to Stimson, 27 April 1945, folder "Memos," Bundy Subject Files, SecWar; draft memorandum, Bundy to Stimson, dated 6 April 1945, RBNS File, NDD; Furer to Hensel, 17 May 1945, attached to Furer Diary entry, 17 May 1945; Forrestal to Truman, 28 July 1945, Official File 330-C, Papers of Harry S. Truman, Harry S. Truman Library.

82. Draft letter, Compton to members of the Research Board, dated 1 August 1945, folder "General," RBNS Files, NAS. Richard N. Chapman provided an analysis of the voting record and political identification of opponents of the academy-sponsored board.

has observed, "but at various points it is by no means certain which party was the aggressor and which the victim." To a degree it was only a marriage of convenience. Some scientists did not relish devising more terrifying weapons, but many welcomed financial support. Military leaders indulged certain of the scientists' demands for autonomy less because they believed in their wisdom than because indulgence appeared the price they had to pay for the scientists' cooperation. Some defense officials viewed the board as a lavish retainer proffered, not in hopes of an immediate payoff, but rather to secure the goodwill and gratitude of the scientific community. The board's scientific members were to be, in Admiral Furer's telling phrase, "ambassadors of national preparedness" to the private scientific community.[83]

But the partnership was not superficial. The scientists' contributions to the war effort impressed military men, many of whom accepted the scientists' argument that the fragility of creative research necessitated their immunity from government controls. Even more important, the military accepted, perhaps too readily, the scientists' long standing claims about the utility of pure research.

Basically, the partnership rested on a shared ideology of national preparedness. Scientists did not drift aimlessly into military research, nor were they duped into it. They espoused its virtues, lobbied hard for it, and rarely questioned it. Perhaps their fastidiousness about their autonomy from controls obscured from them the changing role played by their profession. In agitating themselves over graft, patronage, influence-peddling, and professional standards, most scientists ignored larger questions about the uses to which they were putting their skills. By insistence on their superiority to and aloofness from conventional politics, they sought to persuade themselves of their moral purity. Whatever the case, their commitment and that of the military to peacetime research were fixed by the middle of the war. The devices crafted by OSRD had proved decisive in winning the war, even more so than the atomic bomb, which affected the timing and implications of victory, or Germany's V-weapons, significant as terrifying omens of future war. The new bomb would further dramatize the role of science in modern war, but the lesson taught by that weapon had been learned long before Hiroshima.

---

83. Price, *Government and Science*, p. 57; Greenberg, *Politics of Pure Science*, p. 125; Furer to all bureaus and offices, 23 February 1945, file 39-1-8, SecNav.

6 MEASURING THE RUSSIAN THREAT

The assumption of an identifiable enemy traditionally provided the basis for long-range strategic planning in the United States. From the first such planning in the 1890s through the Joint Board's color plans before World War II, the armed forces shaped their strategy to the requirements of warding off or conquering a specified enemy. The antagonist provided the standard against which to measure American military needs: strategists could compare divisions with divisions, dreadnaughts with dreadnaughts. An enemy also made it possible to formulate a scenario of military action, the essence of strategic planning. Without an enemy, planning lacked focus and direction.[1]

Long-range planners ignored tradition during World War II. Their refusal to name a probable adversary, so notable in the military's public defense of its wartime plans, also represented private conviction. In the preparedness ideology, the primary danger to American security arose from fundamental changes in the conduct of war and international relations, not from the transient threat posed by a particular nation. In addition, the planners' lack of contact with the intelligence community and the State Department, the Joint Chiefs' minimal attention to postwar planning for much of the war, and the difficulties in ascertaining the shape of postwar politics contributed to the paucity of speculation about future enemies.

When officials did speculate, they looked as often as not to Germany or Japan as the most likely threats to world peace, at least until the last year of the war. Apprehension about those nations apparently arose in reaction to past miscalculation of German and Japanese intentions and to the present fury of their aggression. It did not result

1. Davis, *Postwar Defense Policy and the U.S. Navy*, pp. 36, 296. On long-range planning before World War II, see Grenville and Young, *Politics, Strategy, and American Diplomacy*, chaps. 10–11; Matloff, "The American Approach to War, 1919–1945"; Greene, "The Military View of American Foreign Policy"; Miller, "The United States Army During the 1930s," chap. 2.

from a careful projection of their probable future strength and place in the world community. Germany's ability to provoke another world war only twenty years after the defeat of 1918 made planners doubly cautious about the potential threat that nation might pose.[2]

Attitudes toward the Soviet Union, deserving of detailed treatment only because of subsequent events, were ambiguous and rarely elaborated in detail. Though many officers entered the war suspicious of Moscow's expansionist tendencies, for several reasons they paid only limited heed to the Soviet Union for most of the war.

The desperation of the Allies in the first years of the war placed a premium on faith in Soviet cooperativeness. When Germany unleashed Operation Barbarossa against the USSR in June 1941, American military experts predicted early defeat for the Red Army. For months thereafter, Marshall and his colleagues contested, sometimes bitterly, Roosevelt's policy of lavish aid to the newfound ally. However their opposition sprang primarily from anxiety over shortages in American equipment rather than from distrust of the Soviets. Significantly, they also opposed much of the assistance to Great Britain. Defense strategists soon acknowledged the need for aid which would keep the Soviet Union in the war. Equally important, in 1942 they committed themselves to a prompt cross-channel attack. The second front, they believed, was necessary to keep the Soviets fighting.[3]

Even after 1942 the military did not waver in its commitment to a second front, but its motivation for seeking it became more complex. During the winter of 1942–43, as the Red Army slowly ground out victories at Stalingrad and elsewhere, there developed what General Arnold called a "growing uncertainty as to where Russian successes may lead." A sudden German collapse, however unlikely, might allow Stalin's forces to sweep across Europe before the democracies could establish their presence on the continent. A second front appeared desirable not only for winning Soviet cooperation but for curbing Russian ambitions or preventing a separate peace between the Nazis and the Soviets. In addition, an invasion of France might speed the

2. Smith, *Air Force Plans*, pp. 51, 53; Colonel John Weckerling (Deputy for Intelligence, G-2) to Tompkins, 12 February 1944, file "Postwar Army," SPD.

3. George C. Herring, Jr., *Aid to Russia, 1941–1946: Strategy, Diplomacy, the Origins of the Cold War*, pp. 8, 13–15, 51–54; Lukas, *Eagles East*, chaps. 2–3, pp. 59–60, 63–64, 113–15, 164; Mark Alan Stoler, "The Politics of the Second Front: American Military Planning and Diplomacy 1941–1944" (Ph.D. dissertation, University of Wisconsin, 1971), pp. 88–90, 155–57.

end of the war in Europe, thereby accelerating the war against Japan and perhaps facilitating Soviet entry into the Pacific struggle.[4]

The mounting anxiety over potential Soviet domination of Europe surfaced in other ways. An Anglo-American alliance was implicit in many recommendations. We should not, one G-2 agency advised in June 1943, let London fall into an alliance with Moscow "that might eventually align the manpower and resources of Eurasia against us. Our interest demands that the United States, not Great Britain, become the stabilizing wheel of the world." That same summer, as bitterness over the postponement of the second front mounted among the Allies, the Office of Strategic Services (OSS) weighed the merits of an Anglo-American attempt at "turning against her [the Soviet Union] the full strength of a Germany still strong," a possibility briefly mentioned by Marshall at the 1943 Quebec Conference. The OSS rejected that alternative, but made no secret of its distrust of the Soviets. Meanwhile Secretary Knox wanted the British and American navies to unite in "policing all the surfaces of the earth." Many naval officers approved Knox's idea, as apparently did Stimson and Hull, who agreed with Knox in 1943 "to continue the present Anglo-American alliance as far as possible into the post-war dangers and problems." Months later, Admiral William D. Leahy proposed that the "civilized Christian" nations unite to wage war against any new aggressor. "Foreknowledge of certain failure would prevent aggression even by such pagan peoples as are now attempting to enslave the world."[5]

The mood of Americans in Moscow also darkened in 1943. Officials criticized the Soviet Union and warned Washington of communist ambitions. Many were embittered that they had to accept "every rebuff, every refusal of cooperation and every rudeness from the Soviets in the interests of the war effort." The Soviets, argued the

4. Stoler, "Politics of the Second Front," pp. 227–50, 289.
5. "The Changing Power Position of Great Britain as a Factor in the Defense Problem of the United States," prepared by the Analysis Section, G-2, 30 June 1943, copy in Box 4, Earle Papers; Office of Strategic Services study, in JCS Memorandum for Information 121, "Strategy and Policy: Can America and Russia Cooperate?", 22 August 1943, JCS; minutes of CCS meeting, 20 August 1943, in U.S. Department of State, *Foreign Relations of the United States: The Conferences at Washington and Quebec, 1943,* (hereafter cited as *FR: Washington and Quebec, 1943*), p. 911; Pogue, *Organizer of Victory,* pp. 248–49; Frank Knox, speeches of 6 December 1943 and 11 January 1944, copies in Box 8, Knox Papers; Stimson Diary, 11 May 1943; Stimson, memorandum on meeting at State Department, 7 September 1943, Stimson Memos, Stimson Papers; Davis, *Postwar Defense Policy and the U.S. Navy,* pp. 95–96; Leahy speech, 5 June 1944, Leahy Scrapbooks, Box 18, Papers of William D. Leahy, Library of Congress.

American military attaché, "intend to push their claims in Europe even to the extent of resorting to armed force, the day the war with Germany ends." The American ambassador, retired Admiral William Standley, condemned Russian ingratitude for American aid, while in Washington some War Department officials pleaded for a more skeptical attitude toward Soviet requests for support. Yet military officers also remained among the staunchest supporters of no-strings-attached aid to the Red Army. Some hoped that assistance would secure not only Russian collaboration in the war but Soviet friendship after it as well. Disagreement in military circles over unrestricted aid persisted until the last months of the war.[6]

Even in 1943 and 1944, no fixed military view of Soviet intentions emerged. The military's fears, easily aroused, were also easily dissipated. The Moscow and Tehran Conferences, yielding promises of cooperation during and after the war, diminished tensions among the Allies. Scare talk about Soviet expansion faded, and hopes for collaboration in the European theater were high. When Ambassador Averell Harriman questioned the transfer of B-24s to the Red Air Force, General Arnold defended delivery of the bombers by arguing that it would be folly to allow a "single aircraft to sit idle on the ground when it might be smashing the enemy." Furthermore, he stated in August 1944, B-24s could form "the nucleus of a Russian heavy bomber force" and provide transport capability for the Pacific war. Arnold's comment indicated that the army still chased the chimera of Russian cooperation in the war against Japan. Eager to strike the Japanese home islands from American air bases in Siberia or the Maritime Provinces, military officials hoped that a generous lend-lease policy would generate goodwill which the Soviets would repay by collaboration in the Pacific. Military considerations overrode whatever doubts defense officials had about the USSR's long-run objectives.[7]

Those objectives received only passing attention in 1943 and 1944 from the Joint Chiefs, partly because the Roosevelt administration

6. "Interpretation of the attitude of the Soviet Government," report by Brigadier General Joseph A. Michela, Military Attaché, Moscow, 18 February 1943, Box 109, Hopkins Papers; Herring, *Aid to Russia*, pp. 41–42, 80–82, 85–86, 99–101, 121; *FR: Washington and Quebec, 1943*, pp. 624–27.

7. Stoler, "Politics of the Second Front," pp. 308, 362–63; Arnold to Harriman, 21 August 1944, folder "Russia," Official File 1932–1946, Box 51, Arnold Papers; Lukas, *Eagles East*, chaps. 10, 13–14; John R. Deane, *The Strange Alliance*, pp. 225, 252–55.

rarely solicited the chiefs' opinion on postwar political matters.[8] Regarding the configuration of power in the postwar era, the JCS recognized that the changes occurring were "more comparable indeed with that occasioned by the fall of Rome than with any other change occurring during the succeeding fifteen hundred years." With Germany and Japan devastated and demilitarized, and Britain reduced to second-rate status, the United States and the Soviet Union would be the superpowers. Particularly worrisome was the collapse of British power, which meant, a JCS staff committee later remarked, that "the day when the United States can take 'a free ride' in security is over." The United States "must expect to pay its own way." Partly because of the decline of British strength, the JCS doubted that the United States and Britain could challenge Soviet domination of continental Europe, or that either superpower could contest the other's power near the enemy's homeland.[9]

Still, as of the summer of 1944, the Joint Chiefs stressed the priority of winning the war and the dangers of British diplomacy. Learning that a system of international trusteeships for liberated islands and colonies might be discussed in negotiations on postwar international organization, the Joint Chiefs recommended tabling the trusteeship question lest it jeopardize Soviet cooperation in the Pacific. The chiefs did not appear worried about a direct clash between the two allies in the future. Their primary concern was that the United States would become trapped between the expansionist Soviet state and an enfeebled but still grasping Great Britain. The United States, the chiefs advised, should avoid pairing off with Britain, a move which would only arouse Soviet suspicions of a hostile alliance and draw the United States into an Anglo-Soviet struggle.[10]

Military intelligence counseled concern but not alarm about Soviet-American relations after the war. Most intelligence analysts, sensitive to the difficulties of second-guessing the secretive Russians, shied away from dogmatic statements about Soviet postwar policy and Moscow's commitment to a Marxist world revolution. In 1943 and 1944 they

8. Pogue, *Organizer of Victory*, pp. 315, 522.

9. Marshall to Secretary of State, 3 August 1944, in *FR: 1944*, 1, pp. 699–703; excerpts from a letter, JCS to the Secretary of State, 16 May 1944, in U.S. Department of State, *Foreign Relations of the United States: The Conference of Berlin (The Potsdam Conference) 1945* (hereafter cited as *FR: Potsdam*), vol. 1, pp. 264–66; JCS Memorandum for Information 382, "A Security Policy for Post-War America," 29 March 1945, file CCS 092 (7-27-44), JCS.

10. *FR: Potsdam*, 1: 264–66.

believed that Russian policy would be moderately expansionist. The Soviets would dominate, but not necessarily communize, Eastern Europe and Manchuria, and would succeed Germany as the strongest power in Europe. Traditional nationalist objectives and a legitimate fear of Germany would fuel Russian expansion, not a lust for world domination. As the Joint Intelligence Staff put it in January 1945, "the chief aim of Soviet foreign policy is to establish and maintain the security of the U.S.S.R." By Yalta, there even seemed reason to hope that Soviet territorial demands in Europe were already "completely or almost completely met."[11]

Though intelligence experts anticipated conflict between American and Soviet interests, they doubted that the Soviet Union would soon have either the capability or inclination for a war with the United States. The task of reconstruction precluded such a possibility. Nor did the experts worry about a clash of economic interests. They did speculate that Russian expansion could jeopardize the balance of power in Europe and the success of the United Nations Organization, and thereby undermine American security. The "sovietization of eastern and southeastern Europe" would be a "warning to the West to be on its guard," but neither sovietization there nor Russian dominance in "areas adjacent to its Asiatic frontiers" constituted a direct threat to vital American interests, according to some JCS experts. On the other hand, Russian penetration into Germany was regarded as intolerable, and the Allies' success in formulating a common policy on Germany was seen as critical to future Russian-American friendship.[12]

But the services gave little thought to such a policy for Germany or to the implications of American occupation policy for future Soviet-American relations. When Stimson suggested that the USSR "must certainly be included" in any trusteeship for the Saar and the Ruhr,

11. Quotations from Joint Intelligence Committee, "Estimate of Soviet Post War Capabilities and Intentions," "Enclosure D—Soviet Postwar Foreign Policy—General," in Joint Intelligence Committee No. 250/1, 31 January 1945, file ABC 336 (1942–48) Russia Sec. 1-A, OPD; JCS Memorandum for Information 382, 29 March 1945, file CCS 092 (7-27-44), JCS. For other estimates of Soviet policy in Europe, see JCS Memorandum for Information 121, 22 August 1943, JCS; Office of Strategic Services paper, "Russia's Postwar Foreign Policy: By Regions," in unpublished diaries of James Forrestal, pp. 164–86, copy in Naval History Division.

12. Quotations from JCS Memorandum for Information 382, 29 March 1945, file CCS 092 (7-27-44), JCS. See also JIC 250/1, 31 January 1945, Enclosure A, B, and D, file ABC 336 (1942–48) Russia Sec. 1-A, OPD.

he found that "McCloy, much to [his] surprise, was alarmed at giving this addition to Russia's power." Such alarm was apparently rare. Refusing to brook any interference with its pursuit of early victory in the war, the military worried mostly about encroachment from the civilian departments on its prerogatives to make occupation plans, or, in the case of men like Stimson, the danger of a resurgent Germany should the Allies reinstitute the program adopted at Versailles twenty-five years earlier. Reluctant either to make occupation plans or to yield their formulation to others, the services developed no long-range German policy.[13]

Some advisors to the Joint Chiefs appreciated the subtle dangers of miscalculation and misperception as the two superpowers moved into the postwar era. "With the history of foreign attacks upon the U.S.S.R. and the legacy of marxian ideology," observed several scholars in January 1945, "the Soviet leaders will probably over-emphasize any British or American expansionist tendencies and exaggerate the possibility of aggression against the U.S.S.R. from any quarter." Russian overreaction might in turn cause American leaders to misread Soviet intentions and a "dangerous miscalculation" might result. Still, the experts suggested the usefulness of "large capabilities and firm policies . . . in discouraging wide Soviet expansion."[14]

For the most part, the military did not appreciate that the use of American forces for global peacekeeping might alarm the Soviet Union. The military's lack of foresight was due in part to an inability to distinguish between American interests and those of other nations. Many planners proved, in the words of the historian of AAF plans, "unable to grasp the difference between national defense and prevention of all aggression." Navy planners spoke in the same breath of the United States' need to "protect its territories and national interests" and "to suppress any incipient war" by joint or independent action, though the latter was certainly an unprecedented challenge. If America's interests in preserving peace were identical to the interests of other nations, then what country could object? Encouraging that

13. Quotation from Stimson Diary, 7 September 1944. See also Pogue, *Organizer of Victory*, pp. 460–69; John Lewis Gaddis, *The United States and the Origins of the Cold War, 1941–1947*, chap. 4; Paul Y. Hammond, "Directives for the Occupation of Germany: The Washington Controversy," in Harold Stein, ed., *American Civil-Military Decisions*.

14. JIC 250/1, 31 January 1945, Enclosure D, pp. 17–18, file ABC 336 (1942–48) Russia Sec. 1-A, OPD.

outlook was the probability of American participation in an international organization which might legitimize American peacekeeping activity.[15]

Through 1943 and 1944, military views of the Soviet Union remained too volatile and inarticulate to exert much effect on post-war planning, and service leaders apparently made no attempt to impose on their planning staffs a set outlook regarding the Soviets. Inattention to Soviet objectives was evident, for example, in the efforts to develop policy on the nation's peacekeeping role after the war. Military representatives sat on the Advisory Committee on Post-War Foreign Policy, a group established by Roosevelt in 1941 to draft and negotiate American policy for an international organization. The three principal officers detailed to the committee, experienced in disarmament negotiations before the war, were committed to a vigorous disarmament plan. On the organization of a peacekeeping force they were, like Congress and the executive, more cautious. They rejected an international army composed of many national contingents integrated into one force. They preferred that the great powers alone assume responsibility for peacekeeping and merely keep their forces on call for international service, a recommendation later made by the JCS.[16]

At the time of the Tehran Conference in November 1943, the military did not yet have a clear idea of the role American force would play in international organization or in Soviet-American diplomacy. Roosevelt approved a JCS plan for a system of postwar American air bases ostensibly to service American bombers on international peackeeping duty, but no bases were slated for continental Europe or Asia. Since the President stated that American occupation forces would remain in Europe "one year, maybe two," and that the "Four Policemen" might "maintain order in Europe by the 'quarantine' method," the services probably anticipated that aircraft based near Europe would be the primary instrument of American peacekeeping there. At Tehran, there seemed no in-

15. Smith, *Air Force Plans*, p. 47; Cominch-CNO (Admiral King) to Secretary of the Navy, 3 May 1945, file CNO A16-3/EN, CNO-Cominch Records.

16. Lowe, "The Planning and Negotiation of U.S. Post-War Security, 1942–1943"; Leahy (for JCS) to Secretary of War and Secretary of State, 24 April 1945, file CCS 092 (4-14-45) Sec. 1, JCS.

clination by American negotiators to follow up on a statement by
Stalin expressing willingness to see the United States hold bases in
Europe and play a peacekeeping role there. Discussions among the
Allies about postwar bases focused on Germany and Japan as the
most probable future enemies, but gave little attention to the precise
location of bases which might curb their resurgence.[17]

The services appeared to view the prospect of an international
force with indifference or mild enthusiasm. The United Nations
Organization did not seem to threaten their claims to large peacetime forces, since they reasoned that the United States would retain
forces adequate for unilateral defense. Any American contribution
to an international force would comprise only additions to, not
replacements of, national defense forces. At best, an international
force might justify larger American troop strengths and their deployment over a greater part of the globe, a line which Army Air Forces
took. Planners never considered that an effective international army
might so reduce world tensions as to permit a large cut in planned
force levels. Nor did they examine how American power might most
effectively contribute to the successful operation of an international
police body.[18]

Although military officers served on American delegations to
international conferences on the United Nations, only self-interest
sparked close attention by the services to United Nations planning.
Forrestal, for example, became alarmed over reports that air power
might be the primary component of an international force, a prospect
sure to strengthen the AAF's claims to primacy in the postwar
establishment, as aviators recognized. More broadly, the military
responded to persistent criticism that its preparedness programs were
jeopardizing the success of the United Nations. Likewise some defense
leaders became fearful that the State Department's emphasis on the
United Nations as a disarmament organization might, as Forrestal
worried, create "a breach [between State and the services] in our
plans which will be exploited by wishful thinkers of the 'Kellog Pact'

17. U.S. Department of State, *Foreign Relations of the United States: The Conferences at
Cairo and Tehran*, pp. 256, 530–32, 568–71, 595, 845, 846.

18. Smith, *Air Force Plans*, pp. 45–51, and Davis, *Postwar Defense Policy and the U.S. Navy*,
pp. 10, 16, 92, 106, 109, 110, 158; King to Forrestal, 27 April 1945, serial 010045, A1(1) Post
War Plans Files 1, CNO-Cominch Records; minutes of the JCS 116th meeting, 28 September
1943, file ABC 321 (30 July 1943), OPD.

and the 'peace at any price' groups."[19] On the other hand, some officials took heart from the widespread domestic support for international organization, which they saw as a sign of popular repudiation of prewar isolationism and recognition of the need for "the immediate forceful suppression of any form of aggression."[20] Aside from such considerations of public opinion and public relations, the services took a wait-and-see attitude toward international organization.

Soviet policy, a minor concern in the military's international planning, also had little effect on its making of postwar strategy. Bureaucratically isolated, most planners fell prey to a kind of parochialism which discouraged anticipation of the USSR as an enemy. Each service tended to search for an enemy which would justify that service's existence. Army Air Forces planners eyed a renascent Germany or Japan as the most probable enemies because both possessed the technology to develop strategic air power. Certain that only nations with a strategic bombing capability would dare wage war in the future, they dismissed the Soviet Union as a foe because it failed to develop a strategic force during the war and appeared to lack both the technology and the doctrine to do so for at least another twenty or thirty years. The navy also minimized the Russian threat, since the Soviets had demonstrated no more flare for battleships than for bombers. Because the USSR was a great land power, the factor of parochialism was less important in army thinking. But since the Soviets could not use land power to attack the United States, the Red Army did not alarm the army's Special Planning Division. SPD not only failed to single out the Soviet Union but steered clear of any forecasts of future enemies. Elated over the Moscow agreements of autumn 1943, General John McAuley Palmer, advisor to SPD, even went so far as to speculate that "Joe Stalin" might be "the real apostle of future world peace."[21]

19. Forrestal to Secretary of War and Secretary of State, 4 March 1945; Duffield to Forrestal, 15 March 1945; Forrestal to Admiral Willson, 30 March 1945, all in file 2-1-7, SecNav; Smith, *Air Force Plans*, pp. 37, 45.

20. Palmer to Grunert, 9 June 1943, file 370.9 (14 June 1943), Chief of Staff.

21. Smith, *Air Force Plans*, pp. 51–53, 81–82; Davis, *Postwar Defense Policy and the U.S. Navy*, pp. 18, 296; Yarnell to Vice Chief of Naval Operations, 14 June 1944, Series 2, item 2, vol. 1, Papers of H. E. Yarnell, Naval History Division; Palmer to Miles, 9 November 1943, Chronological Files 1942–43, Box 10, Palmer Papers.

Warsaw to Hiroshima

In the war's final year, the military's attitude toward Soviet intentions gradually shifted. Anxiety about Russian aims, always present, crowded out confusion and complacency. The change, checked at times by renewed hopes for cooperation between the two great powers, was irregular. Even at the war's end, the military outlook was in flux. But a fragile trust was giving way to suspicion.

The escalation of suspicion began just when cooperation between Soviet and American armies achieved its greatest success. On June 2, 1944, the Army Air Forces, flying B-17s out of an Italian airfield, conducted the first shuttle-bombing raid. Amid pomp and professions of friendship, American bombers landed at a base in the USSR after striking Axis targets in Hungary. To American officers who for years had battled Soviet opposition to the presence of foreign military men on Russian soil, the start of shuttle bombing that day "marked the high tide of . . . military relations with the Soviet Union." To watch dozens of Flying Fortresses land on Russian soil was "a thrill beyond description." The United States had breached the wall of Russian xenophobia. In a few days, it would seal the alliance by opening the second front against Hitler.[22]

Only weeks later the controversial events at Warsaw dispelled the spirit of cooperation. The Red Army halted within sight of the Polish capital while Polish resistance forces and the Nazi army waged a savage battle. Worse, Stalin denied Britain and the United States the use of shuttle bases in the Ukraine from which to supply the Polish fighters by air drops. Ambassador Harriman and General John Deane, head of the American Military Mission in Moscow, were, in George Kennan's recollection, "shattered by the experience."[23]

The incident sharpened the mistrust of Russian intentions already nursed by Kennan, Harriman, and Deane. For months they had haggled with the Soviets over shuttle-bombing arrangements, lend-lease, and cooperation in the Pacific war. The Warsaw tragedy indicated to Harriman and Kennan that Russian leaders, "bloated

22. Quotations from Deane, *Strange Alliance*, pp. 117, 119. For the story of shuttle bombing, see Lukas, *Eagles East*, chap. 13, and the older but richer account in Deane, chap. 7.
23. George F. Kennan, *Memoirs, 1925–1950*, pp. 210–11.

with power," wished to crush all opposition to Soviet rule in Eastern Europe. American interests in Eastern Europe were not weighty, they acknowledged, but American indifference to Soviet "strong arm methods" there might encourage Russian penetration further west. Kennan wanted a "showdown" with the Soviets. Less belligerent, Harriman and Deane sought, and on their own initiative struck, a tougher attitude in negotiations with the Russians.[24]

The diplomats sent Washington alarmed messages closely heeded by officials there. Despite Kennan's complaint that his views seldom reached home, Harriman and Deane pressed a viewpoint which closely paralleled his. General H. H. Arnold quickly accepted the recommendations of Harriman and Deane. With typical faith in air power, he and Eisenhower recommended to Marshall that American occupation forces in Germany include a "powerful heavy bomber force" capable not only of overawing the defeated Germans but of "instantaneous and effective action in any direction." Hinting at possible Russian misbehavior, though attaching a low priority to his request, Eisenhower deemed the bombers "most desirable" in order to place the nation on "a substantial basis of equality" with the Soviets. Navy Secretary Forrestal, already pursuing his own anti-communist crusade, complained that the American who emphasized the needs of national security was

> apt to be called a god-damned fascist or imperialist, while if Uncle Joe suggests that he needs the Baltic Provinces, half of Poland, all of Bessarabia and access to the Mediterranean, all hands agree that he is a fine, frank, candid and generally delightful fellow.

Forrestal was also stepping up his public campaign for a powerful postwar American military force, a campaign linked in his mind, though not yet publicly, to his suspicions of the USSR.[25]

Harriman's story of Soviet actions in Eastern Europe, told personally to Stimson in October, distressed the secretary of war. What worried him was not simply Soviet expansion westward, but the totalitarian nature of the Stalinist regime. Disbandment of its secret police and establishment of Western-style civil freedoms were

    24. Herring, *Aid to Russia*, pp. 128–37; Lukas, *Eagles East*, p, 207.
    25. Quotations from Alfred D. Chandler, ed., *The Papers of Dwight David Eisenhower: The War Years* (Baltimore, 1970), vol. 4, pp. 2187, 2242–43, and Millis, *Forrestal Diaries*, p. 14. See also Kennan, *Memoirs*, pp. 217, 230–33, 251; Herring, *Aid to Russia*, p. 137.

necessary for peaceful relations between the great powers, he believed. Otherwise, he apparently thought, the Stalinist regime would engage in aggression, since no democratic checks existed to restrain it.[26]

The most powerful indictment of existing policy toward Moscow came on December 2 from General Deane, whose frustration with Russian duplicity and American charity boiled over into a letter to General George Marshall. Deane was no Russophobe. He believed that the USSR and the United States had "few conflicting interests" and saw little reason why the two "should not be friendly now and in the foreseeable future." But he found American generosity during the war self-defeating. After each banquet, he complained, "we send the Soviets another thousand airplanes, and they approve a visa that has been hanging fire for months. We then scratch our heads to see what other gifts we can send, and they scratch theirs to see what else they can ask for." Such charity only sparked Russian contempt and misbehavior. "Gratitude cannot be banked in the Soviet Union," Deane explained, and the nation which tried to amass it would only be regarded as "a sucker." Deane wanted Washington to demand that the Soviets justify any future aid requests, to "insist on a quid pro quo" for any assistance not vital to winning the war. We should "stop pushing ourselves on them and make the Soviet authorities come to us."[27]

Presaging the famous "long telegram" which Kennan sent to Washington fifteen months later, Deane's letter did not so much introduce a new point of view as crystallize an emergent one. Free of the ideological and apocalyptic outlook of Kennan's writings, the letter still reflected much of Kennan's viewpoint on Russian-American relations. Read against the background of Soviet actions in Eastern Europe and elsewhere (and it was quickly fit into that context), it was a disturbing document. It justified a more suspicious attitude toward Soviet intentions and a more demanding diplomacy in dealing with Moscow.

Deane's letter quickly circulated among Washington's highest officials. Marshall, who probably agreed with Deane's warnings, dispatched the letter to Stimson, who in turn discussed it with Forrestal, Secretary of State Stettinius, and the President. The letter

26. Stimson Diary, 23 October 1944.
27. The Deane letter was reprinted in Deane, *Strange Alliance*, pp. 84–86.

strengthened the determination of Stimson and Forrestal to obtain, as Stimson put it, "specific quid pro quo from the Russians as well as a little more mutuality in our relations." Showing the letter to the state and navy secretaries, Stimson discussed how a postwar credit might be used to extract concessions from Moscow regarding military operations against Germany and Japan.[28]

With the President, Stimson went further. On the last day of 1944 the two weighed the Soviet threat to Eastern Europe. Stimson took the occasion "to tell him of Deane's warning to us in the Department that ... we should be more vigorous on insisting upon a quid pro quo." The atomic bomb, Stimson explained, might give Washington the power to implement Deane's recommendation. The secretary knew that the United States could never permanently keep to itself the secret of the bomb or openly brandish such a weapon as a threat. But he hoped to delay sharing the atomic secret until we could be "sure to get a real quid pro quo from our frankness." Apparently he thought the Soviets might relax their grip on Eastern Europe or liberalize their own regime in return for America's sharing of her knowledge.[29]

Stimson recorded that the President "said he thought he agreed" with him, but apparently FDR did not further apprise him of his thoughts on atomic diplomacy. Months earlier Roosevelt had decided, without consulting or informing his scientific and military advisors, to maintain an Anglo-American monopoly on the atomic bomb. He may have shared Prime Minister Churchill's desire to use the weapon to coerce Moscow into diplomatic concessions. He may have indulged hazier notions of the bomb as the club with which the "Four Policemen" could deter aggression and enforce world peace. At the least he had rejected divulging the secret to the Soviets for the time being.[30]

Roosevelt and his military command did little, however, to

28. Quotation from minutes of meeting of Committee of Three, 9 January 1945, Secretary of War's Safe File, SecWar. See also War Department copies of the Deane letter in file ABC 336 Russia (22 August 1943) Sec. 1-A, OPD, and in file 334.8, ASW; Stimson Diary, 31 December 1944 and 9 January 1945; Pogue, *Organizer of Victory*, pp. 291, 530–31. Pogue states, "It is not clear whether the letter had any influence on its recipients," but apparently Pogue did not take note of Stimson's introduction of the letter to the Committee of Three or Stimson's discussion of the letter with the President, described below.

29. Stimson Diary, 31 December 1944.

30. See Sherwin, "The Atomic Bomb and the Origins of the Cold War"; Sherwin, *A World Destroyed*, chaps. 3–5.

formulate new policies toward the Soviet Union in the wake of the autumn warnings from Moscow. Military officials remained out of touch with the political difficulties between the United States and the USSR during the winter of 1944–45. Stimson and Forrestal did not go to Yalta. The Joint Chiefs did, but, with the exception of Admiral Leahy, took no part in political talks there. Roosevelt did not solicit their advice on political matters, and they did not offer it. The President, perhaps hoping that American economic power might moderate Soviet behavior, perhaps just being secretive, did nothing to follow up his December 31 conversation with Stimson.[31]

The Crimean Conference increased the uneasiness of some defense officials about future relations with the Russians. Leahy, although encouraged by Stalin's cooperative attitude at the conference, feared that because the draconian peace terms which the Allies proposed for Germany might "make Russia the dominant power in Europe," the world faced "a certainty of future international disagreements and prospects of another war." On the other hand, the President's chief of staff also worried that a harsh peace carried the "germs of an appalling war of revenge" by the Germans. Significant, too, was the erosion of Leahy's confidence in the United Nations Organization. For that erosion he blamed not the Soviet Union but France, whose possession of a veto dashed Leahy's hopes for an effective United Nations.[32]

The Joint Chiefs did have some success at Yalta in pinning down the Red Army command on the timing of Russian entry into the Pacific war, the coordination of Pacific operations, and American utilization of Siberian air bases. After Yalta the Soviets proved exasperatingly evasive about carrying out the air base agreements. Deane and his staff soon despaired of effective cooperation with the Soviets, and since American advances in the Pacific had reduced the utility of Russian bases, the American military abandoned attempts to secure them.[33]

In March and April, as Soviet and American armies rushed to meet each other along the Elbe, further disagreements developed. Few

31. Pogue, *Organizer of Victory*, pp. 522–35; Herring, *Aid to Russia*, pp. 168–71.

32. Quotations from Leahy Diary, 11 February 1945, Leahy Papers. See also William D. Leahy, *I Was There*, pp. 317–22, which drops the diary reference to "another war."

33. Deane, *Strange Alliance*, pp. 251–66; Lukas, *Eagles East*, pp. 225–27; Millis, *Forrestal Diaries*, pp. 27–28; Leahy, *I Was There*, pp. 302–04, 310–12, 317–19.

actions of Stalin's government infuriated military officials more than Russian obstruction of efforts to assist American prisoners of war freed by the advancing Red Army. Stimson and Marshall rejected Harriman's call for reprisals against the Soviets for their obstruction, but drafted a "red hot" letter to Stalin. "He can only understand rough talk," Stimson thought at the time. But rough talk brought little satisfaction. Disagreement also arose over disposition of Soviet nationals serving in the German army who were captured by American troops. Stalin's indignation over exclusion from Anglo-American negotiations for the surrender of the Nazi army in Italy produced an even more bitter exchange between Russian and American officials. Marshall personally took a hand in drafting a message which conveyed to Stalin Roosevelt's "bitter resentment" over the "vile misrepresentations" of Stalin's informers on the Italian matter. All the time Harriman and Deane kept up a stream of advice urging reprisals, economic pressure, and stern words with the Soviets. The United States, Harriman worried, faced a "barbarian invasion of Europe." No longer did only Eastern Europe appear to be under siege.[34]

The cooperation imposed on the Allies by fear of a common enemy had rarely been warmhearted. Now the impending collapse of the Nazi foe exposed the divergent interests papered over during the war. With the exception of Forrestal, no high military official in Washington became as alarmist as Harriman. But a consensus among the military leadership was taking shape. The United States, they agreed, would have to talk more firmly to the Soviets, view more skeptically their requests for aid, and worry less about securing their help in the Pacific war. All could agree on the need, expressed by Stimson, "to state our facts with perfectly cold-blooded firmness and not to show any temper."[35]

Few were willing as yet to back up talk with action. Marshall, like General Dwight Eisenhower, was determined not to divert American forces from the final destruction of Hitler's armies to a race with the

34. Stimson Diary, 16 March 1945, 17 March 1945. See also Stimson Diary, 2 April 1945; Deane, *Strange Alliance*, chap. 11; U.S. Department of State, *Foreign Relations of the United States: 1945* (hereafter cited as *FR: 1945*), vol. 5 (Europe), pp. 1067–93; Leahy, *I Was There*, pp. 329–36; Pogue, *Organizer of Victory*, pp. 564–67; Herring, *Aid to Russia*, pp. 194–97; Millis, *Forrestal Diaries*, pp. 36, 39–41, 47; Gar Alperovitz, *Atomic Diplomacy: Hiroshima and Potsdam*, pp.22–31.

35. Stimson Diary, 3 April 1945.

Russians for the capture of Central Europe's capital cities. Such a maneuver, proposed by Churchill during the last months of the war, would prejudice Soviet cooperation in the Pacific and delay the redeployment of American forces to the Pacific theater. It would bring American forces into possession of territory they would soon have to vacate to the Soviets anyway, unless the United States assumed the onus of violating wartime agreements. It was as likely to provoke the Soviets as to cow them. And it would cost the Anglo-American forces dearly in casualties. As Marshall told Eisenhower in a statement assented to by the other Joint Chiefs, "I would be loath to hazard American lives for purely political purposes."[36]

An April 23 meeting between Harry Truman and his closest advisors revealed the caution of much of the military leadership. The new President convened the meeting to discuss what he would say to Foreign Minister Vyacheslav Molotov about the Soviet Union's imposition of the Lublin government on Poland and other alleged transgressions of the Yalta agreements. Agitated by Moscow's efforts to secure United Nations recognition of the puppet Polish government, Truman remarked that "if the Russians did not wish to join us they could go to hell."[37]

Among military officials present, only Forrestal and General Deane welcomed the President's belligerence. Contact with Harriman had deepened Forrestal's doubts about Soviet intentions and postwar American security. The navy secretary saw the Soviets' Polish policy as part of a "pattern of unilateral action" and Russian expansion. Acquiescence in such action encouraged Soviet recklessness, he complained. Forrestal insisted that "we had better have a show down with them now than later." Home from Moscow, Deane avoided Forrestal's talk of global patterns but echoed Harriman's call for a hard line on the Polish situation.[38]

Stimson, speaking as a realist who believed in balance-of-power politics, thought otherwise. He welcomed stern language with the Soviets "on minor military matters" in order to "teach them manners." But he shrank from challenging them in their own backyard. Russian interests and power were so great in Poland that Stalin

36. Quotation from Pogue, *Organizer of Victory*, p. 573. See also Pogue, pp. 547–51, 555–57, 564–71, 573–78.
37. *FR: 1945*, 5 (Europe), pp. 252–53.
38. Ibid., pp. 253, 255; Millis, *Forrestal Diaries*, p. 49.

"would not yield on the Polish question," he believed. It was just "too big a question to take chances on."[39]

More than the practical difficulties of contesting Soviet power prompted that counsel of restraint. Stimson accepted the legitimacy of Soviet domination of Poland, most of which, he reminded his younger colleagues, had been Russian until twenty-five years earlier. A frank proponent of America's regional domination, Stimson could understand another great power protecting its sphere of influence. The secretary, probably still smarting over the State Department's advocacy of United Nations trusteeships for the Japanese-mandated islands, suggested to the April 23 gathering that "the Russians perhaps were being more realistic than we were in regard to their own security."[40]

Stimson hoped that Russian-American differences could be adjudicated in frank, private negotiations with Moscow. His optimism sprang from his belief that American interests in Eastern Europe were not great, and from his confidence, unusual among American officials by this time, that Stalin would honor the agreements he made. His hope for Soviet cooperation in establishing prosperity and stability in postwar Europe provided him further cause to trust the Soviets.[41]

Stimson believed that the naive assumptions of American diplomacy had provoked the April crisis over Poland. He implored the April 23 assembly to understand the hopelessness of trying to impose democracy on Eastern Europe, even though he himself at times hoped to impose liberalization on the Soviet regime. With the exception of the United States and Britain, he claimed, "there was no country that understood free elections." Privately he expressed greater exasperation over American attempts at Yalta to insist on democracy for Poland. By making foolish demands on the Soviets and then dragging the issue before the public at San Francisco, the State Department "got public opinion all churned up over it" and now felt "compelled to bull the thing through." Stimson thought it foolish to bluster, especially on secondary issues.[42]

39. Quotations from *FR: 1945*, 5 (Europe), pp. 253–54; Stimson Diary, 23 April 1945. See also Alperovitz, *Atomic Diplomacy*, pp. 49–55, and Pogue, *Organizer of Victory*, pp. 578–80.
40. *FR: 1945*, 5 (Europe), p. 254.
41. Ibid., p. 253; Alperovitz, *Atomic Diplomacy*, pp. 52–53; Stimson Diary, 16 April 1945, 23 April 1945.
42. *FR: 1945*, 5 (Europe), p. 254; Stimson Diary, 23 April 1945.

Admiral Leahy, though a hard-liner on the Polish matter, acknowledged the naivete of expecting the Soviets to institute democracy in Poland. Truman's personal chief of staff repeated a remark made to FDR at Yalta, where he had noted that the Polish accord was "so elastic that the Russians can stretch it all the way from Yalta to Washington without ever technically breaking it." Leahy apparently endorsed neither Stimson's nor Forrestal's stand. Admiral King, as usual, had little to say on political matters.[43]

Marshall sided with Stimson at the April 23 meeting, but built a narrower case for caution in handling the Soviets. Contrary to Leahy's later recollection, the Joint Chiefs had not dismissed the need for Russian participation in the Pacific war. True, they no longer deemed it essential to victory. They had given up hope for bases in Siberia and doubted that Japan could any longer transfer her Manchurian army to the Japanese home islands. They knew that the USSR's interests would ensure Soviet entry into the war no matter what the United States did. But Marshall still believed Soviet entry "useful to us. The Russians," he explained on April 23, "had it within their power to delay their entry into the Far Eastern war until we had done all the dirty work." A showdown over Poland, he feared, might cost American lives in the Pacific and delay final victory. Already disturbed over mounting American casualties and fearful that Americans would have no stomach for a long and bloody campaign against Japan, he wanted no confrontation over Poland which would imperil Soviet cooperation and prolong the Pacific struggle. Less concerned than were some of his colleagues over the Polish matter, he believed that "difficulties with the Russians ... usually straightened out."[44]

The April 23 meeting disclosed that the military, while sharing a vague sense of the need for greater firmness in dealing with the USSR, could reach no consensus on the gravity of the threat posed by Moscow's policies or on specific restraining actions. Military necessity

43. Quotation from Leahy, *I Was There*, pp. 315–16. See also Millis, *Forrestal Diaries*, pp. 49–50; *FR: 1945*, 5 (Europe), pp. 254–55. Leahy's postwar recollections suggested that he had endorsed a tough stand on the Polish issue; Leahy, *I Was There*, p. 351. Too often those recollections have been taken at face value; see Alperovitz, *Atomic Diplomacy*, p. 32. Some credence should be given to Forrestal's contemporary reaction, which was that Leahy had sided with Stimson and Marshall.

44. Leahy, *I Was There*, p. 351; *FR: 1945*, 5 (Europe), p. 254; Pogue, *Organizer of Victory*, p. 552, 580; Lisle A. Rose, *Dubious Victory: The United States and the End of World War II*, pp. 104, 136–43.

—the desire for a speedy victory over the Axis—was one factor dissuading some officials from advocating a harder line. But the decision not to contest the Soviet occupation of Central Europe and the recommendation from Marshall and Stimson not to challenge Stalin on Poland also indicated that many military leaders simply did not regard Soviet behavior or intentions as disturbing enough to warrant a change in the conduct of the war. However irritating, Soviet actions were still too ambiguous to occasion a reversal of wartime policies.

The spring crisis in Soviet-American relations also produced few changes in the postwar plans of the armed services. Forrestal may have communicated to his staff his fears of the Russian giant, but apparently he was not persuasive to the planning officers. For his part, Marshall continued to demand that his staff cut drastically its estimates for postwar active-duty forces. He urged greater reliance on UMT in postwar plans, and apparently said nothing about the deterioration of Russian-American relations or development of the atomic bomb. AAF planning personnel also received no instructions to alter their designs for the postwar air force. The race among the Allies to capture German scientists and military hardware accelerated in the spring, but the haphazard American effort reflected a jumble of motives among which fear of the Soviets played at most a minor role. Clearly, military officials were not greatly alarmed by the spring's squabbles.[45]

Perhaps, as one historian has suggested, Stimson or other officials at the April 23 meeting "agreed with the principle of . . . a showdown, but opposed immediate action" in the hope that the United States could bargain more effectively later with the atomic bomb to back up its demands.[46] However it was not the timing of confrontation that Stimson opposed, but the very need and justification for it. To the secretary and many other military officials, the Polish dispute, about which Marshall and Stimson confessed their ignorance, mattered far less than did the disagreements with Moscow over German surrender in Italy, prisoners of war, and cooperation in the Pacific.[47] Furthermore, because military intelligence had long

45. Davis, *Postwar Defense Policy and the U.S. Navy*, chap. 6; Smith, *Air Force Plans*, pp. 51–53, 81–82; Clarence Lasby, *Project Paperclip: German Scientists and the Cold War*, chaps. 1–2, especially pp. 78–81.
46. Alperovitz, *Atomic Diplomacy*, p. 28.
47. *FR: 1945*, 5 (Europe), pp. 253–54.

predicated Russian hegemony over Eastern Europe, defense officials, unlike other government leaders, were neither shocked nor indignant at Stalin's actions and his interpretation of the Crimean accords.

Stimson had toyed with the possibilities of atomic diplomacy since 1944. He had continued to hope that the Soviets might implement "liberalization [of their regime] in exchange for S-1 [the atomic bomb]." But the secretary's flirtation with atomic diplomacy did not constitute a fixed and steady purpose to employ it. His traditional concept of balance-of-power diplomacy taught him to regard the bomb as another weapon in the diplomatic arsenal, to be used not recklessly but firmly in the pursuit of limited objectives. He also realized that even the cautious use of such a frightening weapon for diplomatic leverage could provoke enormous anxiety and distrust among other nations. He did not resolve the conflict between those two views until his last days in office, when he came out against nuclear intimidation. Until then, he followed no set course. Thus on April 23 he assessed the Polish problem without fitting it into a grand design for nuclear diplomacy. Indeed, he said not a word about the bomb either in his remarks to Truman or in his diary account of the April 23 meeting.[48]

Stimson's views on the Soviet Union hardened in the last three months of the war. Fearful of the communization of Western Europe and Russian penetration into the Far East, moved by Harriman's gloomy predictions of almost boundless Russian expansion, the secretary doubted that the United States could ever live in peace "with a nation . . . systematically controlled from above by Secret Police and in which free speech is not permitted." "I believe," he wrote at Potsdam in July, that "we must not accept the present situation as permanent for the result will then almost inevitably be a new war and the destruction of our civilization." Stimson hoped that the American nuclear monopoly might counter the immediate and long-term dangers which worried him. The bomb, he believed, might force an end to the war before the USSR could complete its seizure of Manchuria and Korea. In return for American disclosure

48. Quotation from Stimson Diary, 15 February 1945. See also "Memorandum discussed with the President, April 25, 1945," found with Stimson Diary entry of 25 April 1945; Elting E. Morison, *Turmoil and Tradition: A Study of the Life and Times of Henry L. Stimson,* especially pp. 513–14. Much of the evidence Alperovitz introduces to indicate that Stimson only wanted to postpone the confrontation postdates by several days or weeks the April 23 meeting; Alperovitz, *Atomic Diplomacy,* pp. 49–55.

of nuclear secrets, Stalin might adhere more scrupulously to the agreements made at Yalta and elsewhere and even liberalize his regime—so Stimson hoped. A combat demonstration of the bomb might dramatize American might and thereby encourage Stalin to behave with more restraint. Stimson opposed crudely threatening the Soviets with nuclear destruction, but he believed the bomb and American economic power comprised "a royal straight flush" and that "we mustn't be a fool about the way we play it."[49]

At the same time, Stimson's suspicions of the Red ally increasingly colored his stance on the negotiations at San Francisco. The issue was an American desire for a free hand to intervene in Latin American affairs under the United Nations charter. In San Francisco, Assistant Secretary of War McCloy worried that the Soviet Union would use the precedent of such a grant of power to press for the same rights in Europe. The effect, he feared, would be to carve up the world into regional blocks and to deny to the United States the right "to intervene in time to avoid a conflagration in Europe." Without that right, the United States would be helpless to prevent the outbreak of another world war. McCloy decided "that we ought to have our cake and eat it too; that we ought to be free to operate under this regional arrangement in South America, [and] at the same time intervene promptly in Europe." Stimson, though pessimistic about the value of any UN agreement and fatalistic about Soviet domination of Eastern Europe, agreed with McCloy on the need for a double standard. The Soviets' position in Europe was not parallel to that of the United States in the Western Hemisphere, he explained to McCloy.

> She's not such an overwhelmingly gigantic power from the ones which she's probably going to make a row about as we are here and on the other hand our fussing around among those little fellow[s] there [in Latin America] doesn't upset any balance in Europe at all. . . . It doesn't upset any balance there where[as] she may upset a balance that affects us.[50]

Though on April 23 he had cautioned restraint in challenging Soviet

---

49. Quotations from memorandum, "Reflections on the Basic Problems which Confront Us," found with 27 July 1945 entry in Stimson Diary; Stimson Diary, 14 May 1945. See Alperovitz, *Atomic Diplomacy*, passim, for a detailed delineation of this aspect of Stimson's thinking.

50. Notes on telephone conversation between Stimson and McCloy, 8 May 1945, Stimson Memos (Europe in Postwar), Stimson Papers.

hegemony along its borders, now the firm approach tempted him.

Stimson, as well as other service leaders, also fought any system of United Nations trusteeships which might include the numerous Pacific islands coveted by the military. They insisted on "unrestricted strategic control by the United States of the Japanese mandated islands and certain islands in the Pacific." Stimson labored to keep the trusteeship issue off the agenda at the San Francisco Conference or confine it to discussion among the great powers. An open discussion, it was feared, might subject the United States to pressure from small powers and embroil the United States in a dispute with the Soviets which would undermine cooperation in the Pacific. Furthermore, should the United States press its claims, the USSR would have grounds to demand trusteeships over neighboring states. After the San Francisco Conference, however, the military saw nothing objectionable in the new United Nations draft charter, although the limits on the UN's ability to enforce peace through military means were probably increasingly apparent.[51]

Some War Department experts indulged graver doubts about the Soviet Union than did Stimson and his staff. Moscow's postwar aims might be limited and acceptable, an April 2 staff paper acknowledged; but, it said, "we cannot possibly wait until Russia's policy is fully revealed before taking" certain "countermeasures in anticipation of another world war." Those countermeasures were "imperative at once." Otherwise, the USSR might soon overrun Europe and Asia, proceed to "outbuild us in every phase of military production," and then successfully attack the United States. The authors granted the need "to convince Russia of our own unaggressive intentions," but proposed a program sure to have the opposite effect. The American government would have to build a "West-European-American power system" as a "counterweight to Russia." It would have to support the European colonial empires while also encouraging "liberalization of the colonial regimes . . . to check Soviet influence in the stimulation of colonial revolt." Even then, Europe might succumb and the United States might have to fall back in "hemisphere defense."[52]

51. Leahy (for JCS) to Secretary of War and Secretary of the Navy, 24 April 1945 (quotation source) and 23 June 1945, both in file CCS 092 (4-14-45) Sec. 1, JCS; Millis, *Forrestal Diaries*, pp. 28–29, 33, 37, 38, 45; Stimson Diary, 21 January 1945, 18 April 1945.

52. "Problems and Objectives of United States Policy," unsigned paper, 2 April 1945, file 336 (Russia), ASW. See also Smith, *Air Force Plans*, pp. 110–13.

G-2 was scarcely more encouraging. Earlier intelligence estimates had stressed that the Soviet government's postwar goals were expansionist but limited and based on security needs. A G-2 paper of July 6, 1945, ignored those needs and stripped Soviet motives down to a naked lust for world conquest. "The limit has been reached to which the United States can subscribe to Soviet expansion," the paper advised.[53]

The Joint Chiefs took some actions which indicated skepticism about the USSR's postwar intentions. After V-E day the JCS sought cuts in lend-lease to the Soviet Union, although they were no more sympathetic toward lavish aid to the British. When the USSR probed for bases on the Spitzbergen Archipelago and Bear Island off the coast of Norway, the JCS recommended stiff opposition. "From the long-range security point of view, and until the post-war situation and Soviet policy can be seen more clearly, we should, in so far as practicable, resist demands and policies which tend to improve [the] Soviet position in Western Europe."[54]

But the alarmist outlook advanced by some in the military and State Department staffs did not panic the top command. Firm about resisting Soviet penetration into Western Europe, in May and June many service leaders still showed little concern about Russian influence in Eastern Europe. More broadly, those leaders still clung, though less confidently, to their hopes for Soviet cooperation in the Pacific war and the enlistment of the USSR in the cause of world peace.

In rapid sequence during the late spring of 1945, the armed services rejected pleas from Churchill and the State Department for a challenge to Soviet policies in Europe. Churchill begged for retention of the Anglo-American joint command until the United States and Britain could wring certain concessions from Stalin, but Stimson and his staff were loath to lock arms with the British in an anti-Russian crusade. The United States, Stimson told McCloy on May 19, should stick to Roosevelt's pursuit of an independent path between the USSR and England. The Soviets, Stimson said, distrusted England more than the United States.

---

53. "Soviet Intentions," unsigned G-2 paper, 6 July 1945, file ABC 092 USSR (15 November 1944), OPD.
54. Herring, *Aid to Russia*, pp. 224–29; Rose, *Dubious Victory*, pp. 188–92. Quotations from *FR: 1945*, 5 (Europe), pp. 96–97.

Any steps we took now in immediate reversal of our agreement with the Russians would be construed by them as a definite alignment of the Anglo-Americans against the Russians and make it all the more difficult for us to work out an effective relationship with them.

Marshall and the JCS joined Stimson in approving the prompt dissolution of Eisenhower's joint command post. Likewise, the services rejected Churchill's entreaties that the Anglo-American forces refuse to withdraw to agreed-on occupation zones in Europe until Stalin proved more cooperative in Austria. Such tactics, Eisenhower warned, "would wreck the whole cooperative attempt" to achieve harmonious relations with the Russians.[55]

The service heads also shied away from a clash between Anglo-American troops and Tito's triumphant partisan army. Churchill and the American State Department, fearful that Tito's advance on Trieste represented the opening wedge of Soviet expansion, urged forcible Anglo-American occupation of the Adriatic city. Truman weighed a tough stand against Tito's bold moves. Partly at the urging of Stimson and Marshall, diplomacy prevailed. Confrontation in Europe would slow victory in the Pacific, the two army chieftains feared. Stimson may also have thought a showdown with the USSR premature. Marshall's objections were more fundamental. He believed, Truman later recalled, that "if we were to win the peace after winning the war, we had to have Russian help."[56]

Marshall, on whose advice Truman relied heavily, emerged as the guardian of the frazzled hopes for mutual trust between the two superpowers. The State Department, headed by Stettinius and the Russophobe under secretary, Joseph Grew, and galvanized by Harriman's dire predictions, argued for an unyielding stand against supposed Soviet expansion. Stimson, Forrestal, Leahy, and King in

55. Quotations from McCloy, Memorandum of Telephone Conversation with the Secretary of War, 19 May 1945, file 334.8 (Committee of Three Minutes), ASW; Eisenhower, quoted in Alperovitz, *Atomic Diplomacy*, p. 46. See also Marshall to McCloy, 3 July 1945, and Dorr to McCloy, 8 June 1945, both in file 336 (Russia), ASW; Harry S. Truman, *Memoirs*, 1: 298, 300–01; Alperovitz, *Atomic Diplomacy*, pp. 42–43, 45–46, 83–84.

56. Quotation from Truman, *Memoirs*, 1: 246. See also Alperovitz, *Atomic Diplomacy*, p. 137, 138n.; Rose, *Dubious Victory*, pp. 121–27; Gabriel Kolko, *The Politics of War: The World and United States Foreign Policy, 1943–1945*, pp. 414–20. Kolko's claim that the American military feared "a new war in Europe that would delay the resolution of the Pacific conflict" may be doubted, but the military did fear the tying down of American troops in Europe and the strain on the Soviet-American alliance.

various degrees endorsed a firm stand. Marshall, himself troubled, dissented.

Marshall's views on Soviet-American relations were less precise and well formed than those of many of his colleagues. His belief in military subordination to civilian control discouraged expansive comment on those relations. His anxiety about the apparent remoteness of final victory over Japan dissuaded him from considering long-run Soviet intentions or dwelling on political differences between the two allies which might jeopardize a combined effort against Tokyo. More important, the chief of staff continued to see little reason to distrust the Red ally. Speaking on May 31 to the Interim Committee weighing the future of atomic weaponry, Marshall argued that the "allegations" of secretiveness or duplicity made against the Soviets during the war had "proven unfounded. The seemingly uncooperative attitude of Russia in military matters stemmed from the necessity of maintaining security." Marshall had "accepted this reason for their attitude in his dealings with the Russians and had acted accordingly." He even suggested inviting "two prominent Russian scientists" to witness the test of the nuclear device at Alamogordo. The committee ignored the proposal.[57]

Marshall's faith in postwar Soviet-American cooperation was not blind. He "was inclined," as paraphrased in the Interim Committee minutes, "to favor the building up of a combination among like-minded powers" after the war, "thereby forcing Russia to fall in line by the very force of this coalition."[58] By "force" Marshall most likely meant diplomatic pressure rather than overt military power. In combination with frank efforts to secure Soviet friendship, such pressure, he probably hoped, might induce the Soviet Union to join collective efforts to maintain peace. Firmness and trust were, to him, compatible.

Others in the War Department also tried to restrain the hard-liners. Stimson's old friend and advisor, Goldthwaite Dorr, ridiculed sug-

57. Notes of the Interim Committee meeting, 31 May 1945, pp. 11–12, Harvey Bundy File No. 160, Manhattan Engineer District Records.
58. Ibid., pp. 10–12. Arthur Holly Compton's recollections of the May 31 meeting were that Marshall posed a number of objections to the use of the bomb, objections not mentioned in the committee notes. It is unclear from Compton's account whether Marshall suggested that refraining from using the bomb might prevent an arms race, or whether he hoped that abstinence might enable the United States to retain the nuclear secret. See Arthur Holly Compton, *Atomic Quest*, pp. 237–38.

gestions for a showdown with the USSR. "I do not know," Dorr wrote McCloy, "how we can expect to receive from the Russians a tolerance for the existence of a capitalist system and for the freedom of any area to live under it or adopt it, if we cannot feel the same tolerance with regard to the socialist form of economy." He doubted that the Soviet system threatened the West, since "from its very nature the socialist economy may prove to be less aggressive than the capitalist because it tends to be self-sufficient." The great danger, Dorr explained, was not Soviet expansion but the misperceptions and miscalculations of the superpowers. Many Soviet actions gave Americans "a natural sense of grave apprehension," Dorr acknowledged. But it might be, "if we had the eyes to see it," that American actions and statements, if seen "against the background of Murmansk, eastern Siberia, and the 'Cordon Sanitaire,'" also frightened the Soviets. The United States, Dorr knew, must not incite the very behavior it feared. McCloy, though expressing doubts about Moscow's German policy, agreed "wholeheartedly" with the Dorr analysis.[59]

The immediate concern of service leaders, however, remained the war in the Pacific and the Soviet Union's role in it. In May and June fresh evidence of Japanese exhaustion and growing confidence that the atomic bomb would work stirred hopes among American policymakers that Japan might collapse before an invasion proved necessary or progressed too far. Several measures, singly or in combination, might induce an early surrender: blockade, atomic or conventional bombing, a Russian declaration of war, or a stern warning to the Japanese coupled with assurances of the Emperor's status. If such measures succeeded, the Americans might avoid not only a bloody invasion of the home islands but Russian occupation of North China and Korea. Such a possibility must have intrigued those American military leaders who were wary of Soviet intentions, reluctant to share credit with any ally for victory over Japan, and perhaps eager to show the United States' overwhelming military power to the Soviets. At the least, there seemed little reason to solicit Russian entry, since Stalin appeared determined to fight soon anyway.[60]

59. Dorr to McCloy (memorandum on Hoover paper), 8 June 1945, with handwritten note by McCloy, file 336 (Russia), ASW.

60. Stimson memorandum with 27 July 1945 diary entry; Stimson Diary, 14 May 1945; Alperovitz, *Atomic Diplomacy*, chap. 4.

In May Harriman and Grew urged the military to back a policy of resistance to Soviet expansion. Believing that victory over Japan was now possible without Russian help, they wanted Washington to renegotiate the Yalta agreements on the Far East as part of a plan to forestall Soviet expansion there. The navy was tantalized by the prospect of ending the Pacific war before Russian entry, and Forrestal, more than ever brooding over the "Marxian dialectic," may well have wished to endorse the State Department's tough policy on the Soviets. Stimson, McCloy, and Marshall were all willing to see the State Department reopen negotiations with Moscow on the tangled matter of a Far Eastern settlement.[61]

Neither the army nor the navy wanted to push the Soviets too hard, however. For one thing, as the War Department explained in its May 21 reply to Grew, Soviet expansion in the Far East would soon be a *fait accompli*. Short of going to war, the United States could do little to stop it. Although Stimson hoped that possession of the bomb would later strengthen the American bargaining position and end the war before the Red Army swept southward, the military never figured out how nuclear diplomacy could slow the Soviet advance. Even should the bomb force a sudden end to the war before Russian entry, Stalin's armies could still invade China and Korea— and face no opposition in doing so. The success of the nuclear test in July did not change that condition. As Marshall argued to Stimson on July 23, "even if we went ahead in the war without the Russians, and compelled the Japanese to surrender, that would not prevent the Russians from marching into Manchuria anyhow and striking, thus permitting them to get virtually what they wanted in the surrender terms." It is therefore unlikely that the military saw much point in trying to force any early Japanese surrender in order to arrest Soviet expansion. The Yalta accords, the War Department told Grew, were acceptable insofar as they only ratified what Stalin would in any event accomplish.[62]

61. Herbert Feis, *Between War and Peace: The Potsdam Conference*, pp. 80–81. Alperovitz, *Atomic Diplomacy*, pp. 98–99; Rose, *Dubious Victory*, pp. 157–61; Millis, *Forrestal Diaries*, pp. 55–58; memorandum, War Department to Grew, 21 May 1945, in Joseph C. Grew, *Turbulent Era: A Diplomatic Record of Forty Years, 1904–1945*, 1: 1457–59.

62. Quotation from Stimson Diary, 23 July 1945. See also Grew, *Turbulent Era*, 2: 1457–59; Feis, *Between War and Peace*, pp. 80–81; Alperovitz, *Atomic Diplomacy*, pp. 98–99. The Joint Staff Planners did consider placing a token American force in China to offset Soviet influence; see Alperovitz, *Atomic Diplomacy*, p. 94.

Furthermore, the army advised, if the United States chose to challenge Soviet designs in the Far East or elsewhere, Stalin could delay Soviet entry into the war. He could thereby diminish his casualties and increase those of American forces. That prospect was worrisome indeed to military planners still impressed by Japanese fanaticism and afraid that only an invasion of the Japanese home islands would force surrender. In an invasion attempt, the timing of Soviet entry into the war would be a critical concern.[63]

The military still took its invasion plans seriously. In a long meeting on June 18, the service heads and the President considered the casualties which might be suffered in a bloody assault on Kyushu in November. Mindful of Okinawa, where casualties soared as Americans flushed out dug-in Japanese defenders, "the President expressed the view that it was practically creating another Okinawa closer to Japan, to which the Chiefs of Staff agreed." The Joint Chiefs, worried that Americans might not tolerate more Okinawas, warned that "any irresolution in the leaders may result in costly weakening and indecision in the subordinates." Such fears indicated how firm the expectation of an invasion remained. Even King, Leahy, Forrestal, and General Eaker from the AAF approved the invasion plans, whatever their hopes that a naval and aerial siege might alone defeat Japan. The navy secretary "pointed out that even if we wished to besiege Japan for a year or a year and a half, the capture of Kyushu would still be essential." While Marshall and his colleagues believed that Japan might eventually succumb even without invasion, they may well have regarded invasion as the quick alternative to a long and protracted siege which would tax the patience of the American people and perhaps afford the Soviet Union more time to assemble a large force and expand southward.[64]

The best hope for an early end to the war, Marshall explained on June 18, was that the multiple threats of continued blockade and bombardment (perhaps with nuclear weapons), invasion, and a Russian declaration of war might shock the Japanese into surrender "short of complete military defeat in the field." In the weeks ahead

63. Grew, *Turbulent Era*, 2: 1457–59. For a different view, see Alperovitz, *Atomic Diplomacy*, pp. 105–06, 110–13.
64. Quotations from *FR: Potsdam*, 1, pp. 903–10. See also Stimson to the President, 2 July 1945, in *FR: 1945*, 1, pp. 889–902; *FR: Potsdam*, 1, pp. 888, 902; Leahy, *I Was There*, pp. 384–85; Ernest J. King and Walter Muir Whitehill, *Fleet Admiral King: A Naval Record*, pp. 598, 605–06.

the military never settled the timing of the various measures it hoped to take against Japan. The goal, however, as Stimson wrote on June 19 after a further talk with Marshall, was "to coordinate all the threats possible to Japan." Far from regarding Russian entry into the war as an alternative to other methods of forcing surrender, the military hoped to assemble all possible means to convince Japanese leaders to submit.[65]

Therefore, as Marshall made clear at the June 18 meeting, Soviet participation in the war remained vital to American plans. Even if it failed to force an early Japanese surrender, it could minimize American casualties. If a Soviet attack from Siberia were launched "sufficiently ahead of our target date to commit the enemy to major combat," the American task would be easier. King, Leahy, and Forrestal fought off their doubts about the wisdom of soliciting Soviet cooperation. After listening to his service chiefs give their opinions, Truman pledged that at Potsdam he would seek "to get from Russia all the assistance in the war that is possible."[66]

The successful test of an atomic device at Alamogordo on July 16 emboldened the opposition to Soviet diplomacy of Truman and his advisors, now gathered at Potsdam, a few miles from Hitler's devastated capital. But the news from New Mexico did not, despite Stimson's efforts, alter official policy about Soviet entry into the war. Stimson found himself in a trap because use of the bomb—the most promising instrument for securing victory before Russian entry—might prove "such a wanton act" as to "make it impossible during the long post war period to reconcile the Japanese to us in that area rather than to the Russians." Despite these doubts, Stimson on July 23 discussed with Marshall the chance that the bomb might end the war promptly. Marshall "could not answer directly or explicitly," but Stimson "inferred," as he told the President on July 24, that the chief of staff believed that the new bomb made the Soviet Union's help unnecessary. Stimson exaggerated the importance of Marshall's statements. Not for several months had the general said that Soviet entry was necessary for victory. He had only argued that it would speed surrender and minimize American casualties. If the United

65. *FR: Potsdam*, 1, pp. 904–05; Stimson Diary, 19 June 1945. The point is missed by Alperovitz, who tends to claim that American policymakers looked on the various means of ending the war as mutually exclusive; see *Atomic Diplomacy*, especially pp. 110, 113–15.
66. *FR: Potsdam*, 1, pp. 904–06, 909, 910.

States paid the price, it could secure victory on its own, but Marshall recoiled at the costs. Stimson, in any event, changed nobody's mind on the question of Soviet entry. He raised the matter with the President on the morning of July 24, but later that day Truman, Churchill, and the Combined Chiefs of Staff reaffirmed their intent to "encourage Russian entry into the war against Japan" and assist "her war-making capacity."[67]

Meanwhile Stimson feebly pursued a policy of openness with the Soviets, even as he hoped to squeeze them out of participating in victory over Tokyo. Worried that use of the bomb without prior disclosure to Stalin "might have a serious effect on the relations of frankness between the three great Allies," Stimson advised Truman to inform the Soviet premier at Potsdam of the new weapon. He did not endorse a frank discussion of the bomb. Stimson's advice was more a sop to his conscience than a wholehearted effort to avoid the pitfalls of nuclear diplomacy.[68]

As two of its B-29s wiped out Hiroshima and Nagasaki, the military command still had no fixed outlook on American-Soviet relations. For months the State Department and some of the military staff had warned of Russian aggrandizement. Stimson, Leahy, and above all Forrestal deeply distrusted Soviet intentions. General Arnold later claimed that at Potsdam he "believed our next enemy would be Russia," a conviction certainly shared by some operational commanders, most notably George C. Patton. The general with the notorious tongue regarded the Russians contemptuously as a "scurvy race" of "Mongolian savages," every one of them "an all out son of a bitch, a barbarian, and a chronic drunk," who would conspire with Jews and others to communize Europe and America.[69] But Patton was an eccentric, more amusing to his colleagues than persuasive. In Washington, Admiral King was largely noncommittal on the whole Russian matter, and Stimson was optimistic about accommodation despite (or perhaps because of) his faith in nuclear diplomacy. Marshall, long wary of rash interpretations of Soviet objectives, apparently retained his cautious hopes for the perpetuation of the

---

67. Stimson Diary, 23 July 1945, 24 July 1945; *FR: Potsdam*, 2, pp. 339–44, 1463.

68. Stimson Diary, 3 July 1945; *FR: Potsdam*, 1, p. 942; Alperovitz, *Atomic Diplomacy*, pp. 154–56.

69. Henry H. Arnold, *Global Mission*, p. 586; Martin Blumenson, ed., *The Patton Papers, 1940–1945*, pp. 712, 731, 734, 735.

Grand Alliance. The military still lacked a consensus on what threat the Soviet ally posed.

Fat Boy, Thin Man, and the Russian declaration of war ended the Pacific struggle with a suddenness that surprised the high command. To the last moment they still considered invasion a possibility, did not foresee fully the impact of the atomic weapon, and did not appreciate the significance the Japanese had attached to the now-severed negotiations with the Soviet Union.[70] The services had, of course, made contingency plans for an early end to the war, but that was a customary step which did not imply expectation of a quick surrender. The bomb was so secret that the Joint Chiefs had not even discussed it in their meetings.[71]

Service leaders undoubtedly surmised that their use of the atomic bomb would alarm Soviet leaders and might carry at least the collateral benefit of stiffening American policy toward the USSR. Yet none had ascertained how to use the nation's newfound power to contest Soviet ambitions in Europe or the Far East. Indeed, they had not yet decided how threatening those ambitions were, or whether Japan or Germany might not still pose the greater danger. Increasingly wary of the USSR, the services had fixed no policy regarding the possibility of future war with the Russians, the place of the bomb in Soviet-American relations, or the effect of the bomb on postwar American defense needs. Now facing the postwar world, they needed a policy to deal with it.

70. Arnold later recalled that the Japanese surrender "came more or less as a surprise." He had figured that it would take at least four atomic bombs or increased B-29 raids to force capitulation; see Arnold, *Global Mission*, p. 598, and, for a contrasting recollection, Maxwell D. Taylor, *Swords and Plowshares* (New York, 1972), p. 110. On the importance of the Japanese-Russian negotiations, see Paul Kecskemeti, *Strategic Surrender: The Politics of Victory and Defeat*, pp. 176–210.

71. King, *Fleet Admiral King*, pp. 611, 621; Rose, *Dubious Victory*, pp. 337–38. The Combined Chiefs of Staff agreed on July 19 that for manpower and planning purposes November 15, 1946, was to be considered the date for an end to organized Japanese resistance, though the chiefs thought an earlier victory almost certain; see *FR: Potsdam*, 2, p. 115.

7   PREVENTING WORLD WAR III

The news from Japan should have evoked jubilation. Hiroshima lay in ruins. Its sudden destruction marked a transcendent technological achievement, one sure to speed victory and awe friend and foe alike. Instead of exalting, Admiral William Leahy, who only weeks earlier had doubted that the device would even work, confided worriedly to his diary his fear that the bomb would "in the future be developed by potential enemies and . . . used against us."[1]

Given such forebodings, victory over Japan prompted little elation among American military leaders. Though triumphant in war, they faced an unpredictable future without firm plans and policies, the need for which was now, suddenly, urgent. The instrument of American triumph, the atomic bomb, instilled anxiety rather than confidence about future security. Unprecedented occupational duties confronted the army and navy. And the approach of peace was widening the breach between the members of the Grand Alliance.

Perhaps most worrisome was the response of the American people to victory. For years the two military departments had been bracing themselves for popular demands to bring the boys home. The leadership hoped that its elaborate point system for demobilization, instituted only after extensive polling of servicemen, would minimize the confusion and inequities which enraged so many soldiers and civilians after the First World War. Delays in discharging troops would, Generals Marshall and Handy warned their staff, cause "a loss of the good will built up by the Army in its successful campaigns."[2]

Wanting congratulations, the army instead found condemnation. Even before Hiroshima some grumbling over the speed of demobilization was evident. By August 9, Stimson complained, it seemed "as if everybody in the country was getting impatient to get his or

1. Leahy Diary, 8 August 1945. For a similar expression by Patton see Blumenson, *Patton Papers*, p. 741.
2. Handy remarks, in General Council Minutes, 14 May 1945.

her particular soldier out of the Army." Calls rang out for the blanket release of all fathers lest, as a New Jersey congressman warned, "a generation of fatherless children" turn the nation into "a second rate power." Soldiers with low point ratings were, along with their families, disappointed to find that peace did not bring them speedy release. Facing manpower shortages, certain powerful interest groups, especially the rail and coal industries and unions, demanded exemption from the point system for their workers. Scientists and educators, fearful of another year of half-empty classrooms, waged a vigorous campaign to change the point system. The list of claimants grew daily.[3]

Just as distressing were charges that the army abused the point system. Demobilization regulations provided that commanders could withhold from release soldiers whose skills were deemed essential. Men who found that their critical task was peeling potatoes or chauffeuring generals thought that the military made a mockery of the point system.

To harsher critics, the lumbering pace of demobilization in August and September indicated a conspiracy within the military establishment to aggrandize itself. The army, some congressmen suggested, held on to its draftees in order to justify continuation of the swollen officer corps. Other politicians disputed the need for large occupation forces and the draft calls they would require. Critics alleged that a prolonged occupation of defeated and liberated countries would antagonize the United States' allies or serve to prop up the tottering colonial regimes of Europe's imperial powers. Besides, other argued, the atomic bomb could be counted on to provide the nation whatever military muscle it needed.

The army refused to change its demobilization procedures. On August 9, Stimson rushed to disabuse the public of any notion that the bomb would affect the army's manpower needs. The bomb's effect on the army's size had been "in our minds for many months," he assured the press, though in fact the War Department had given the matter no formal study. The army would not exempt men from the point system for fear that it compromise the "integrity of the discharge system." Capitulation to a few demands, the army sup-

3. Quotations from Stimson Diary, 9 August 1945; Ross, *Preparing for Ulysses*, p. 176. See also Sparrow, *History of Personnel Demobilization*, pp. 112–17, 125–35, 141–60, 317–19, and Ross, *Preparing for Ulysses*, pp. 159–62, 170–80.

posed, would encourage the same sort of interest-group pressures which threatened the UMT campaign.[4]

Although angered by public criticism, the Pentagon recognized privately that its demobilization machinery was badly fouled. The navy was illprepared for the job of mustering out its men. The sudden collapse of the Japanese caught the army with all its men in all the wrong places just when the public expected a quick return of its sons. Thousands of low-point soldiers were in the United States, in transit from Europe to the Pacific for the invasion of Japan, now called off. High-point men, who deserved immediate release, were in Europe because the army had exempted them from the invasion. As a matter of efficiency, Marshall later ruefully admitted, the War Department would almost have been better off had the war gone on longer.[5]

More than circumstance snarled demobilization. Repeatedly the army's commanders had to admonish their staffs to "see that our house is in order and that we keep it in order." Under Secretary Patterson discovered that "thousands of men" eligible for mustering out were kept in the army—victims of officers who attached the "essential" label to "cutting grass, washing windows, driving staff cars or doing other relatively unimportant jobs." Such abuses, he advised, threatened "to destroy the confidence of the soldiers, the public and Congress" in the demobilization system. Marshall, ever mindful of events after World War I, ordered his staff to demobilize the army "with the greatest rapidity consistent with national commitments for occupation forces." Congress, he cautioned on August 15, would insist on economy with the war's end. But Marshall, who acknowledged that the "natural tendencies" of his staff were to hold on to all the men and equipment they could, must have been pessimistic about the effectiveness of his orders.[6]

The armed forces aggravated the crisis of public confidence by failing to prepare soldiers and their families for the manpower

4. Stimson Diary, 9 August 1945; Stimson, Memorandum for the Press, 9 August 1945, and Memorandum of Conference with the President, August 8, 1945, at 10:45 a.m., both attached to 9 August 1945 Stimson Diary entry; Sparrow, *History of Personnel Demobilization*, p. 130.

5. Davis, *Postwar Defense Policy and the U.S. Navy*, p. 122; Robert W. Coakley and Richard W. Leighton, *Global Logistics and Strategy, 1943–1945*, pp. 610–15; Truman, *Memoirs*, 1:506–07; Ross, *Preparing for Ulysses*, pp. 164–66; personal communication from Forrest Pogue.

6. Handy remarks, in General Council Minutes, 6 August 1945; Sparrow *History of Personnel Demobilization*, pp. 131–32 (Patterson), 230–31 (Marshall). See also Sparrow, pp. 132–38.

demands of the occupation period. In misleading statements during the last year of the war, War Department and Veterans Administration officials indicated that occupation would be short and painless. The army, perhaps fearful of undermining combat morale, rejected proposals for a more frank explanation of the postvictory task. Not surprisingly, many Americans then were stunned when in August the army, now 8,000,000 strong, released plans to keep millions of men in uniform—over 2,500,000 men through July 1, 1946, a figure soon scaled·down to 1,950,000. For a time the cabinet doubted that Congress would support a temporary extension of the draft, a measure needed to man the occupation forces.[7]

The gravest aspect of the August clamor for speedy demobilization was that it seemed to portend a lasting popular hostility toward the military. Impatience to get the boys home was understandable, but the swift reversal in press and congressional attitudes toward basic policies like universal training was alarming. Only months earlier UMT had seemed within grasp. By August, the press and radio reported, congressional backers of UMT were "privately admitting" that they had "lost their fight."[8]

Journalists pointed to army "brasshattedness" to explain the demise of UMT. The army's refusal to speed up demobilization and pare occupation forces indicated to some critics an "unnecessary ramrod-type stubbornness" in the Pentagon. To hold on to their forces the militarists were even whipping up fear of another war, one paper charged. "By necessity in war the military had been in the saddle. They do not want to get off their high horse and walk." The administration's request for an extension of the draft fueled such speculation and undercut the UMT campaign, since critics now suspected that the army, contrary to earlier promises, wanted both selective service and UMT.[9]

Opponents of UMT also scoffed at the military utility of citizens' training. The atomic bomb would "blow up peacetime conscription"

7. Sparrow, *History of Personnel Demobilization*, pp. 108–11, 141, 238; Millis, *Forrestal Diaries*, p. 90; Stimson Diary, 11 August 1945.

8. Robert St. John, NBC radio network broadcast, 6 August 1945, transcription in War Department Bureau of Public Relations, *Universal Military Training, Including Post-War Military Establishment* . . ., Series 30–55 (hereafter cited as War Department, *UMT*): see also *New York Times*, 7 August 1945.

9. Quotations from *Danbury New Times*, 14 August 1945; *Shreveport Times*, 9 August 1945; *Raleigh News and Observer*, undated editorial [August 1945], all in War Department, *UMT*. See also Ward, "Movement for Universal Military Training," pp. 113–14.

and "mean the end of big armies and militarism as bred from big armies," a Colorado senator was quoted as saying. Some columnists urged caution in assessing the effects of the bomb, but many were certain that nuclear weapons rendered land armies obsolete and made strategic air power all important. More broadly, science itself appeared to have replaced the mass conscript army as "the first front" in warfare and the best hope for winning wars "cheaply and easily." "The Postwar army," reported one Washington paper, "will be a compact, extremely mobile force with nightmarishly destructive weapons stemming, like the atom bomb, straight from the laboratories of science." Well-publicized predictions, such as one made by General H. H. Arnold on August 2, hurt the UMT case.

> The next sneak attack may not come 2,000 miles from our shores. It may be centralized on Michigan Boulevard, Biscayne Boulevard, Sunset Boulevard or on Main Streets in your home town. We may not have a comfortable cushion of time to plan and build and train. It bodes fair to be sudden death out of a clear sky.

Air power and the atomic bomb did not alone undermine support for UMT. What they did do was deepen public faith in science as an alternative to the traditional sacrifices of war.[10]

Alarmed by popular reaction to the war's end and the advent of nuclear energy, the military grew increasingly pessimistic about the chances that Congress would approve its UMT plans.[11] The services' belief that the coming of peace and the atomic bomb jeopardized UMT was arguable in light of the strong opposition to UMT which already existed before the war's end. But the army and navy were convinced that a peacetime backlash against them had set in.

The services themselves were also still at odds on postwar policy. Throughout the war, long-range planning had been fragmented

10. Quotations from NBC radio network broadcast, 7 August 1945, in War Department, *UMT*; "Scientific Research Is Our First Defense," *Saturday Evening Post*, 25 August 1945, p. 108; *Washington Times-Herald*, 19 August 1945, and *Pittsburgh Sun Telegram*, 2 August 1945 (Arnold), both in War Department, *UMT*. For cautionary comment about the effect of the bomb, see "Are Armies Obsolete?" *New York Herald Tribune*, 11 August 1945; for the opposite view, see Sidney Shallet, "Pattern of Future War is Changed," *New York Times*, 12 August 1945, and Josephine Ripley, "Truman and Atomic Bomb Upset Peacetime Draft," *Christian Science Monitor*, 7 August 1945; all in War Department, *UMT*.

11. Carpenter to Deputy Director, SPD, 15 August 1945, file 353 (July–Sept 1945), SPD; Persons to Marshall, 1 August 1945, file 353 (157), Chief of Staff; H.A.G. [Colonel Harrison A. Gerhardt] to McCloy, 22 August 1945, file 353 UMT (June 1 '45–), ASW; Arnold, *Global Mission*, pp. 598–99.

among them. Unprepared for the war's abrupt end, the War Department had no firm postwar plan at all. Marshall had tentatively approved an active army of 330,000 men (including 16 air groups), backed by a reserve of 4,500,000 personnel. But the AAF, seeking a 75-group air force of 485,000 regulars, stubbornly fought the economy-minded scheme and by June forced a virtual suspension of the army's efforts at long-range planning. In contrast, the navy had settled on a definite figure—50,000 officers and 500,000 enlisted men, plus trainees, reserves, and 110,000 marines.

Aggravating the disagreement over force levels was a bitter argument over proposals to unify the armed services. Under a merger plan offered by a Joint Chiefs of Staff committee in April 1945, the air force would achieve status equal with that of the army and navy, and a single defense secretary and chief of staff would preside over a unified general staff and defense department. Certain that in such a department the army and air force would gang up to strip the navy of its air power and marines, Forrestal and the admirals fought the JCS staff recommendation. As part of a public relations battle with the AAF, they sought to strengthen the public image of the navy as a modern strategic force. Forrestal also enlisted Ferdinand Eberstadt, a friend and fellow New York investment banker, to develop a plan for the coordination of defense policymaking which would stop short of full unification. At the same time, Forrestal and Admiral King jumped the gun in the race for postwar appropriations by submitting their plan for a 660,000-man navy to a special joint session of the Senate and House Naval Affairs Committees. The reception was gratifying. The congressmen's only criticism of the June 19 presentation was that the navy asked for too little. Finally—unknown to the War Department or the Joint Chiefs—Forrestal sought White House approval for the navy's peacetime plans. After preliminary liaison with James Byrnes and Budget Director Harold Smith, the naval command secured a private audience with the President and pleaded for a quick decision on its proposals.[12]

12. Davis, *Postwar Defense Policy and the U.S. Navy*, pp. 138–53, 157–67; Demetrios Caraley, *The Politics of Military Unification*, pp. 38–44; Lawrence A. Legere, Jr., "Unification of the Armed Forces" (Ph. D. dissertation, Harvard University, 1950), pp. 288–89; "Presentation, *Post War Navy*, 7 June 1945," folder "Post-War Navy (2)," Box 23, Forrestal Papers; "Revised Report of the Special Committee on the Permanent Military Establishment of the Army of the United States," 29 November 1945, p. 1, file 320 (78) 1945, OPD; Smith, Daily Record, 16 July 1945, Smith Papers; Forrestal to Vinson, 26 May 1945; Vinson to Forrestal, 29 May 1945, and King to Forrestal, 5 June 1945, all in General Correspondence, SecNav.

The rivalry among the services continued through the last days of the war. On May 12 the Joint Chiefs did agree to formulate a "United States Military Policy and Strategic Plan," the first such joint examination of basic postwar strategic needs. This study was incomplete at war's end, however, and though the Joint Chiefs recognized the wisdom of joint planning, only outside pressures finally forced them into it.[13]

By August, the services sensed the need to close ranks if they were to succeed with Congress and the President. "Certainly if the Joint Chiefs of Staff haven't a clear-cut conception of what our post-war requirements are we can't expect any higher echelons to have one," Arnold pointed out on August 22.[14] The Joint Chiefs suspected that the longer they delayed in drawing up their plans, the more intense would be the postwar backlash of popular and congressional opinion against their requests. Failure of the services to curb extravagant programs and present a unified front would also invite the charge that service politics, rather than real strategic needs, dictated their plans. Renewed political agitation for an investigation of the Pearl Harbor disaster probably reminded the military of the danger of divisiveness within its ranks. Finally, worsening Soviet-American relations and the advent of nuclear weaponry compelled attention at the joint level.

With the dangers of disunity in mind, Marshall recommended on August 19 that the JCS planners "initiate immediately ... a study of the post-war requirements for military forces," including the "size, composition and deployment of the forces required." Before the Joint Chiefs could act on Marshall's request, the White House intervened to order a broader study of postwar military needs. Budget Director Smith, angered by the navy's unilateral bid for postwar forces, wanted joint planning by the services and an active role for the White House in postwar policy. On August 20 Smith advised Truman to ask the JCS for a review of "the over-all peacetime requirements of the Armed Services ... in the light of our international commitments for the post-war world, the development of

13. King, memorandum for JCS, 5 May 1945, file CCS 660.2 Alaska (3-23-45) Sec. 2, JCS; extract from JCS 1295; extract from JCS minutes, 12 May 1945; extract from JPS minutes of 25 July 1945 and 3 August 1945; JPS 633/4, JWPC 385/2/D, and JWPC 394/d, all in CCS 381 (5-13-45) Sec. 1, JCS.

14. Arnold to Norstad, 22 August 1945, Jacket 144, Official File (1932–46), Box 44, Arnold Papers. See also Moore to McFarland, 7 August 1945, file CCS 334 (Joint Postwar Survey Committee), JCS.

new weapons, and the relative position of the services as a result of these factors." Smith's advice constituted precisely the broad view of planning which the services seemed so slow to take.[15]

On August 21 Truman ordered the Joint Chiefs to prepare for him the report sought by Smith. Since the President's order and Marshall's recommendation had similar objectives, the Joint Chiefs combined the two into a single study of the size and composition of the postwar defense establishment. Through Truman's request the War Department also learned for the first time of the navy's submission two months earlier of its requests to the White House. Meanwhile, on August 20 Truman met personally with Marshall, reviewed the problems of demobilization and postwar planning, and discussed UMT. At an August 31 cabinet meeting the President finally promised to seek some form of universal training.[16]

By the end of August the Joint Chiefs had initiated a broad examination of the services' postwar needs. In addition, the JCS staff was analyzing the impact of the atomic bomb on strategy, continuing its work on unification and overseas bases, and reexamining American policy toward the Soviet Union. The events of August ended the fragmentation of planning and forced the services at last to assign top priority to postwar policy.

The Strategic Consensus

Military leaders reached speedy agreement in August and September on a strategy for postwar America. Unanimity was possible because the war had already shaped a common strategic outlook. Their task was not to formulate a new strategy but to systematize and codify one which had already emerged.

The effort, begun in May, accelerated after the atomic strikes against Japan. In the last days of summer, staff planners sent to the

15. Marshall to JCS, 19 August 1945, JCS 1478, and Smith to the President, 20 August 1945, found as enclosure to JCS 1482, both in file ABC 040 (2 November 1943), Sec. 5-a, OPD.
16. Legere, "Unification of the Armed Forces," pp. 289–90; Truman to Leahy, 21 August 1945, JCS 1482; King to JCS, 25 August 1945, JCS 1478/1; note by the JCS Secretaries, 30 August 1945; JPS 745/D and JWPC 405/D, all in file ABC 040 (2 November 1943) Sec. 5-a, OPD; Marshall to President, 23 August 1945, with enclosed draft letters and statement, as enclosure to memorandum, Hull to Under Secretary of War, 31 August 1945; Truman, "Memorandum on Postwar Military Training," as enclosure to memorandum, Matthew J. Connelly to Stimson, 4 September 1945, both in file ABC 353 Universal (1 May 45) Sec. 1-a, OPD.

Joint Chiefs the completed drafts of their studies on postwar strategy. The Joint Chiefs approved JCS 1496/2, "Basis for the Formulation of a Military Policy," on September 18 and dispatched it to the service secretaries. On October 9 the chiefs approved JCS 1518, "Strategic Concept and Plan for the Employment of United States Armed Forces." The service secretaries, who endorsed both papers, tried with some success in the last months of 1945 to secure State Department approbation of the JCS policies, a move which delayed presentation of the papers to the President. Fear of public condemnation of some of the JCS statements, especially those on the relationship of the United States to the UN, killed plans to use the papers "for official publicity on policy matters." Still, the approval of JCS 1496 and 1518 gave the armed forces for the first time a common policy on postwar strategy.[17]

The Joint Chiefs' view of their peacetime responsibilities was in some ways conventional. Their job was to uphold national policies established by civilian authority: the territorial integrity of the United States and its possessions, the integrity and independence of the Philippines, the imposition of peace terms on the defeated states, and "full support of the United Nations Organization." More broadly, they were also to assist in "advancing the political, economic and social well-being of the United States," and to keep themselves "ready when necessary to take military action abroad to maintain the security and integrity of the United States." But the Joint Chiefs also defined a much more ambitious goal, one not hitherto assumed: "the maintenance of world peace, under conditions which insure the security, well-being and advancement of our country."[18]

The obstacles to achieving that goal seemed large and novel. The United States, naked before an enemy attack, lay stripped of its natural defenses by revolutionary changes in weapons.

---

17. For the development of JCS 1496 and 1518, see file CCS 381 (5-13-45) Sec. 1–2, JCS; Lincoln to Stilwell, 20 December 1945, file ABC 092 (18 July 1945) Sec. 1-a, OPD; Secretary's Staff Committee (Department of State), "Action on Joint Chiefs of Staff Statement of United States Military Policy," 16 November, 1945, file ABC 092 (18 July 1945) Sec. 1-a, OPD; Marshall to McCloy, 2 October 1945, file 336 (192/4) Top Secret, OPD; extract from JCS "Status of Papers," n.d., file ABC 040 (2 November 1943) Sec. 5-a, OPD; Colonel Florence Newsome to Marshall, 15 October 1945, and Patterson to Forrestal, 17 October 1945, both in file 370.01 (8) Top Secret, Chief of Staff.

18. JCS 1496/3, 20 September 1945, file CCS 381 (5-13-45) Sec. 2, JCS.

> For probably the last time in the history of warfare those ocean distances [which aided American defense in World War II] were a vital factor in our defense. We may elect again to depend on others and the whim and error of potential enemies, but if we do we will be carrying the treasure and freedom of this great Nation in a paper bag.

Aggravating the disappearance of geographical defenses was the loss of strong allies to absorb the first blows of a future aggressor. The British navy could no longer shield America. The future enemy, realizing the decisive role played by the United States in the first two world wars, "will not ... give us time to mobilize our forces and productive capacity; the United States will be attacked first." The JCS did not fully agree on the extent to which geographical isolation had declined—King minimized the danger somewhat. But it seemed clear that "another major war, at worst, would destroy the United States; at best would be won only at a terrible cost in blood and treasure."[19]

With wars too costly to fight, the imperative need was to prevent them. The JCS wanted the United States to have "sufficient military power to make it unwise for any major aggressor nation to initiate a major war against the opposition of the United States." Stimson made the same point more simply. Some people, he complained to the cabinet, discussed UMT "from the point of view of what it will do or not do in regard to the defense of the country in wartime. I prefer," he said, "to look at it from another angle. I do not want war to come. I want to prevent it from ever coming." The United States would prevent future Pearl Harbors, Forrestal told inquiring congressmen, if it were strong enough to "make it obvious that nobody can hope to win a war against us." Overwhelming strength, it was hoped, could pacify the globe.[20]

Should deterrence fail, the more drastic action of preventive war appeared justified. "When it becomes evident that forces of aggression are being arrayed against us by a potential enemy," argued the Joint Chiefs, "we cannot afford, through any misguided and perilous idea of avoiding an aggressive attitude, to permit the first blow to be struck

19. Marshall, *Biennial Report, 1943–1945*, in *War Reports*, p. 290; JPS 633/4, 18 July 1945; King to JCS, 7 September 1945, JCS 1496/1, all in file CCS 381 (5-13-45) Sec. 1, JCS.
20. JCS 1496/3, 20 September 1945, file CCS 381 (5-13-45) Sec. 2, JCS; Statement to the Cabinet on UMT, 7 September 1945, Stimson Diary, 7 September 1945; U.S. Congress, House Committee on Naval Affairs, *Hearings, Sundry Legislation Affecting the Naval Establishment 1945*, 79/1, 1945, Item 110, *Composition of the Postwar Navy*, Hearings pursuant to House Concurrent Resolution 80, p. 1174.

against us." In such a situation, the United States should press for a diplomatic settlement "while making all preparations to strike the first blow if necessary." "We are not going to deliver the first blow," Eisenhower reassured Congress late in the fall; but secret plans suggested otherwise, and even in public testimony some officers hinted strongly at the wisdom of preemptive attacks. The legitimacy of preemptive strikes, only implied in earlier plans, now received the Joint Chiefs' explicit endorsement.[21]

The advocacy of deterrence and preventive war overturned traditional American defense policy. National leaders had always hoped that America's skeletal navy, coastal fortifications, and latent strength would discourage an attack on the homeland. But the nation's feeling of security before World War II arose primarily from its sense of geographical remoteness from the cockpits of conflict, not from confidence in its modest professional military forces. The nation usually built a large war machine only after hostilities began, and then in order to punish aggression or pursue other national goals rather than to deter an attack. Theodore Roosevelt and Woodrow Wilson did hope that their naval policies would deter war, but even those policies were hemispheric in orientation. Only the aerial rearmament and dispatch of B-17s to the Philippines in 1941 foretold the full sweep of postwar policy, whose intent was to deter not merely attack against the United States but the outbreak of any major conflict. Global deterrence was a policy of the 1940s.[22]

Staff planners were aware of how sharply their recommendations departed from earlier practice. The goal they pursued was "one of active—as contrasted to our traditional policy of passive—defense," they wrote in a July 18 draft of JCS 1496. Successive staff discussion sharpened the emphasis on deterrent and preventive action. Navy planners moved to insert into JCS 1496 an explicit reference to striking "the first blow," and insisted that "this point should be emphasized to make it clear that this is a new concept of policy, different than the American attitude toward war in the past."[23]

Staff planners recognized the risks of deterrence or preemptive

21. JCS 1496/3, 20 September 1945, file CCS 381 (5-13-45) Sec. 2, JCS. For Eisenhower's testimony, see U.S. Congress, House Committee on Military Affairs, *Hearings, Universal Military Training*, 79/1, 1945, p. 63. For testimony hinting at use of preemptive attacks, see the same *Hearings*, p. 614, testimony of General Ray Porter.

22. On this point, see also Weigley, *American Way of War*, pp. 365–67.

23. Extract from minutes of the Joint Staff Planners' 216th meeting, 29 August 1945, file CCS 381 (5-13-45) Sec. 1, JCS.

attack: the danger "that if we were to make sudden moves to build up and reinforce outer bases during a time of strained relations we would precipitate the very thing we would want to avoid." In a September 12 meeting, one key officer, General George A. Lincoln, expressed doubt that a first strike would be decisive enough to prevent large-scale retaliation by an enemy. Lincoln acknowledged that "it might be desirable to strike the first blow," but contended that "it is not politically feasible under our system to do so or to state that we will do so." But while the staff acknowledged Lincoln's objections, it did not deem them persuasive enough to retract its recommendations. The nation, one officer argued, "should be prepared to implement a militarily desirable course."[24]

The services' recommendations on deterrence and preventive war constituted a brief for the United States to become the world's policeman and peacemaker. The nature of modern weaponry and the facts of international life gave the United States no other choice, defense experts believed. As Marshall explained:

> It no longer appears practical to continue what we once conceived as hemispheric defense as a satisfactory basis for our security. We are now concerned with the peace of the entire world. And the peace can only be maintained by the strong.

Rejecting geographical restrictions on American power, the defense chiefs, as Forrestal declared, were determined to use American "power wherever aggression arises in the world." Even as modern weaponry made America more vulnerable to attack, it enabled the United States to project her power further and further outward. As a result, "we will possess the means for retaliatory or punitive attack against other powers who may threaten the United States or the international peace structure in general." The Joint Chiefs were quick to assert that American power would not be used as "an international threat" or instrument of "world domination," but they did not always appreciate that other nations might so regard it.[25]

Defense officials doubted that the United Nations could assist the

24. Extract from minutes of the Joint Staff Planners' 219th meeting, 12 September 1945, file CCS 381 (5-13-45) Sec. 1, JCS.

25. Marshall, *Biennial Report, 1943–1945,* in *War Reports,* p. 291; House Naval Affairs Committee, *Hearings, Composition of the Postwar Navy,* p. 1175 (Forrestal); JCS 1496/3, 20 September 1945, file CCS 381 (5-13-45) Sec. 2, JCS. On plans for global peacekeeping, see also Smith, *Air Force Plans,* pp. 46, 48–49, 104–05.

United States in policing aggression. Provisions for the veto in the Security Council and the developing tensions with the Soviet Union confirmed the long-held suspicion among military and other planners that the UN would never take military action against a major world power. The UN might evolve into a useful instrument of international peace, the military acknowledged, by performing minor police functions, enforcing nonmilitary sanctions, and marshalling international support for American policies. Furthermore, the military recognized that it must not antagonize domestic opinion or undermine international faith in the UN by permitting "any defeatist or cynical note to creep into ... papers or public discussions about it." Such pessimism about the UN would be self-fulfilling, Assistant Secretary of War McCloy warned, and Marshall and his advisors on the subject, General Lincoln and Colonel Dean Rusk, agreed. However, the armed services believed that the UN would not mobilize substantial police forces, and they no longer used the possibility of a UN police force to justify their force levels for the postwar.[26]

Dismissing the possibility of collective efforts, the military planned for unilateral enforcement of world peace. But the task would be difficult, the Joint Chiefs knew, because "the maintenance of overwhelmingly strong forces in time of peace is politically and economically unacceptable to the people of the United States." To minimize the burden of national defense, they proposed reliance on small but technologically sophisticated forces capable of rapid movement "to thwart attack by a potential aggressor" or hold off an attack already initiated. Probably to preserve interservice harmony, final plans for JCS 1496 and JCS 1518 downplayed the importance of air power, but the military wanted, as an early draft emphasized, the capacity for "rapid concentration and application of air power, both land- and carrier-based, in a decisive area." As in previous plans, land

26. Quotation from McCloy to Marshall, 23 September 1945, file 336 (192/4) Top Secret, OPD. See also JCS 1496/3, 20 September 1945, pp. 2–3, file CCS 381 (5-13-45) Sec. 2, JCS; Proceedings, meeting of the Joint Strategic Survey Committee, Joint War Plans Committee, Joint Staff Planners, and Joint Post War Committee, 3 August 1945, file ABC 381 United Nations (23 January 1942) Sec. 3-d, OPD; unsigned memorandum [probably OPD staff] to Lincoln, 3 August 1945, file ABC 092 (18 July 1945) Sec. 1-a, OPD; Report by the Joint Staff Planners, "U.S. Quota of Armed Forces for the United Nations," 13 September 1945, and Lincoln to Assistant Secretary, War Department General Staff, 30 September 1945, both in file ABC 040 (2 November 1943) Sec. 5-a, OPD; Marshall to McCloy, 2 October 1945, file 336 (192/4) Top Secret, OPD. War Department spokesmen did hint that UMT trainees might serve in an international force; see House Military Affairs Committee, *Hearings, UMT*, p. 47.

forces would garrison and hold bases. But they would not perform the primary strategic mission of destroying the enemy's capacity to wage war—unless or until air power proved incapable of forcing the conflict to a decision.[27]

The use of air power for global peacekeeping necessitated an extensive system of bases. In the fall of 1945 the Joint Chiefs continued refining the plans for postwar air bases first drawn up in 1943, although interdepartmental misunderstandings prevented the completion of base plans in 1945. As in 1943, the chiefs set their sights mainly on the Pacific and Atlantic ocean basins and apparently did not contemplate permanent installations on the European or Asiatic mainland. They were probably still confident that future long-range aircraft would make intervention possible from the peripheries of those continents. However in 1945 they did expand the proposed system of bases, most notably by adding outposts in New Zealand and the Ryukyus. Furthermore, their interests in the arctic air approaches to North America signified a new awareness of the Soviet Union, its capacity to develop strategic air power, and the probable paths of attack in the air age.[28]

If the worst happened and air power failed to deter, preempt, or throttle an attack, then preparation for a protracted major war would be necessary. Therefore the defense chiefs did not abandon the concept of mobilization. But the time factor required a new scheme of mobilization. The nation would not have time to mobilize its latent industrial and man power. It would need universal training for its young men so that they could be readied for action in weeks rather than years. Critical materials would have to be stockpiled. A close military relationship with industry would speed conversion to war production. Dispersion or concealment of some industries might be necessary, while other key industries, especially aircraft plants, might have to maintain war production even in peacetime. Weapons research would have to be entirely a peacetime operation, so long was the lead time

27. JCS 1496/3, 20 September 1945, file CCS 381 (5-13-45) Sec. 2, JCS; JPS 633/4, 18 July 1945, file CCS 381 (5-13-45) Sec. 1, JCS. See also Marshall, *Biennial Report, 1943–1945,* in *War Reports,* pp. 151–52, 294–95.

28. Extract from minutes of the Joint Staff Planners' 215th meeting, 22 August 1945, and Lovett to JCS, 24 August 1945, JCS 570/28, both in file CCS 360 (12-9-42) Sec. 7, JCS; undated tables of postwar air bases [October 1945], file CCS 360 (12-9-42) Sec. 9, JCS; JCS 1518, 19 September 1945, p. 7, file CCS 381 (5-13-45) Sec. 2, JCS; House Naval Affairs Committee, *Hearings, Composition of the Postwar Navy,* pp. 1168, 1238.

for scientific discoveries. Finally, with every minute's warning critical to a nation's chances of mobilizing against attack, a sophisticated intelligence system and the close coordination of all government departments would be essential. Modern war demanded not merely military preparedness but national readiness as well.[29]

In the event of a major war, certain objectives were clear. The United States should follow "what has been our one and only basic policy in the last thirty years. This is that we prefer to fight our wars, if they be necessary, in some one else's territory." Through its far-flung system of bases and the mobility of its forces, the United States would shield itself, to the limited extent possible, from direct attack. As General Lincoln explained, "we will have to intervene militarily in Europe or Asia because we certainly don't envisage getting set back on our heels where the military operation[s] are going to start in the United States."[30]

The ultimate objective in a major conflict was not so clear. Drafts of JCS 1518 indicated doubt about the desirability of attempting full conquest or destruction of a major enemy like the Soviet Union. But General Lincoln argued that the objective in a war with the USSR "should not be to drive her back within her frontiers but to destroy her war making capabilities; otherwise a long war or a stalemate would result." Marshall's view was even stronger. "The nature of war," he pointed out in his biennial report, "is such that once it now begins it can end only as this one is ending, in the destruction of the vanquished." If the United States adhered to that viewpoint, it would pursue total victory in a future conflict, as it did in World War II.[31]

The Search for Credible Deterrence

The advent of nuclear weapons cast a shadow over all strategic plans of this period. The atomic bomb appeared certain to revolutionize

29. JCS 1496/3, 20 September 1945, file CCS 381 (5-13-45) Sec. 2, JCS; JPS 633/4, 18 July 1945, file CCS 381 (5-13-45) Sec. 1, JCS; C.H.B. [General Charles H. Bonesteel] to Lincoln, 28 August 1945, file ABC 092 (18 July 1945) Sec. 1-a, OPD; Marshall, *Biennial Report, 1943–1945*, in *War Reports*, pp. 294–99; Smith, *Air Force Plans*, pp. 105–06.

30. C.H.B. [Bonesteel] to Lincoln, 28 August 1945, file ABC 092 (18 July 1945) Sec. 1-a, OPD; Proceedings, meeting of JSSC, JWPC, JPS, JPWC, 3 August 1945, file ABC 381 United Nations (23 January 1942), Sec. 3-d, OPD.

31. See JPS 744/1, file CCS 381 (5-13-45) Sec. 1, JCS; JCS 1518 (before amendments of October 10), file CCS 381 (5-13-45) Sec. 2, JCS; minutes of the Joint Staff Planners' 219th meeting (Lincoln), 12 September 1945, file CCS 381 (5-13-45) Sec. 1, JCS; Marshall, *Biennial Report, 1943–1945*, in *War Reports*, p. 299.

warfare and enlarge beyond calculation the already swollen military power of the United States. Yet possession of this ultimate weapon did not ease the anxiety of military commanders about the nation's future security nor greatly alter their strategic outlook. The most monumental development in weaponry proved most ambiguous in its effect on policy.

Nowhere was this more evident than in the field of military research. Despite fears among both soldiers and scientists, neither the use of atomic weapons nor the demise of the Research Board for National Security ruptured the alliance between science and the military. Denied the Research Board, the services assumed direct responsibility for the funding of research. The navy, acting first, established the Office of Naval Research, an agency which provided the bulk of federal support for basic research in the late 1940s and thereby earned the gratitude of scientists. Soon the other services expanded their funding of research, while also enlarging their program to capture and utilize German scientists.[32] The military, through its own agencies and through the Atomic Energy Commission, became the primary patron of scientific research in the postwar era.

Scientists and the armed services continued their collaboration in part because the military retained the spirit of the defunct Research Board by farming out its research to private laboratories and by employing advisory committees of scientists to award contracts. At the same time, scientists learned to accept a minimum of government control over their activities.[33]

The alliance also persisted because many leaders of science remained committed to the preparedness ideology, whatever the doubts raised among them by the use of nuclear weapons on Japan. Intimately familiar with radar, the use of prototype computers in gunnery, and other recent innovations in weaponry, men like James Conant and Vannevar Bush did not regard the atomic bomb as quite the novel development in warfare that many Americans believed it was. Nor did they desire any abrupt change in national security policy. Undoubtedly the specter of nuclear war strengthened their determination to "end war as an accepted instrument of nations," as Bush said. But

32. "The History of United States Naval Research," vol. 10, pp. 1602–05; Lasby, *Project Paperclip*.
33. "The History of United States Naval Research," vol. 10, pp. 1602–50. For good introductions to the postwar relationship between science and the military, see Price, *Government and Science*, chaps. 2–6; Greenberg, *Politics of Pure Science*, chap. 7; Robert Gilpin and Christopher Wright, eds., *Scientists and National Policy-Making*.

in order to "prevent future wars" Bush believed the nation had to rely on military strength.

> In my opinion, as an immediate step we want to be sure that this country is very strong in every way, because only if we are thoroughly strong ourselves can we approach the problem of international collaboration with any hope of achieving success.

Bush saw no conflict between military strength and the goals of peace and international control of atomic energy. American power was not an obstacle but the key to international agreement—"the surest guarantee of peace in the world." A strong United States would not have to terrorize or bully the world. The mere existence of American power, not its use, would secure peace.[34]

Science was now in the forefront of the fight against irresolution and appeasement, deserving support, so Patterson told Congress in October, because "weakness on the part of those who love peace invites war." The bomb had not altered the course of science policy set long before the end of the war. Research remained, in the army view, "the keystone of the whole security structure."[35]

Initially the effect of the bomb on strategic thinking appeared greater. Public reaction to Hiroshima alarmed the army and navy, each stung by allegations that the new weapon made conventional forces obsolete. In contrast, the Army Air Forces, calculating an obvious opportunity, launched a hard-sell campaign to prove that the bomb made strategic air power "all-important" in future warfare. Arnold was so eager to prove the bomb's effect on conventional installations that he proposed another test of the weapon. "I suggested that we evacuate a Japanese harbor after the war, put ships at dock and at anchor, and then try it," he later recalled.[36]

The army and navy swiftly contested the aviators' claims. The bomb and other recent technical developments, Marshall claimed, might shrink the size of combat forces, but they necessitated an

34. Bush, *New York Herald Tribune* Forum Speech, 31 October 1945, copy in file 3048, Bush Papers; Senate Military Affairs Committee, *Hearings on Science Legislation, 1945*, pp. 145, 221.

35. Senate Military Affairs Committee, *Hearings on Science Legislation, 1945*, p. 228; Committee on the Permanent Military Establishment of the Army of the United States, "Outline of Report" (draft 7), 31 August 1945, p. 2, file 71 "Permanent Postwar Army," General Correspondence 1943–47 (Top Secret), G-1.

36. Quotations from Arnold, *Third Report*, in *War Reports*, p. 462; Arnold, *Global Mission*, p. 590. See also Smith, *Air Force Plans*, pp. 16–17; Davis, *Postwar Defense Policy and the U.S. Navy*, pp. 190–92.

expansion of supporting personnel. Therefore no cut in the overall size of the army was foreseeable.[37] The navy fought back more aggressively. Secretary Forrestal argued in September that since delivery of atomic weapons had to occur through air space over the seas, both defense against the bomb and offensive use of it would require naval superiority. He questioned the effectiveness of atomic weapons against surface fleets dispersed and prepared for offensive action. Most important, the navy set about studying how it might use atomic energy for ship propulsion or for its own nuclear arsenal. If the navy delivered the new weapon, Forrestal told Congress, its carrier task forces could "give this Nation and the world a swift and effective means of dealing with arrogance wherever it might raise its head."[38]

With varying degrees of conviction, each service could argue that the atomic bomb enhanced its importance. Given the resulting stalemate, the staff of the Joint Chiefs avoided any claim for the bomb which might appear to favor one service. The bomb, the staff noted, was primarily a strategic weapon for use against industrial and civilian targets. It was relatively ineffective against ground and naval forces, which could be widely dispersed, although military experts theorized that nuclear weapons might some day be reduced in size for use as tactical weapons. "The advent of the weapons," the Joint Strategic Survey Committee concluded in October, "does not at this time justify elimination of the conventional armaments or major modification of the services that employ them." Even Bush, though a persistent critic of sluggish military response to technological change, counseled the JCS staff that the "atomic bomb should be considered only as a supplement to conventional armament and established methods of warfare." Nuclear weaponry would not revolutionize the conduct of national defense, not immediately at any rate.[39]

37. Marshall, *Biennial Report, 1943–1945*, in *War Reports*, p. 293; Patterson testimony, House Military Affairs Committee, *Hearings, UMT*, pp. 4–6; "Notes on Universal Military Training," submitted by General Marshall to President Truman, 13 September 1945, folder on Universal Military Training, Secretary of War Patterson's Safe File, SecWar.

38. Forrestal before the House Naval Affairs Committee, as quoted in Davis, *Postwar Defense Policy and the U.S. Navy*, p. 195. See also Davis, pp. 192–95, 240–45; Richard G. Hewlett and Francis Duncan, *Nuclear Navy, 1946–1952*, pp. 24–27.

39. JCS 1477/1, "Over-All Effect of Atomic Bomb on Warfare and Military Organization," report by the Joint Strategic Survey Committee, 30 October 1945, p. 46, file ABC 471.6 Atom (17 August 1945) Sec. 2, OPD. See also minutes of the Joint Staff Planners' 215th meeting, 22 August 1945, file CCS 381 (5-13-45) Sec. 1, JCS.

But the armed forces could hardly be complacent. They knew that the new weapon would in the long run only weaken American security, despite the Anglo-American monopoly on the bomb. The reason was clear: the monopoly would be short-lived, perhaps five to fifteen years, and then other nations could attack the United States. Even if the United States retained "hegemony" in nuclear weapons, it might still suffer "the most terrible destruction" in a war, the Interim Committee's Scientific Panel advised Stimson. The United States would be peculiarly vulnerable to nuclear annihilation because of the bomb's effectiveness against concentrated industrial and urban targets and its "exposure to attack by bombs launched from the sea." In contrast, the panel reported, "Russia is inaccessible from the sea and its industry and population are widely dispersed over vast areas." The bomb, originally built to enhance national security, would soon subvert it.[40]

In that sense, the bomb was not in itself a revolutionary weapon, defense officials agreed. It only confirmed and accelerated the revolutionary trends in warfare already obvious to military experts. Like other new weapons, the bomb placed "a greater premium than ever before upon the value of surprise in the initiation of war." The United States faced the "probability that a future major war will be opened by an attempt on the part of the aggressor nation to achieve the effects of Pearl Harbor on a vast and relatively complete scale." Against a "surprise assault," especially one launched by rockets on the nation's major cities, no real defense or retaliation appeared possible. Only Bush dissented from this view. He argued that the nation able to protect a few bombs from a first strike "could wreak greater destruction on its enemy" and thus presumably deter attack.[41]

The bomb heightened the necessity of "striking first, if necessary, against the source of threatened attack." The nation would need to project its bases even farther out from the homeland in order to maximize the surprise of its attacks and minimize the surprise which an enemy could achieve. The bomb also indicated "the cardinal impor-

40. J. Robert Oppenheimer to Secretary of War, 17 August 1945, Harrison-Bundy File No. 77, Manhattan Engineer District Records; JCS 1477/1, p. 2, file ABC 471.4 Atom (17 August 1945) Sec. 2, OPD. Military estimates of the time necessary for the Soviet Union or other powers to develop an atomic bomb varied widely, but generally fell within the five to fifteen year range.

41. JCS 1477/1; minutes of the Joint Staff Planners' 215th meeting, 22 August 1945, p. 4, file CCS 381 (5-13-45) Sec. 1, JCS.

tance of dispersion of vital targets," especially naval forces and industrial concentrations. Pushing that point further, James Conant, a sometime advisor to the services, insisted on "a drastic change in our industrialized pattern" and a vigorous civil defense program, so that "survivors of a holocaust could carry on some sort of national life in spite of the devastation." General Leslie Groves worried that the bomb might "be assembled in the cellar of a city building" by persons bent on sabotage or international blackmail. Nuclear weapons would also force nations to speed up defense research, expand their technological base, and enlarge intelligence operations.[42]

Perhaps most significant, the atomic bomb enhanced the importance of deterrence. With nuclear warfare too terrible to contemplate and a first strike too politically risky to venture, prevention of war was the first priority. The atomic bomb tempted policymakers as the ultimate weapon of deterrence.

Yet its very horror seemed to diminish its usefulness, as Budget Director Smith learned in conversation with the President. Trying to allay the President's anxiety over the rapid demobilization of the nation's conventional forces, Smith reminded Truman, "you have an atomic bomb up your sleeves." "Yes," Truman replied, "but I am not sure it can ever be used."[43] Truman apparently feared domestic or international reaction to further employment of the weapon. Looking ahead to the day when other nations would develop the bomb, he may even have imagined his own nation's destruction should it start a nuclear war. Whatever the case, the administration found itself in the quandary which would for decades confound American military planners: how credible was the bomb as a deterrent if its destructiveness precluded its use?

A related question bothered Stimson as he addressed the cabinet on September 7. The retiring secretary argued that the gravest failing of the United States in foreign relations had been its inability to demonstrate its resolve to keep the world peaceful. The nation's image in peacetime was

> a picture painted by our movies and our newspapers and it is not a flattering one. The people of other nations during those times have regularly got the impression of this nation as a frivolous, selfish,

42. JCS 1477/1; Conant to Grenville Clark, "Some thoughts on international control of atomic energy," 8 October 1945, file 614, Bush Papers; minutes of the Joint Staff Planners' 215th meeting (Groves), 22 August 1945, p. 6, file CCS 381 (5-13-45) Sec. 1, JCS.

43. Smith, Memorandum on Conference with the President, 5 October 1945, Smith Papers.

pleasure loving country which did not take the stern business of living in a rough international world seriously.

Twice in his lifetime, Stimson said, the appearance of American irresponsibility had led to war.[44]

Could the bomb dispel the image of irresponsibility? Stimson probably thought it could not. Precisely because technological achievement came so easily for Americans, possession of the bomb could not convince other countries of the nation's peacekeeping resolve. Effective deterrence, Stimson implied, required a dramatic gesture of national sacrifice. The bomb was only a substitute for sacrifice. Stimson's solution to the problem was hardly novel. To maintain credibility, he argued, the nation needed UMT. As a commitment of manpower rather than just money and technology, UMT would "combat this dangerous misconception" that Americans are "too irresponsible to take the trouble to prepare or to defend themselves." Universal training would work a "tremendous effect" on other states, and strengthen the UN enormously. Marshall and others agreed. Following Stimson's reasoning and even his wording, the chief of staff advised Truman that UMT would "establish a national policy which will encourage the other world powers to believe the United States is not only desirous but is prepared to enforce its determination to outlaw aggression."[45]

The United States now faced a paradox: the credibility of military systems might soon stand in inverse ratio to their destructiveness. The bomb gave America enormous military power which it could not translate into political power. As a deterrent, it could at most supplement more conventional demonstrations of national will. In contrast, the political utility of UMT seemed to increase even as its military usefulness declined.

Because he appreciated the paradox, Stimson by September favored sharing the nuclear secret with Moscow. Atomic diplomacy, with which he had long flirted, now appeared to him pointless. Brandishing the atomic weapon while fearing to use it would provoke suspicion without instilling respect—a dangerous bluff in the view

44. Statement to Cabinet on UMT, 7 September 1945, Stimson Diary, 7 September 1945.
45. Ibid. (Stimson); Marshall, "Notes on Universal Military Training," 13 September 1945, UMT folder, Secretary of War Patterson's Safe File, SecWar. See also Marshall's draft of the President's proposed message on UMT to Congress, 13 September 1945, UMT folder, Secretary of War Patterson's Safe File, SecWar; Marshall, *Biennial Report, 1943–1945*, in *War Reports*, pp. 294–97.

of this disciple of Theodore Roosevelt. In his final hours as secretary of war, Stimson had not turned soft. He had not abandoned his fears of the Soviet Union nor his faith in military strength; he had balanced his plea for nuclear sanity with an impassioned call for UMT. But he sought to liquidate a policy of nuclear coercion whose risks were many and rewards were few. Backed for the moment by some scientists, his civilian assistants, and his successor, Robert Patterson, Stimson argued before the cabinet and the President that the United States must approach Moscow in an attitude of trust on the nuclear matter, lest relations between the two nations become "irretrievably embittered."[46]

Where Stimson tried to lead, few followed. Though cautious, his proposals found little favor in the armed services. Believing themselves "on a road where we can neither stop nor turn back," military leaders stumbled forward on their course. Although recognizing that a contest for atomic weapons could only erode American security and that negotiations for international control of atomic energy were desirable, they could envision no real alternative to an arms race. Forrestal regarded sharing nuclear information as equivalent to the appeasement tried with Hitler. The Joint Chiefs recommended secrecy on nuclear energy until the major powers settled all their fundamental differences. In October, a JCS committee proposed an accelerated effort at research and production of atomic weapons, the maintenance of maximum secrecy, and the "refusal to give these secrets to any other nation or the United Nations Organization." To hasten progress down the chosen path, the War Department led an effort to insure military control over future atomic research and development. Aided by the chieftains of science, Bush and Conant, the services would win a substantial victory in the final legislation for the Atomic Energy Commission, though the new agency would force them to forgo some of the ironclad authority over nuclear matters they had enjoyed in wartime.[47]

Certain that it could choose no other course, the military now made

46. Alperovitz, *Atomic Diplomacy*, pp. 276–79, reprints the documents containing Stimson's recommendations. See also Truman, *Memoirs*, 1:524–25, Hewlett and Anderson, *The New World*, pp. 417–20, 424–25; Gaddis, *The United States and the Origins of the Cold War*, p. 248; unpublished Forrestal diaries, pp. 493–98, Naval History Division.

47. Quotations from JCS 1477/1, pp. 3–4. See also Leahy to President, 23 October 1945, Leahy File 125, JCS; Robert G. Albion and Robert H. Connery, *Forrestal and the Navy*, pp. 181–82; Millis, *Forrestal Diaries*, pp. 94–96; Truman, *Memoirs*, 1:526–28; Hewlett and Anderson, *The New World*, p. 420; John Morton Blum, *V Was For Victory: Politics and American Culture During World War II*, pp. 320–22.

plans to use the bomb as its primary instrument of massive deterrence and retaliation. That policy was no secret. In his November 1945 published report to the secretary of war, Arnold asserted that the nation must make it "apparent to a potential aggressor that an attack on the United States would be immediately followed by an immensely devastating air-atomic attack on him." Going beyond Arnold, a secret JCS staff study weighed the advisability of both retaliatory and preventive atomic strikes against the Soviet Union. The Joint Intelligence Committee suggested twenty Soviet cities suitable for atomic bombing in case "the U.S.S.R. has either initiated aggression [in Europe or Asia] or has clearly indicated that aggression against the United States is imminent." The committee recommended an atomic attack not only in case of an imminent Soviet attack but in the contingency that enemy industrial and scientific progress suggested a capability for an "eventual attack against the United States or defense against our attack." The committee advised "that use of strategic air power should be given highest priority" in any effort to arrest Russian progress toward an attack capability. The committee added that atomic bombing was relatively ineffective against conventional military forces and transportation systems—an admission that the bomb really would be useful only for mass destruction of urban targets.[48]

The doctrines of massive deterrence and retaliation, as the new policies would later be called, had begun to receive the emphasis that would be given them throughout the cold war. Their adoption indicated the bankruptcy of strategic planning. The military committed itself to an arms race which it recognized could in the long run only weaken national security. It advocated a deterrent whose credibility it had cause to doubt. It could find no practical use for the new weapon—no way to utilize the bomb in a manner limited in destructiveness but decisive in warfare. It could only propose enlarging the destruction so lavishly practiced in the war just fought.

The New Enemy

The formulation of a contingency plan for an atomic attack against the Soviet Union indicated that military suspicions of the Red ally

48. Arnold, *Third Report*, in *War Reports*, p. 464; Joint Intelligence Committee Paper 329, "Strategic Vulnerability of the U.S.S.R. to a Limited Air Attack," November 1945, file ABC 336 Russia (22 August 1945), OPD.

had intensified. While the military was not ready to go public with its fears of the Soviets, by the fall G-2's secret reports designated "the U.S.S.R. and its satellite states or a coalition of [the] U.S.S.R. and other powers" as the only force with "the capacity to threaten us militarily." Just a few months earlier, considerable confusion had still marked the military outlook on possible postwar enemies.[49]

The end of the war had dispelled the confusion. Severing the fragile bonds of cooperation between the superpowers, it freed defense officials to articulate latent suspicions toward the Soviet Union or to nurture new ones. The prostration of the defeated Axis powers and the Allied determination to enforce a draconian peace on them diminished the likelihood of their resurgence. With Germany and Japan devastated, British strength sapped, and China torn by civil war, the Soviet Union took first place on the enemies list partly by default. Too, the services could not fail to notice the alarm over Russian policy in Eastern Europe and the Middle East evinced by Truman and his civilian advisors, and the breakdown in harmony evident at the September meeting in London of the Council of Foreign Ministers.

The Soviet Union presented no immediate threat, the services acknowledged. Its economy and manpower were exhausted by the war, its technology was primitive by American standards, and its immediate goals were being achieved through occupation and wartime agreements. Consequently, the USSR would concentrate on internal reconstruction and limited diplomatic objectives for the next several years.[50]

Moscow's long-run aims were less predictable. As during the war, most experts who speculated on those aims avoided dogmatic predictions and downplayed the role of Marxist ideology in Soviet policy. G-2 characterized the Soviets' long-range objectives as "progressive expansion wherever practicable," a phrase it did not further define. A JCS committee described the "extreme toward which

49. Quotations from Bissell to Handy, 14 September 1945, with enclosed paper, "United States Military Situation 1945–55," file 381 Top Secret, Chief of Staff. On secrecy, see Davis, *Postwar Defense Policy and the U.S. Navy*, pp. 86–87; House Naval Affairs Committee, *Hearings, Composition of the Postwar Navy*, pp. 1174–75.

50. Bissell to Handy, 14 September 1945, file 381 Top Secret, Chief of Staff; Joint Intelligence Staff 80/15, 9 November 1945, file CCS 092 USSR (3-27-45) Sec. 3, JCS; "Postwar Economic Policies and Capabilities of the U.S.S.R.," with enclosures, 30 October 1945, Project No. 2566, Box 1206, Intelligence (G-2) Library "P" File 1946–51, Records of the Military Intelligence Division (G-2), Records of the Army Staff, RG 319, Washington National Records Center.

Russian policy may conceivably be heading" as "domination of Europe, comparable with that which inspired the Germans," and "control of the eastern Mediterranean, the Persian Gulf, Manchuria, Northern China, and Korea." A top army planner described the USSR as having "in effect two parallel foreign policies": an aggressive policy which might "evolve into a bid for world domination," and a sincere interest in the preservation of world peace and the success of the United Nations Organization. At a minimum, a Soviet thrust into Western Europe appeared possible to defense officials.[51]

Seen through the prism of a decade's struggle with the Axis, the Soviet threat appeared more alarming. The USSR fit a preconceived image of what constituted a threat to the United States, an image seared into the military consciousness by the war experience. Worried only about another world war, American strategists ignored the many possibilities for conflict spawned by disintegrating colonial empires and aspiring nationalities. The sole enemy which could seriously trouble the United States was the superpower, the successor to Germany and Japan—the nation capable of matching technology and manpower with the United States. Only the Soviet Union fit that definition. Already, experts feared, the Soviet Union was capable of overrunning Europe, an act which would insure it the resources for an eventual attack against the United States. Even without conquering Europe, the Soviets might in five to ten years develop both the atomic bomb and a strategic capability to deliver it. The USSR would be slower to develop an oceangoing navy, and would thus be sharply limited in its ability to conduct offensive landings overseas. But the potential nuclear threat seemed menacing enough, especially in light of America's relative vulnerability to nuclear attack. Soviet capabilities alone, regardless of what was thought of Russian intentions, appeared sufficient cause to designate the USSR as a potential enemy.[52]

51. Bissell to Handy, 14 September 1945, file 381 Top Secret, Chief of Staff; JCS 1545, "Military Position of the United States in the Light of Russian Policy," report by the Joint Strategic Survey Committee, 9 October 1945, file ABC 384 United Nations (14 July 1944) Sec. 1-c, OPD; C.H.B. [Bonesteel?], memorandum, "Presidential Commission on Russia," 7 November 1945, file 336 (Russia), ASW.

52. On estimates of Soviet military capabilities, see JIC 329, "Strategic Vulnerability of the U.S.S.R. to a Limited Air Attack," November 1945, file ABC 336 Russia (22 August 1945), OPD; JCS 1477/1, file ABC 471.6 Atom (17 August 1945) Sec. 2, OPD; "Postwar Economic Policies and Capabilities of the U.S.S.R.," 30 October 1945, Box 1206, G-2; JIS 80/15, 9 November 1945, file CCS 092 USSR (3-27-45) Sec. 3, JCS; Weckerling to Assistant Chief of Staff, OPD (Attn: Bissell), 17 December 1945, "Estimates of the World Situation Three Years after Termination of Occupation by American Forces," an enclosure to the "Revised Report of the Special Committee on the Permanent Military Establishment of the Army of the United States," 21 December 1945, file 370.01 Top Secret, Army Ground Forces.

As for Moscow's foreseeable aims, they might seem limited, but so it had appeared with Germany and Japan in the 1930s, military officials recalled. Implicitly and sometimes explicitly, the military equated Stalinist Russia to Nazi Germany and used the pattern of German expansion to forecast Soviet aims. In September 1945, G-2 listed the similarities between the Soviets' current policy and Germany's path in the 1930s. Both operated as totalitarian regimes, engaged in propaganda and subversion, and maintained a closed economy, G-2 noted. Both made temporary deals with their enemies "to gain time": the Germans with the Nazi-Soviet Pact of 1939, the Soviets in subscribing to the United Nations Charter. Both sought domination of Europe. Both followed a similar timetable for conquest: the USSR's takeover of the Baltic states paralleled Germany's occupation of the Ruhr, and the Russian attack on Finland matched the Nazi seizure of Czechoslovakia. The facile equation between Nazism and Stalinism made the USSR appear an ominous threat and fostered an expectation that history would repeat itself in the form of a Soviet bid for continental or world domination.[53]

The scientific elite made the same equation between Nazism and Stalinism. As in other areas of policy, the putative Soviet threat served to justify proposals before Congress for science legislation. For Bush, the Russian menace fit into a model of the postwar world based on his reading of recent history:

> We must grasp the tough fact that the very emphasis on peace in the great democracies, in the interval between the last two wars, undoubtedly fostered the aggressors' conviction that the democracies were soft and decadent, and encouraged Hitler to strike. Talk of peace must this time be realistic; we shall need to maintain our full strength as a military power if we are to be respected and listened to.

In private Bush elaborated the historical analogy. He confided to Conant his anxiety that the United States under the "labor government" of the Roosevelt and Truman administrations might be going down the path of internal "disintegration" traveled by France in the 1930s. Bush feared that Stalin was taking Hitler's place and the

53. Bissell to Handy, 14 September 1945, file 381 Top Secret, Chief of Staff. For a suggestive essay on the tendency of Americans to equate the Soviets and the Nazis, see Les K. Adler and Thomas G. Paterson, "Red Fascism: The Merger of Nazi Germany and Soviet Russia in the American Image of Totalitarianism, 1930's–1950's," *American Historical Review* 75 (April 1970): 1046–64.

United States was succumbing to the weakness which rendered France impotent against the Nazis.[54]

Conant, harboring a similar fear of weakness, urged Bush to be tough on the issue of atomic energy control. Chiding Bush for his concern about "threatening the world with our present power," he asserted: "You do essentially threaten or bargain if you do anything short of 'blandly giving away the secret.' ... I think we should bargain very hard with Russia, and do it pretty soon."[55] Bush, Conant, and many of their colleagues were sincere advocates of international control of atomic energy facing perhaps insoluble diplomatic problems. But their fears of a recurrence of totalitarian aggression may have led them to offer their proposals less in the spirit of generosity than of compelling the world to do what the United States knew was best for it.

The fear of internal weakness voiced by Bush also intensified the apprehension felt by military men. Firm resistance to Soviet expansion might curb Moscow's appetite for world hegemony, just as it could have checked the ambitions of Germany and Japan. But popular pressure for rapid demobilization convinced military leaders that Americans were determined to recommit the follies of the 1920s and 1930s. Marshall believed the country to be "in a widespread emotional crisis" during which demobilization has become, "in effect, disintegration, not only of the armed forces but apparently of all conception of world responsibility." Forrestal's fears were identical. The country was "going back to bed at a frightening rate, which is the best way I know to be sure of the coming of World War III." Truman, too, feared that demobilization was robbing the United States of the means "to enforce our demands—a just and fair peace—and unless we have that means we are heading directly for a third world war." In military eyes, the navy had "shrunk to about the dimensions of two small task groups," the Army Air Forces were nothing more than "*a symbolic instrument of National Defense,*" and the morale of troops still in service appeared poor. Serious doubt existed about whether the United States Army could take offensive or even defensive military action in Europe. Unless arrested, the collapse of American will would

54. Senate Military Affairs Committee, *Hearings on Science Legislation, 1945*, pp. 216, 220; Bush, *Tribune* Speech, 31 October 1945, file 3048, Bush Papers; Bush to Conant, 20 October 1945, file 614, Bush Papers.
55. Conant to Bush, 27 September 1945, file 614, Bush Papers.

turn the Soviet Union into an enemy, whatever Stalin's immediate intentions—or so the military believed.[56]

If national irresolution gave the services cause to designate the Soviet Union a potential enemy, so too did considerations of military strategy and self-interest. Throughout the war, adherence to a Mahanian concept of navies had weakened the navy's planning and its claim on postwar budgets. If navies existed only to do battle against a rival sea power, then there appeared little reason to maintain a large American fleet after the war, since no naval rival appeared imminent. The coming of nuclear weapons exacerbated the threat of naval obsolescence.

The perfection of carrier air power proved the navy's salvation. Encouraged by Forrestal and at times by King, carrier commanders returning from the Pacific in the fall of 1945 argued that naval power need no longer be limited to the seas. The navy's future mission, they urged, would be to strike with carrier planes against tactical and strategic targets deep within the great landmasses of the world. Shouldering aside the battleship admirals, the carrier officers envisioned a postwar navy able to compete against the air force for popularity, funds, and utilization of the atomic bomb, and therefore for strategic importance. Their conception also allowed the navy at last to identify an enemy against which its weapons might be useful and whose existence would justify its schemes. The Soviet Union, with its relatively short shoreline and modest navy, was impervious to conventional naval attack, but carrier aircraft might tear at the vitals of the former ally. Thus self-interest encouraged the navy to magnify the Russian threat, while in turn the emergence of the Soviet Union as a putative enemy invited the navy to concentrate on carrier development.[57]

56. Quotations from Marshall speech, "Responsibility of Victory: Strength of Cooperators tied to the Strength of United States," delivered before the *New York Herald Tribune* Forum, 20 October 1945, in *Vital Speeches of the Day*, 15 November 1945, pp. 76–78; Millis, *Forrestal Diaries*, p. 100; Truman to Representative John M. Folger, 16 November 1945, quoted in Ross, *Preparing for Ulysses*, p. 187; Sparrow, *History of Personnel Demobilization*, pp. 268, 273 (Sparrow's italics). See also Duffield to Forrestal, 18 October 1945, file 8-1-20, SecNav; minutes of the Committee of Three meetings, 16 October 1945 and 20 November 1945, Secretary of War Patterson's Safe File, SecWar. The civilian heads of the services were also worried by November about the inability of American forces to bolster Chiang Kai-shek's regime in China; see Forrestal's account of the Committee of Three meetings of 6 November 1945 and 20 November 1945, in unpublished Forrestal diaries, pp. 591–92, 639, Naval History Division.

57. Davis, *Postwar Defense Policy and the U.S. Navy*, pp. 147–50, 163–66, 181–206, 225–31.

For the AAF, the motivation to identify the USSR as an enemy was simpler. The new urgency about Soviet-American relations strengthened the case for air power. Given the might of the Russian ground army, it appeared that only air power could be effective against the Soviet Union. Furthermore, the Soviet Union itself might develop a strategic bombing capability. During the war the AAF believed that the Soviets could not create a large bomber force for at least twenty years. Fall estimates, however, pared that figure down to five to ten years. The AAF, which once denigrated Soviet techno-logy, now began to fear it.[58]

The army had the least political stake in regarding the USSR as an enemy, since the Russian and American ground armies could not contest each other in the enemy's homeland. A clash of ground forces in Western or Central Europe was plausible, yet the overwhelming numerical superiority of the Red Army made it doubtful that the United States would rely on ground forces to combat Soviet expansion there.

Service interests were one of several factors in military thinking which coalesced during the first autumn of peace. The military was called upon to formulate postwar policy just when the atomic bomb dramatized the possibility of extinction for the underdefended nation, just as Soviet-American relations were disintegrating, and just when the return of overseas commanders brought a new aggressiveness into military planning and politics. At the same time, the battle over unification of the services and public pressure for rapid demobilization intensified competition among the armed services for men and money and threatened to reduce America's military power. If this confluence of factors had not occurred, the military still would have worried about postwar defense. But each element in the military outlook served to reinforce the others. The military viewed the fall's events not in isolation but as part of an alarming pattern which portended peril for the nation's security. Fit into that pattern, Stalinist Russia appeared to more and more military men as an enemy bent on world domination.

58. JIS 80/15, appendix C, 9 November 1945, file CCS 092 USSR (3-27-45) Sec. 3, JCS; Weckerling to Bissell, 17 December 1945, "Estimates of the World Situation . . . ," as enclosure to the "Revised Report of the Special Committee . . . ," 21 December 1945, file 370.01 Top Secret, Army Ground Forces.

Politics Again

By the first days of autumn, the military had identified its prospective antagonist and formulated a tentative strategy for postwar security. The armed services still had to determine the mix of forces necessary for implementing their strategy, a task which had produced only stalemate during the war. Victory over Japan and the President's own directive made agreement on the force levels question urgent, but victory also ended the wartime moratorium on open combat between the services.

The navy continued its independent course. When Congress reconvened in September, Representative Carl Vinson, the navy's most powerful sponsor on Capital Hill, introduced a concurrent resolution which enumerated the numbers and types of ships which would comprise the postwar navy. Vinson proposed a large fleet reliant on carrier air power and requiring, in line with Navy Department plans, over a half million men to operate it. The resolution was a device to commit Congress on the size of the peacetime navy before the lawmakers' zeal for military preparedness had time to cool. Vinson chose the expedient of a concurrent resolution, which was nonbinding on Congress and the President, because the navy's final plans were not ready, and because formal legislation would have to pass through the Budget Bureau and would stir greater controversy.[59]

The resolution, for which the navy unconvincingly denied any responsibility, irritated Truman and his Budget Director. Vinson's maneuver challenged Smith's insistence on joint planning for force levels and budgets and his design for centralizing economic and budgetary policymaking in the White House. He and the President also regarded the navy's proposal as "entirely too ambitious and . . . utterly out of the question in relation to the total Government program." The navy responded that budgets should be determined by "the new role of the United States in world affairs," in Smith's eyes a hopelessly vague yardstick for determining budgets. Truman further thought that the navy was bungling the job of demobilization and "double-crossing the Administration in connection with unification of the Army and the Navy." He was scarcely less suspicious of

---

59. *Congressional Record*, 79/1, 1945, p. 10207; Davis, *Postwar Defense Policy and the U.S. Navy*, pp. 182–83.

the War Department leadership, who he thought "would spend every nickel that they could get their hands on unless we did draw the line rather closely."[60]

The navy's aggressiveness also alarmed and embarrassed the army. Even before submission of Vinson's resolution, the War Department worried that the navy was "way ahead of us on the post-war organization." In order to catch up with the admirals and to carry out Truman's order for a joint postwar plan, Marshall hastily convened a Special Committee on the Permanent Military Establishment. Marshall charged its officers with fixing the size and composition of the postwar army.[61] The committee in effect superseded the Special Planning Division, which had tried unsuccessfully during the war to draw up postwar force levels.

The committee's first report, sent to Marshall on September 15, proposed a counterattack against the navy. Certain that the army would fare better in budgetary matters in a single defense department, the committee urged the army to force the unification issue before fixing its postwar size. Since unification would yield many "economies and efficiencies" in defense, the group argued that it could not establish a definitive figure on force levels while the unification issue remained unresolved. McCloy and Assistant Secretary of War for Air Robert Lovett, believing the President sympathetic to unification, encouraged the committee in its arguments. [62]

Still, pending unification, the Special Committee had to make some interim plans. Unwilling to see the army smaller than the navy, the committee wanted a postwar army of 778,548 active-duty personnel, plus universal military training. That figure—more than twice the

60. Quotations from Smith, Memorandum of Conference with President Truman, 13 September 1945; Memorandum of Conference attended by Truman, Forrestal, Smith, Walsh, Vinson, Gates and others, 14 September 1945; Memorandum of Conference with the President, 30 October 1945; Memorandum of Conference with the President, 19 September 1945; Memorandum of Conference with the President, 5 October 1945, all in Smith Papers. See also Smith, Daily Record, 10 September 1945, 14 September 1945; Smith, Memorandum for the President, 11 September 1945, White House Memoranda; "Excerpts from Telephone Conversation Between the Secretary of the Navy and the Director of the Budget—10 September 1945," and Forrestal to Sheldon Clark, 24 September 1945, both in file 70-1-1, SecNav; Millis, *Forrestal Diaries*, pp. 115–16.

61. Hull to Craig and Lincoln, 24 August 1945, file 320 (102), OPD; Hodes to Bessell and others, 27 August 1945, file 320 (30), Chief of Staff.

62. "Interim Plan for the Permanent Military Establishment of the Army of the United States," JCS 1520, 15 September 1945; Lovett to Marshall, 24 August 1945; McCloy to Marshall, 31 August 1945; Marshall to McCloy, n.d. [sent 4 September 1945], all in file ABC 040 (2 November 1943) Sec. 5-a, OPD.

number tentatively approved by the chief of staff the previous winter
—would provide an air force of 45 groups. When the AAF protested
that figure, the committee quickly reversed itself and recommended
a 70-group air force, which would raise total strength to 958,548.[63]

Marshall not only damned the committee's force level recommendation, but took the extraordinary step of rebuking his own staff, as
well as the navy, before the Joint Chiefs. Forwarding the Special
Committee's report to the chiefs on September 19,1945, Marshall
noted that pending army and navy requests came to "a grand total
of 1,617,000" men, a figure he believed unrealistic given "the inability
to obtain the necessary volunteers . . . [and] the financial burden this
would impose upon the country." By keeping in mind the economies
made possible by unification and UMT, the JCS staff could come
up with much more modest figures for both services, he believed.
On the other hand, submission of the bloated figures to a peace-
minded Congress would backfire against the services and might
"eliminate entirely the chances of obtaining universal military
training."[64]

Marshall further vented his anger over the services' ambitions in
a blunt letter to Eisenhower, commander of American forces in
Europe. The chief of staff described himself as "in general disagreement with almost the unanimous opinion" of his own Special Committee. The committee's recommendations and the attempt to outbid
the navy sprang from "tragically bad judgment," he told Eisenhower.
The General Staff, oblivious to the treatment the army received after
World War I, sought a course of action which he felt would "not
only ruin the confidence of the Congress in the War Department's
wisdom but . . . defeat Universal Military Training." Taken together,
the army and navy recommendations constituted "a demand for
annual appropriations" which was "wholly unreasonable in relation
to the national budget" and "illogical in relation to the state of the
world, assuming we have Universal Military Training." Yet, Marshall
declared, he was reluctant to act strongly on the matter because he
considered it unfair to tie the hands of Eisenhower, his probable
successor as chief of staff.[65]

63. "Interim Plan," JCS 1520, file ABC 040 (2 November 1943) Sec. 5-a, OPD.
64. Marshall to JCS, 28 September 1945, file ABC 040 (2 November 1943) Sec. 5-a, OPD.
See also drafts of this memorandum in file 353 (795), OPD.
65. Marshall to Eisenhower, 20 September 1945, file ABC 040 (2 November 1943) Sec. 5-a,
OPD.

Replying to Marshall, Eisenhower was reassuring. If the services rigorously eliminated duplicate functions and relied on UMT, he wrote, the army might need only 325,000 men. Eisenhower's message gave the green light for his superior to proceed with his desired course.[66]

Nonetheless, the obstacles to Marshall's program were formidable. Popular pressure for rapid demobilization suggested the correctness of his cautious handling of Congress. But the worsening of American-Soviet relations and the growing conviction that only military strength would arrest Soviet expansion encouraged the military, including Marshall, to buck popular attitudes and press for a powerful military establishment. The chief of staff himself remained alarmed by "the present emotional move to tear down our military power without regard to the lessons of history and again waste the victory and imperil our future."[67] Could he fight his staff's recommendations in the face of a Soviet menace aggravated by the dissipation of American strength?

To Marshall, the only solution to such a dilemma was, as it had been for a quarter century, to slash expenses by using UMT to back up a small professional force. Two events in October briefly raised army hopes for the training program it sought. One occurrence was the "extraordinarily wide and eminently favorable" press reaction to the publication of Marshall's biennial report, which included a powerful brief for UMT. The second was Truman's announcement of his unqualified support for UMT, spelled out in a special message delivered in person to Congress on October 23. "Our geographical security is now gone—gone with the advent of the rocket bomb, the rocket, aircraft carriers, and modern airborne armies," the President claimed. "The surest guaranty that no nation will dare again to attack us is to remain strong in the only kind of strength an aggressor can understand—military power." The President had followed precisely the military's argument for deterrence.[68]

66. Eisenhower to Marshall, 24 September 1945, file ABC 040 (2 November 1943) Sec. 5-a, OPD.

67. G.C.M. [Marshall] to Porter, 21 October 1945, file 353 (219), Chief of Staff.

68. Quotations from General Council Minutes, 15 October 1945; *Congressional Record*, 79/1, 1945, pp. 9934–37. See also, Ward, "Movement for Universal Military Training," pp. 113–15, 120–23, 125–29. For the military's input into Truman's address, see Marshall, "Notes on Universal Military Training," 13 September 1945, and "Draft of President's proposed message on universal military training to Congress, 13 September 1945," both in UMT folder, Secretary of War Patterson's Safe File, SecWar; General Vaughan to Secretary of War, 17 October 1945, and Marshall to Secretary of War, 18 October 1945, both in file 353 (255), Chief of Staff.

224 PREPARING FOR THE NEXT WAR

Still, UMT was going nowhere. The atomic bomb and the army's unexpected success with voluntary enlistments undercut the case for mandatory peacetime training, while the continuation of draft calls compromised the military's claims for UMT as an alternative to a large standing army. Support for UMT continued high in opinion polls—Americans did not believe the bomb made UMT obsolete. But UMT was anathema to congressmen. In the House, fall hearings on UMT showed that the army and navy had done little to polish their tarnished arguments for training. The hearings only made the War Department's political strategists more pessimistic about success. At the same time, the political alliance on UMT was shattering on the issue of the length of training. Veterans and reserve organizations advocated a reduced training period of four months, after which the trainee would work off his obligation in the National Guard, the Organized Reserves, or ROTC—a scheme also deliberated on at the White House. For years the War Department had fought off compromise and insisted on a year's training. Marshall continued to do so, contending that less than eight months' training would be a "waste" which would "give a false sense of security and be an unwarranted load on the taxpayer and the individual."[69]

The military's own support of UMT was also collapsing. Marshall's staff had already let it be known that it cared less about his UMT plan than about the size of the professional force. The Army Air Forces remained lukewarm to UMT. Now the navy hedged on its support. In October Forrestal put the critical question to Admiral King: "How much support should we invest in the UMT drive?" Noting the proposals for a shortened training period, the chief of naval operations advised Forrestal to tell Truman that anything less than a year's training would be worse than useless to the navy. "If this is impolitic or if universal military training is a lost cause," King added, then the navy should refrain from supporting any watered-

69. Quotation from G.A.L. [George A. Lincoln], memorandum for the record, 16 October 1945, file ABC 353 Universal (1 May 45) Sec. 1-a, OPD. See also Ward, "Movement for Universal Military Training," pp. 103–15, 132–35, 138–42; Cantril, *Public Opinion*, p. 472; General Council Minutes, 13 November 1945; Connelly to Secretary of War, enclosing President's draft memorandum, "Memorandum on Postwar Military Training," 4 September 1945, file ABC 353 Universal (1 May 45) Sec. 1-a, OPD; Vaughan to Secretary of War, 16 October 1945, and Marshall to Secretary of War, 18 October 1945, both in file 353 (225), Chief of Staff; Commodore James K. Vardaman, Jr. (naval aide to the President) to Forrestal, 16 October 1945, and Horne to Forrestal, n.d. [October 1945], both in file 45-1-10, SecNav; unpublished Forrestal diaries, 7 September 1945 entry, p. 462, Naval History Division.

down training measure. Forrestal, though still favoring UMT, advised Secretary Patterson a few days later that he was "extremely dubious as to the possibility of getting any such legislation passed by Congress." Stiffening competition among the services for funds may have further cooled the navy's ardor for UMT, since a costly training program would divert appropriations away from the regular navy. Nor was the navy's need for UMT as pressing as the army's, since the admirals were confident that the navy could recruit its 660,000 men on a volunteer basis.[70]

By November, UMT was doomed. Disappearing with it was any chance that Marshall could impose on either the JCS or his own staff his vision of an economical, citizen force. Marshall had little success in getting the Joint Chiefs to reduce force levels on the basis of savings anticipated from UMT. Nor would the JCS agree to reductions that might result from unification. King opposed operating on the assumption that the services would be unified and insisted that force levels be determined on the basis not of financial considerations but of the nation's "military policy, strategic concept and overseas base requirements."[71] The JCS reached a compromise on force levels which, settling nothing, only dragged the service secretaries into the squabble. Meanwhile the House passed Vinson's resolution on the postwar navy, though Truman halted the measure in the Senate, and on December 4 the House enacted legislation authorizing a 660,000-man navy. The Joint Chiefs, locked in disagreement and finding the whole matter of long-range planning overtaken by legislative developments, failed to heed Truman's order for a joint recommendation on postwar forces.[72] That failure set the pattern for the postwar, when the chiefs

70. Forrestal to King, n.d. [October 1945], and King to Forrestal, 9 October 1945, file 45-1-10, SecNav; Forrestal to Secretary of War, 13 October 1945, file 320 (119), OPD; testimony of Admiral Louis Denfield, House Naval Affairs Committee, *Hearings, Composition of the Postwar Navy*, pp. 1386–87.

71. King to JCS, 25 September 1945, JCS 1478/2, file ABC 040 (2 November 1943) Sec. 5-a, OPD.

72. Marshall to JCS, 28 September 1945, JCS 1478/3; Decision Amending JCS 1478/3, 11 October 1945; JPS 764/D, 12 October 1945; JCS 743/2, 19 October 1945; JCS 1520/2, 26 October 1945; JCS 1478/5, 7 November 1945; Decision on JCS 1478/5, 16 November 1945; "Brief of JCS Papers," n.d. [1946], all in file ABC 040 (2 November 1943) Sec. 5-a, OPD; Secretary, Joint Staff Planners, to Joint Strategic Survey Committee, 24 October 1945; minutes of Joint Staff Planners' 223rd meeting, 24 October 1945; Arnold to JCS, 2 October 1945, JCS 1478/4, all in file CCS 370 (8-19-45) Sec. 1, JCS; Forrestal to Patterson, 7 November 1945, and Patterson to Forrestal, 12 November 1945, both in file 320 (78/53), OPD; Smith, Memorandum of Conference with the President, 28 November 1945, Smith Papers; Davis, *Postwar Defense Policy and the U.S. Navy*, p. 212.

would fight their budgetary battles to a standstill and dump the problem on civilian authority.

While the Joint Chiefs were deliberating fruitlessly, Marshall ordered the War Department's Special Committee to draw up a new plan for army and AAF postwar strengths. The committee grudgingly complied. It advised that if cost restrictions and the limitations of voluntary recruitment governed the size of the regular army, as Marshall instructed, then an active-duty force of only 562,700 men would be feasible. Such a force would limit the AAF to 34 groups, in spite of Arnold's warning of "tragic possibilities" if the AAF get fewer than 70 groups. The peacetime army could mobilize to 4,500,000 men for a major war, the committee stated, if backed by an effective program of citizens' training and an intelligence system capable of giving a year's warning of attack. The 562,700-man force would cost $2.7 billion annually, plus $1.75 billion for the UMT system.[73]

The committee's heart was not in its own report. It complained that the revised figures provided only one full-strength reserve division in the United States ready for combat overseas. Furthermore, it tacitly endorsed a stinging dissent to its own report by the AAF representative on the committee. The AAF trotted out the now commonplace arguments against budgetary restrictions on its size.

> V-1 and V-2 type missiles, atomic power, and 5,000 mile bombers—in enemy hands—would leave us no time for even miraculous manpower and materiel mobilizations. . . a sudden strike against the U.S. requires *immediate* action by an Air Force in being.

Belittling the notion that the United States would have a year's time in which to mobilize, the AAF insisted that it had to be ready "to meet aggression with immediate destruction of the aggressor's vitals." To be able to strike "immediately anywhere in the world," a "bedrock minimum" of seventy groups was necessary. The seventy groups might swell the federal budget; but, the AAF hinted, the money could come from other appropriations, since the AAF now had first call on federal monies. The services could also frighten Americans into spending more: "the nation, given the awareness of the real

73. Hodes to Bessell and other committee members, 15 October 1945, file 320 (30), Chief of Staff; Arnold to JCS, 2 October 1945, JCS 1478/4, file CCS 370 (8-19-45) Sec. 1, JCS; "Revised Report of the Special Committee on the Military Establishment of the Army of the United States," with memorandum from the committee to Chief of Staff, 29 November 1945, file 320 (78), OPD.

threat to its security, will approve and find the means to meet such a threat." And if the War Department did not secure the mission of strategic air power, the AAF warned, then the navy might seize it with its carrier aircraft.[74]

The pattern was now familiar. Each of Marshall's attempts to introduce financial and political considerations into planning met with a melodramatic AAF appeal to the needs of national security. However sound, Marshall's position was vulnerable because it rested on budgetary more than strategic considerations. Arnold, King, and many other officers maintained that their job was simply to tell Congress and the President what the military needed to uphold national security. To do as Marshall suggested—to trim their sails to the winds of popular and congressional opinion—would, they claimed, imperil national security.

In fact, the force levels they recommended had only the most tenuous grounding in an analysis of security needs. Arnold later admitted as much:

> Who knows whether 70 groups of airplanes is the right or wrong number to prevent another war? Was not that number selected in relation to costs and expenditures, rather than with regard to the composition and strength necessary to our armed forces in the world picture?

The AAF was asking for what it thought it could get, though protesting Marshall's attempt to deal frankly with financial and recruiting limitations. Recognizing the value of a simple figure easily remembered by the public, the AAF seized on the 70-group number, refused to deviate from it, and sought to make it appear indispensable to national defense.[75]

Similar considerations governed the War Department and the navy, each driven by jealousy of its rival. The head of the army's Special Planning Division, citing the admirals' request for 660,000 men, argued that if the army asked for fewer personnel it "would patently be in an embarrassing position, vis-a-vis the Navy." Despite the urging of some officers, the force level recommendations made by the services in the fall of 1945 represented not a careful compilation

---

74. "Minority Report of AAF Member" (italics in the original), in "Revised Report," with memorandum, committee to Chief of Staff, 29 November 1945, file 320 (78), OPD.

75. Arnold, *Global Mission*, pp. 614–15; Smith, *Air Force Plans*, pp. 71–74.

of personnel needs, but a response to competitive urges and a guess as to what the nation would support.[76]

Marshall, though himself vulnerable to air power arguments, had imposed some restraint on the competition. But he was no longer available to do so by the time the AAF lodged its protest against the proposed 562,000-man army. After serving more than six years as chief of staff, he retired in November, soon to embark on a frustrating diplomatic mission to China. Succeeding him on November 20 was General Eisenhower, a man of more flexible views on budgetary matters.

On December 11 Eisenhower and his staff reviewed the Special Committee's recommendations. He reached no decisions, but he made it clear that, despite his pledges to Marshall to economize, he regarded the 562,700-man program "generally inadequate" in both ground and air forces. He doubted the value of a year's warning of attack assumed by the committee "in view of the apathy of the American people prior to World War II and our traditional reluctance to prepare before we are actually kicked into war." The army, he indicated, needed forces-in-being. Accordingly, he questioned the usefulness of UMT and approved the AAF's plan for seventy groups, while his top aides repudiated cost as a legitimate determinant of military strength.[77]

Finally, the new chief of staff and his assistants agreed that they "should present separate plans for the Army Air Forces and the Army Ground Forces thereby strengthening our position vis a vis the Navy, particularly its Air and Marine Corps plans."[78] The ploy was obvious enough: submission of separate plans for air and ground forces would enable the War Department to avoid using a large cost

76. Porter to Deputy Chief of Staff, 2 November 1945, file 350.06 (Study 115), SPD. See also Bessell to Lincoln, 29 September 1945, and Lincoln to Strategy Section, 15 September 1945, both in file ABC 040 (2 November 1943) Sec. 5-a, OPD; Smith, *Air Force Plans*, pp. 71–74, and Davis, *Postwar Defense Policy and the U.S. Navy*, p. 176.

77. M.M.B., memorandum for the record, 12 December 1945, file 334 (Special War Department Committee on the Permanent Military Establishment), SPD. The December 11 meeting was attended by the Special Committee members, by Deputy Chief of Staff Handy, and by Generals Hull, Lincoln, and Nelson. Significantly, while Patterson used a figure of 500,000 for the postwar regular army in hearings on UMT in November 1945, by December, after Eisenhower had taken over as chief of staff, the War Department was hedging on Patterson's statement and suggesting a higher figure; see House Military Affairs Committee, *Hearings, UMT*, pp. 6, 646.

78. M.M.B., memorandum for the record, 12 December 1945, file 334 (Special War Department Committee), SPD.

figure that might upset congressmen. It would also alter the rules of the fiscal game. Whereas Congress might naturally tend to divide the fiscal pie equally between the War and Navy Departments, if judging three requests it might grant the navy only one-third.

Eisenhower's elevation to chief of staff marked a critical turn in military strategy and politics. In one of his first actions, the new army head encouraged the ambitions of his officers for a large peacetime establishment, especially air forces. He invited them into a keener rivalry with the navy, undermined the effort to secure UMT, and downplayed the financial considerations so important to Marshall. In short, he moved toward reliance on strategic air power for massive deterrence and retaliation—the posture which the American government would assume during much of the cold war and during his presidency in particular.

The New Dogma

The strategic air power argument triumphed in part because the airmen were shrewd propagandists, skillful at invoking all the terrifying developments of the war to dramatize their case. It triumphed also because the primacy of strategic air power was dogma which few officers thought to contest. Though Marshall and King made briefs for ground and naval power in their final reports, Marshall himself was receptive to air power arguments.

The AAF's foresight into future technology was often strikingly prophetic. While some scientists and officers doubted that atomic power could be readily harnassed to rocketry, Hap Arnold was convinced that the V-2 was "ideally suited to deliver atomic explosives" and was eager to press a development program. He foresaw the day when atomic bombs would be launched "from true space ships, capable of operating outside the earth's atmosphere."[79]

But if farsighted about new weapons, the AAF was often blind to the impact of technology on the conduct of war. Air power doctrine asserted that Pearl Harbor proved the necessity of air-forces-in-being able to respond instantly to an enemy attack and carry the knockout blow to the aggressor. A closer look at the December 7 disaster might have countered such facile conclusions, for Pearl Harbor raised

79. Arnold, *Third Report*, in *War Reports*, p. 463.

doubts about the ability of a military command to anticipate a surprise attack in time to throw its forces into battle before they were destroyed. The new chief of staff himself acknowledged as much. "You cannot be ready on M-day," Eisenhower told a House committee. "For one thing, you cannot be ready psychologically on M-day. It takes a Pearl Harbor to inspire us to face the necessity of fighting, and we cannot be ready on that day."[80] If the enemy struck too swiftly, if constant readiness were impossible, if adequate warning were unlikely, then an American counterstrike by air might never materialize or might prove too weak to decide the conflict. There could ensue a protracted struggle in which the decisive factor might be not M-day readiness but the nation's capacity rapidly to mobilize its total resources, including its navy and ground army. The nation which relied too heavily on a powerful M-day force would then confront the dilemma faced by the United States in 1941: whether to throw its small professional army immediately into battle or to use it as a training cadre for building up a force adequate to defeat the enemy. Such a dilemma would be even more excruciating if, as all predicted, the course of war were swifter in the future. By failing sufficiently to explore the possibility of an indecisive M-day battle, UMT defenders neglected perhaps the most convincing argument for citizens' training. Of course air power experts were disinclined to entertain objections that cast doubt on their theories.

Postwar planners also ignored the mixed results of the strategic air offensives of World War II. "The Strategic Theory," Arnold wrote at the end of the war, "postulates that air attack on internal enemy vitals can so deplete specific industrial and economic resources, and on occasion the will to resist, as to make continued resistance by the enemy impossible." Arnold continued:

> Examination of *any* national economy will disclose several specific industries or other national activities whithout which the nation cannot effectively carry on modern warfare. It is conceivable that there will always be one so necessary to all phases of the national warmaking ability that its destruction would be fatal to the nation.[81]

80. House Military Affairs Committee, *Hearings, UMT*, p. 76. The classic study is Roberta Wohlstetter, *Pearl Harbor: Warning and Decision.*

81. Arnold, *Third Report*, in *War Reports*, p. 457 (italics added). Arnold's thinking had been changed little by the war. He had written in 1942: "The schooled air strategist will study the enemy nation to determine his solar plexus, his vital nerve centers. He will then locate these and determine what is required for their destruction." From Henry H. Arnold and Ira G. Eaker, *Army Flyer* (New York, 1942), p. 264.

The existence and vulnerability of such an industry was questionable even in highly advanced industrial states, much less in more rudimentary economies. Indeed, planners had already commented on the relative imperviousness of the Soviet economy to strategic attack. Furthermore, the AAF's frustrating experience in bombing Germany and its switch to night area bombing of Japan might have been taken as its own tacit confession of the inadequacies of precision bombing. But the AAF clung stubbornly to a simplistic theory of air power developed in the 1920s and 1930s.

A dispassionate reading of the studies of the United States Strategic Bombing Survey would have dispelled some of the excessive confidence in the bomber. By the fall of 1945, the survey, established at the AAF's initiative, was completing its reports on Germany and beginning those on Japan. The reports emphasized the difficulties involved in ascertaining and attacking "bottleneck" targets in an enemy economy. The survey staff found that "even in the case of a very concentrated industry very heavy and continuous attack must be made," and that civilian morale stabilized after initial urban attacks. Attacks on urban and industrial targets in Germany proved less useful than those on Nazi transportation, the survey showed. German war production peaked in 1944 despite relentless bombing, but much material never reached the front. Taken together, the survey reports suggested air power was relatively ineffective unless used to incinerate enemy cities on an indiscriminate scale, as in Japan, or employed in concert with ground and naval forces, or delivered with a precision attainable only after months of effort and the destruction of enemy fighter forces. As Walter Millis later wrote, the decisive factor in World War II was not independent air power but rather "the mechanization of the ground battlefield with automotive transport, with the 'tactical' airplane and above all with the tank." The war punctured the dream of air power as capable of swift, decisive attack on the enemy's jugular.[82]

Understandably the AAF, bent on justifying an independent strategic mission, did not appreciate the significance for future strategy

82. Quotations from United States Strategic Bombing Survey, *Over-all Report (European War)*, p. 29; Millis, *Arms and Men*, p. 253. For the formation of the survey, the AAF's attitude toward it, the dates of reports, and some of the survey's findings, see David MacIssaac, "The United States Strategic Bombing Survey, 1944–1947" (Ph.D. dissertation, Duke University, 1970). For further discussion of the weaknesses in the AAF's arguments for strategic air power, see Millis, *Arms and Men*, pp. 252–60; Smith, *Air Force Plans*, chaps. 2–3; Legere, "Unification of the Armed Forces," pp. 408–22, an older but still useful study.

of the survey's findings. More surprisingly, neither did the Army General Staff, which might presumably have welcomed ammunition for use against the AAF's claims. Perhaps all parties felt that the atomic bomb settled the air power question once and for all, though the JCS staff doubted that was the case. Whatever the reason, the AAF's only concession to the war experience was to propose a large force of long-range fighters which could protect its bomber force. Ever since the devastating losses of American bombers over Germany in 1943, the vision of a bomber so bristling with armaments that it could sweep past enemy defenses had faded. That concession represented little doctrinal change, however. The close support of ground and amphibious troops, the interdiction of enemy supplies and reinforcements, and defense against enemy aviation received little attention from the AAF high command.[83]

Finally, the military might have questioned, as it had begun to do with the atomic bomb, whether the very destructiveness of strategic bombing might preclude its future use. If incineration were the only feasible objective of strategic air power, then how readily could the United States unleash the bomber? The military was too confident of deterrence to address that question. The AAF saw its planes as forming the core of a global police force which would deter or preempt an attack rather than fight it off. If American power could prevent war, there was no urgency in discussing how to wage it.

83. Smith, *Air Force Plans*, pp. 24–25, 35–37, 58.

EPILOGUE: THE LEGACY

World War II marked a revolution in the power of the American armed forces. Before the war the United States had been a modest power; though endowed with the potential of a giant, it had remained wedded to a hemispheric and defensive strategy and had confined the military to a minor role in politics. After the war the United States possessed the power to destroy entire nations, positioned its forces throughout the globe, used them repeatedly to impose the nation's will, and allowed them a commanding position in the American government and economy.

At one, superficial level, wartime military officials responsible for postwar plans played only a small role in the transformation of American military power. Bureaucratic tangles and mutual jealousies often obstructed their efforts. Divided among themselves, the services also took little initiative to coordinate their programs with other governmental agencies or to confirm them with higher authority. Eager to advance service interests, they screened out those strategic considerations which failed to justify their hopes, a practice so transparent that it only sabotaged the military's ability to defend its programs before Congress and the president.

By their own standards, army and navy planners had failed by 1945. Service leaders had built their political strategy, like their military program, on the supposed lessons of their prewar experience. Suspicious of the layman's wisdom and of his willingness to support national defense in peacetime, both the military and scientific elites tried either to bypass Congress or at least to secure congressional approval of their plans before the end of the war dissipated the martial spirit. The strategy of early approval did not work. Political differences within the military, the weakness of the planning staffs, and objections to military programs from Congress and the White House, especially the Budget Bureau, all hampered the military's efforts. Preoccupation with fighting the war, and then the war's abrupt termination, also upset military timetables. On V-J day, Congress had not enacted a single major plank of the services' postwar program. Indeed, it had not even received all of that program.

Nonetheless, despite their handwringing over popular antipathy to their requests, the services eventually got most of what they wanted. While, for example, the Research Board for National Security had to disband, Congress appropriated lavish research funds for the services to dispense directly. Under military sponsorship, the growth of federal science spending was exponential. By 1967, research and development funding, more than two hundred times larger than the 1940 figure, had reached $17 billion, of which the Defense Department spent over $8 billion. Counting research expenditures for atomic energy and space exploration, defense-related research seized an even larger portion of the federal science budget: 91 percent in 1960, 76 percent in 1974. Even for basic research, from which it could expect few quick dividends, the Department of Defense spent more than $250 million annually through fiscal 1974.[1] Since World War II, the partnership of soldiers and scientists, though damned at times by both parties as well as by their critics, has been vital to each.

The services prospered in other ways as well. Postwar force levels and expenditures, though rarely high enough to please the Defense Department, became enormous by prewar standards. Military spending, never above $650 million between 1931 and 1940, leaped from $12 billion in fiscal 1948 to $80 billion by the 1970s. Total military strength, which hovered between a quarter million and a third of a million men in the 1920s and 1930s, never dipped far below one and one half million men after the war, or below two and one-quarter million men after the Korean War.[2] Congress refused to enact UMT legislation, but until 1973 selective service usually kept military ranks full. Further, most officers preferred the selective draft. They had advocated UMT in 1945 primarily because they mistakenly calculated that selective service would offend the nation's egalitarian and antimilitarist sensibilities.

The causes of the stunning growth in America's military machine were several. The nation's pursuit of an Open Door economic system

1. National Science Foundation, *Federal Funds for Research, Development and Other Scientific Activities*, vol. 22, pp. 6, 17.
2. U.S. Bureau of the Census, *Historical Statistics of the United States: Colonial Times to 1957*, pp. 718, 736; U.S. Bureau of the Census, *Statistical Abstract of the United States: 1973*, 94th ed., pp. 257, 265–66.

and its rivalry with and suspicions of the Soviet Union, factors cited by other historians, were important. But the course of military planning indicates a third component. By the close of World War II, military and science policymakers had formulated and propagated an ideology of preparedness. The premises of the ideology were simple. Believing that American weakness had encouraged Axis ambitions in the 1930s, strategic planners thought that powerful military forces could deter or subdue future troublemakers. Pearl Harbor and the new weapons developed subsequent to it demonstrated the nation's nakedness to sudden attack and its need for unprecedented forces-in-being to ward off the coming blitzkrieg. If attack were to come without warning, the war machine had to be ever ready.

Those arguments were not new. The novelty of the ideology lay not in the originality of its premises but in the pervasiveness of its acceptance. More a mood than a fixed doctrine, the ideology was not embraced by everyone in the military, nor reflected in all postwar plans. But the ideology provided a unity to the outlook of the often quarrelsome armed services. Just as important, civilian administrators, scientists, academicians, and businessmen, among others, frequently campaigned for preparedness more vigorously than the officer corps. Both wartime presidents also wanted a powerful military establishment which could overawe potential aggressors, as did many congressmen. Before the cold war developed, there had arisen a cold war mentality, an anxiety about the nation's security and an insistence on mobilizing full resources to protect it.

That mentality emerged primarily in reaction to the war experience. It developed before the war's end, and therefore before the onset of the rivalry between the USSR and the United States or the alarm set off by the explosion of the atomic bomb. Soviet-American hostility and the nuclear weapons race, later so easily regarded as catalysts of a cold war mentality, were in fact, also products of it. Soviet policy and the advent of nuclear weapons appeared threatening partly because policymakers saw them in the context of the grave historical and technological patterns they had already observed. In turn, the emergence of a powerful Soviet state served to validate and intensify the fears for national safety which the war had bred.

In addition to Soviet behavior, ideological considerations seemed to validate the preparedness faith. To its proponents, the preparedness ideology did not conflict with the other "second chance" programs developed during the war, those for extension of free trade or establishment of a more effective international organization. At bottom, all the second-chance ideologies shared a common historical prespective and rationale. Americans were determined to prevent a repetition of the holocaust they had witnessed. Probably many, including military men, saw the various remedies as complementary rather than competitive. Suspect in American eyes for decades, Soviet diplomacy at the end of the war appeared threatening not merely to one scheme but to the entire program of Open Door economics, international organization, and national defense.

More than ideology moved these men, of course. Preparedness served not only complementary ideologies, but interlocking interests as well, and not merely the vested interests which faced severe contraction at war's end—the services themselves, defense industries and dependent unions and communities, and academic science. Those interests, many of them long present, had never succeeded in greatly altering government policy. Alone, their influence would have been limited, and blunted in part by opposing interests. But a cold war also served the interests of the capitalist economy as a whole, at least as those interests were interpreted by leading Americans, many of them worried about a repetition of the Great Depression. Preparedness would help nourish the scientific infrastructure needed for economic expansion, strengthen ties between the corporate and political elites, and defend access to the markets and materials deemed necessary for continued economic growth. And preparedness could stimulate gross investment at a time when other forms of government spending were anathema to powerful interests. To military men these were, at most, collateral benefits to their policy, more often not considered at all. But they probably enhanced the appeal and the utility of the preparedness program, and its acceptance as the cold war went on.

It is difficult to fault American soldiers and scientists for the urgency they attached to peacekeeping and the alarm they shared about the nation's future security. While much of their planning simply represented bureaucratic self-interest and inertia, the fears of the planners sprang from real and frightening changes in the technology of war and the conduct of international diplomacy. The makers of postwar policy would have been derelict in their duty had they failed to incorporate those changes into their strategic thinking. All too often, their plans and predictions were appropriate and prophetic.

They were also simplistic. Always preparing for a world war between great powers, the military disregarded developments in the nonwestern world—the crumbling colonial empires in Southeast Asia and elsewhere to which American power would later be drawn and often misapplied. Certain that armed force could have deterred Axis aggression, they overrated the usefulness of military solutions for postwar political problems. Obsessed by the pattern of Axis aggrandizement, they were primed to see that pattern in the activities of other nations. The frequency with which they drew upon analogies to combating disease and crime suggested their naive faith that the world could be frozen in its current political state and protected against the ebb and flow of national power. The American cop, on a world beat, could deter the international criminal. The conviction was firm that, as Robert Patterson said, "the military position of the United States will determine the maintenance of world peace."[3] The belief was just as firm that most other nations trusted American power and welcomed an American prophylactic against war. Most of all, policymakers developed a misguided faith in the capacity of American technology, especially air power and nuclear weapons, to deter or check future aggressors.

The supporters of universal military training—Stimson, Marshall, and Palmer—dimly perceived the fallibility of American technology. They sensed that the nation could not enforce a *pax Americana* cheaply. To keep other nations in their place would, they felt, require the sacrifice of American men rather than merely the expenditure of American money. By doubting whether nuclear power alone could be a credible deterrent, they obliquely raised one of the most persistent questions of the cold war. They also warned of the dangers of a swollen professional military establishment immune to popular control and corrosive to the nation's democratic traditions and institutions. And they noted that failure to train new manpower would exact an unfair burden on the veterans of World War II, a prophecy proven true in the Korean War. But the advocates of UMT presented their case poorly and allowed the army aviators successfully to exploit the threat of "instant" war.

3. House Military Affairs Committee, *Hearings, UMT*, p. 13.

In the postwar era, the preparedness ideology helped to encourage and excuse America's activities as a global policeman. The facile references to "appeasement" and Pearl Harbor could justify nuclear deterrence, global intervention, peacetime conscription, and the spinning of an intricate web of relationships among the military and those institutions—industry, science, education, labor—which supported or profited from preparedness. The experience of World War II spawned much of the reasoning and rhetoric of the cold war.

Whatever the long-term consequences of the preparedness mentality, clearly the nation's soldiers and scientists left an ironic legacy at the close of World War II. Resolved to prevent war, they risked creating the very conditions they feared most. Alarmed by a technological revolution, they chose to develop even more terrifying instruments of annihilation, a course which, as some feebly understood, could only intensify competition for new weapons and thereby diminish further the nation's security. Determined never again to by caught off guard by a Hitler, they set out to patrol the world in the interests of peace. They seemed unaware that they might provoke other nations as much as pacify them. In 1945 the alternative to preparedness and global peacekeeping appeared to the policymakers to invite national suicide. The course they ultimately followed became for the world, including the United States, substantially as dangerous.

SELECTED BIBLIOGRAPHY

Manuscripts and Archives

Kept mostly secret, postwar military planning during World War II generated little coverage in published sources of the time, and has received little attention from historians. Therefore, manuscript and archival records, listed here by the abbreviations used (after the first reference) in the text, are the most important sources for this study. Security restrictions slow but rarely bar final access to some records. The disorganized state of military records, especially the confusing and eccentric filing systems used by the services, poses a greater obstacle. Of military records, those of the Joint Chiefs of Staff are vital, but primarily for 1945. For the army, the records of the War Department General and Special Staffs, especially the files of the Special Planning Division, the Operations Division, and the Chief of Staff, are the most important. For the navy, the most useful sources are the secretary of the navy's records and the files of the coordinator of research and development. Many private collections are useful, but especially those of Bush, Furer, and the National Academy of Sciences on scientific matters; the Forrestal, Stimson, and Palmer collections for the military; and the Smith Papers for the White House.

Adm. Asst. SecWar	Records, Office of the Administrative Assistant to the Secretary of War, Record Group 107, National Archives Building, Washington, D.C.
Army Ground Forces	Records, Headquarters Army Ground Forces, Record Group 337, National Archives Building, Washington, D.C.
Arnold Papers	Papers of Henry Harley Arnold, Library of Congress, Washington, D.C.
ASW	Records, Assistant Secretary of War, Record Group 107, National Archives Building, Washington, D.C.
Baldwin Papers	Papers of Hanson Baldwin, Yale University Library, New Haven, Connecticut.
Bowen Papers	Papers of Harold G. Bowen, Princeton University Library, Princeton, New Jersey.

Budget Division — Records, Budget Division, War Department General and Special Staffs, Record Group 165, National Archives Building, Washington, D.C.

BuPers — Records, Bureau of Naval Personnel, Record Group 24, National Archives Building, Washington, D.C., and Washington National Records Center, Suitland, Maryland.

Bureau of the Budget — Records, Bureau of the Budget, Record Group 51, National Archives Building, Washington, D.C.

Bush Papers — Papers of Vannevar Bush, Library of Congress, Washington, D.C.

Chief of Staff — Records, Office of the Chief of Staff, War Department General and Special Staffs, Record Group 165, National Archives Building, Washington, D.C.

CNO-Cominch Records — Records, Chief of Naval Operations—Commander-in-Chief, United States Navy, Naval History Division, Washington, D.C.

Coordinator's Records — Records, Coordinator of Research and Development, Executive Office of the Secretary of the Navy, Record Group 80, Washington National Records Center, Suitland, Maryland.

Earle Papers — Papers of Edward Mead Earle, Princeton University Library, Princeton, New Jersey.

FDR Papers — Papers of Franklin D. Roosevelt, Franklin D. Roosevelt Library, Hyde Park, New York.

Forrestal Diaries — Unpublished diaries of James V. Forrestal, copies at Naval History Division, Washington, D.C., and at Princeton University Library, Princeton, New Jersey.

Forrestal Papers — Papers of James V. Forrestal, Princeton University Library, Princeton, New Jersey.

Furer Papers and Diary — Papers of Julius A. Furer, Library of Congress, Washington, D.C.

G-1 — Records, G-1 (Personnel) Division, War Department General and Special Staffs, Record Group 165, National Archives Building, Washington, D.C.

G-2	Records, G-2 (Intelligence) Division, War Department General and Special Staffs, Record Group 319, Washington National Records Center, Suitland, Maryland.
G-3	Records, G-3 (Organization and Training) Division, War Department General and Special Staffs, Record Group 165, National Archives Building, Washington, D.C.
General Board-Secretary of the Navy	Records, General Board-Secretary of the Navy Files, Naval History Division, Washington, D.C.
General Council Minutes	Minutes of the War Department General Council, Document 262, Reference Collection, Modern Military Branch, National Archives Building, Washington, D.C.
Hopkins Papers	Papers of Harry Hopkins, Franklin D. Roosevelt Library, Hyde Park, New York.
JCS	Records, United States Joint Chiefs of Staff, Record Group 218, National Archives Building, Washington, D.C.
King Papers	Papers of Ernest J. King, Library of Congress, Washington, D.C.
Knox Papers	Papers of Frank Knox, Library of Congress, Washington, D.C.
Leahy Papers	Papers of William D. Leahy, Library of Congress, Washington, D.C.
L&LD	Records, Legislative and Liaison Division, War Department General and Special Staffs, Record Group 165, Washington, D.C.
Manhattan Engineer District Records	Records, Manhattan Engineer District, Office of the Chief of Engineers, Record Group 77, National Archives Building, Washington, D.C.
NAS	Archives, National Academy of Sciences, Washington, D.C.
NDD	Records, New Developments Division, War Department General and Special Staffs, Record Group 165, National Archives Building, Washington, D.C.
OPD	Records, Operations Division, War Department General and Special Staffs, Record Group 165, National Archives Building, Washington, D.C.

Palmer Papers	Papers of John McAuley Palmer, Library of Congress, Washington, D.C.
Patterson Papers	Papers of Robert P. Patterson, Library of Congress, Washington, D.C.
Rosenman Papers	Papers of Samuel Rosenman, Franklin D. Roosevelt Library, Hyde Park, New York.
SecNav	Records, Secretary of the Navy James Forrestal, General Records of the Department of the Navy, Record Group 80, National Archives Building, Washington, D.C.
SecWar	Records, Office of the Secretary of War, Record Group 107, National Archives Building, Washington, D.C.
Smith Papers	Papers of Harold D. Smith, Franklin D. Roosevelt Library, Hyde Park, New York.
SPD	Records, Special Planning Division, War Department General and Special Staffs, Record Group 165, National Archives Building, Washington, D.C.
Stimson Papers and Diary	Papers of Henry L. Stimson, Yale University Library, New Haven, Connecticut.
Truman Papers	Papers of Harry S. Truman, Harry S. Truman Library, Independence, Missouri.
Yarnell Papers	Papers of H.E. Yarnell, Naval History Division, Washington, D.C.
War Plans Division	Records, War Plans Division, War Department General and Special Staffs, Record Group 165, Washington, D.C.

Public Documents

The government has published few documents on postwar military planning. The most useful are the wartime hearings of a few committees, especially those of the House Select Committee on Postwar Military Policy.

National Science Foundation. *Federal Funds for Research, Development and Other Scientific Activities.* vols. 17–24. Washington, D.C., 1968–74.
U.S. Bureau of the Census. *Historical Statistics of the United States: Colonial Times to 1957.* Washington, D.C., 1960.
———. *Statistical Abstract of the United States: 1973.* Washington, D.C., 1973.

U.S. Congress, House. Committee on Military Affairs. *Hearings on H.R. 2946 (Research and Development)*, 79/1, 1945.

———. *Hearings, Universal Military Training*, 79/1, 1945.

U.S. Congress, House. Committee on Naval Affairs. *Hearings, Sundry Legislation Affecting the Naval Establishment 1945*, 79/1, 1945, Item 110, *Composition of the Postwar Navy*, Hearings pursuant to House Concurrent Resolution 80.

U.S. Congress, House. Select Committee on Postwar Military Policy. *Hearings, Proposal to Establish a Single Department of the Armed Forces*, 78/2, 1944.

———. *Hearings, Surplus Material—Research and Development*, 78/2, 1944.

———. *Hearings, Universal Military Training*, 79/1, 1945.

U.S. Congress, House. *House Report 505*. Report of the Chairman of the House Select Committee on Postwar Military Policy, 79/1, 1945.

U.S. Congress, House. *House Report 857*. Report of the Chairman of the House Select Committee on Postwar Military Policy, 79/1, 1945.

U.S. Congress, Senate. Committee on Military Affairs, Subcommittee of the Committee. *Hearings on Science Legislation*, 79/1, 1945.

U.S. Congress, Senate. Committee on Naval Affairs. *Hearings, Establishing a Research Board for National Security*, 79/1, 1945.

U.S. Department of State. *Foreign Relations of the United States: 1944*. Washington, D.C., 1966.

———. *Foreign Relations of the United States: 1945*. Washington, D.C., 1967.

———. *Foreign Relations of the United States: The Conferences at Cairo and Tehran, 1943*. Washington, D.C., 1961.

———. *Foreign Relations of the United States: The Conferences at Washington and Quebec, 1943*. Washington, D.C., 1970.

———. *Foreign Relations of the United States: The Conference of Berlin (The Potsdam Conference), 1945*. Washington, D.C., 1960.

U.S. Strategic Bombing Survey. *Over-all Report (European War)*. Washington, D.C., 1945.

U.S. War Department. Bureau of Public Relations. *Universal Military Training, Including Post-War Military Establishment* (title varies). Washington, D.C., 1945.

U.S. *Congressional Record*, 79/1, 1945.

The War Reports of General of the Army George C. Marshall ... General of the Army H. H. Arnold ... Fleet Admiral Ernest J. King, foreword by Walter Millis. Philadelphia and New York, 1947.

Unpublished Studies and Histories

The unpublished official military histories are not very useful, but the dissertations are helpful, especially those by Stoler and Ward.

"The Army-Navy Proposal for Universal Military Training: A Preliminary

Analysis of the Problem and the Program." Study prepared by the Bureau of the Budget, November 1944. Copy in file 353 (March 44), Records of the Special Planning Division, RG 165, National Archives Building, Washington, D.C.

Furer, Julius A. "Narrative History, Office of the Secretary of the Navy, Office of the Coordinator of Research and Development, July, 1945." Manuscript history at the Naval History Division, Washington, D.C.

"History of Research and Development Division, 1 July 1940–1 July 1945 with Supplements to 1 January 1946." Manuscript prepared by Research and Development Division, Army Service Forces, 1946. Office of the Chief of Military History, Washington, D.C.

"The History of United States Naval Research and Development in World War II." Prepared by the University of Pittsburgh Historical Staff at the Office of Naval Research. Naval History Division, Washington, D.C.

Legere, Lawrence A., Jr. "Unification of the Armed Forces." Ph.D. dissertation, Harvard University, 1950.

Lowe, Henry Jackson. "The Planning and Negotiation of U.S. Post-War Security, 1942–1943." Ph. D. dissertation, University of Virginia, 1971.

McCracken, George W. "The Army Ground Forces and Universal Military Training." Washington, 1948. Office of the Chief of Military History, Washington, D.C.

MacIssaac, David. "The United States Strategic Bombing Survey, 1944–1947." Ph. D. dissertation, Duke University, 1970.

Miller, John Andrew. "Air Diplomacy: The Chicago Civil Aviation Conference of 1944 in Anglo-American Wartime Relations and Post-War Planning." Ph. D. dissertation, Yale University, 1971.

Miller, Robert A. "The United States Army During the 1930s." Ph. D. dissertation, Princeton University, 1973.

"Scientists in Uniform, World War II." A Report to the Deputy Director for Research and Development, Logistics Division, General Staff, U.S. Army, 1948. Office of the Chief of Military History, Washington, D.C.

Stoler, Mark Alan. "The Politics of the Second Front: American Military Planning and Diplomacy 1941–1944." Ph. D. dissertation, University of Wisconsin, 1971.

Ward, Robert David. "The Movement for Universal Military Training in the United States, 1942–1952." Ph. D. dissertation, University of North Carolina, 1957.

Books

The critical secondary works are the studies of Army Air Forces and navy postwar plans by Perry McCoy Smith and Vincent Davis, each a thorough if parochial analysis as well as an excellent guide to archival material. With few exceptions, notably George C. Marshall, the subject of Forrest Pogue's superb multivolume study, the major figures in postwar planning have not yet received definitive biographical treatment. There are many autobiographies, diaries, and memoirs, especially among scientists. The best are those of Vannevar Bush, General John R. Deane, and James Forrestal. The official military histories of the war are not very useful, with the exception of John C. Sparrow's work.

Albion, Robert Greenhalgh, and Connery, Robert Howe. *Forrestal and the Navy*. New York, 1962.

Alperovitz, Gar. *Atomic Diplomacy: Hiroshima and Potsdam*. New York: Vintage, 1971. Dated but still a provocative study.

Ambrose, Stephen E. *Duty, Honor, Country: A History of West Point*. Baltimore, 1966.

————. *Rise to Globalism: American Foreign Policy Since 1938*. Baltimore, 1971. One of the best surveys of the war and the cold war.

Arnold, Henry Harley. *Global Mission*. New York, 1949. By the AAF's head, it says little about postwar planning.

Baxter, James Phinney. *Scientists Against Time*. Boston, 1946. Chronicles their wartime achievements.

Blum, John Morton. *V Was For Victory: Politics and American Culture During World War II*. New York, 1976. Valuable overview of postwar planning and other facets of the American wartime experience.

Blumenson, Martin. *The Patton Papers, 1940–1945*. Boston, 1974. Colorful, but hardly typical views.

Bruner, Jerome. *Mandate from the People*. New York, 1944. On public opinion during the war.

Burns, James MacGregor. *Roosevelt: The Soldier of Freedom*. New York, 1970.

Bush, Vannevar. *Pieces of the Action*. New York, 1970. A most enjoyable and useful scientist's memoir.

Cantril, Hadley, *Public Opinion, 1935–1946*. Princeton, 1951.

Caraley, Demetrios. *The Politics of Military Unification*. New York, 1966.

Cline, Ray S. *Washington Command Post: The Operations Division*. Washington, D.C., 1951.

Coakley, Robert W., and Leighton, Richard W. *Global Logistics and Strategy, 1943–1945*. Washington, D.C., 1968.

Compton, Arthur Holly. *Atomic Quest*. New York, 1956.

Conant, James B. *My Several Lives*. New York, 1970.

Craven, Wesley Frank, and Cate, James Lea, eds. *The Army Air Forces in World War II*. 7 vols. Chicago, 1948–58.

Davis, Vincent. *The Admirals' Lobby*. Chapel Hill, 1967.

————. *Postwar Defense Policy and the U.S. Navy, 1943–1946*. The definitive study on navy plans.

Deane, John R. *The Strange Alliance*. New York, 1947. An important general's account of his wartime experiences in and with the Soviet Union.

Derthick, Martha. *The National Guard in Politics*. Cambridge, 1965. An excellent monograph on this topic.

Divine, Robert A. *Roosevelt and World War II*. Baltimore, 1961.

————. *Second Chance: The Triumph of Internationalism in America During World War II*. New York, 1967. A definitive account of one important current of wartime planning.

Eisenhower, Dwight D. *Crusade in Europe*. Garden City, N.Y., 1948.

Fairchild, Byron, and Grossman, Jonathan. *The Army and Industrial Manpower*. Washington, D.C., 1959.

Fausold, Martin L. *James W. Wadsworth, Jr.: The Gentleman from New York*. Syracuse, 1975. Wadsworth was the key Republican congressman in matters of postwar national security, given too little attention in this study.

Feis, Herbert. *Between War and Peace: The Potsdam Conference*. Princeton, 1960.

Frye, William. *Marshall, Citizen Soldier*. New York, 1947.

Gaddis, John Lewis. *The United States and the Origins of the Cold War, 1941–1947*. New York, 1972. A good survey appreciative of the complex factors involved.

Gilpin, Robert, and Wright, Christopher, eds. *Scientists and National Policy-Making*. New York, 1964.

Gray, George W. *Science at War*. New York, 1943.

Green, Constance M.; Thomson, Harry C.; and Roots, Peter C. *The Ordnance Department: Planning Munitions for War*. Washington, D.C., 1955.

Greenberg, Daniel S. *The Politics of Pure Science*. New York, 1967. Journalistic but insightful.

Grenville, John, and Young, George. *Politics, Strategy, and American Diplomacy, 1873–1917*. New York, 1966.

Grew, Joseph C. *Turbulent Era: A Diplomatic Record of Forty Years, 1904–1945*. 2 vols. Boston, 1952. A useful primary source by a militant State Department anticommunist.

Halberstam, David. *The Best and the Brightest*. Greenwich, Conn.: Fawcett, 1972.

Harriman, W. Averell, and Abel, Elie. *Special Envoy to Churchill and Stalin, 1941–1946*. New York, 1975.

Herring, George C., Jr. *Aid to Russia, 1941–1946: Strategy, Diplomacy, the Origins of the Cold War*. New York, 1973. An excellent study and a rich source on military thinking.

Hewlet, Richard G., and Anderson, Oscar E., Jr. *The New World, 1939/1946*. University Park, Pa., 1962. Definitive account of development of bomb and nuclear policy.

Hewlett, Richard G., and Duncan, Francis. *Nuclear Navy, 1946–1952*. Chicago, 1974.

Huntington, Samuel P. *The Soldier and the State: The Theory and Politics of Civil-Military Relations*. Cambridge, 1957.

Huzar, Elias. *The Purse and the Sword: Control of the Army by Congress through Military Appropriations, 1933–1950*. Ithaca, 1950.

Janowitz, Morris. *The Professional Soldier.* New York, 1960.

Kecskemeti, Paul. *Strategic Surrender: The Politics of Victory and Defeat.* Stanford, 1958.

Kennan, George F. *Memoirs, 1925–1950.* Valuable source on the development of suspicions of the Soviet Union.

King, Ernest J., and Whitehill, Walter Muir. *Fleet Admiral King: A Naval Record.* New York, 1952. Okay on the man but has little on his thinking about the postwar.

Kolko, Gabriel. *The Politics of War: The World and United States Foreign Policy, 1943–1945.* New York, 1968. A pioneer revisionist account, exhaustive, often poorly argued, sometimes ill informed about military policy and planning.

Lasby, Clarence. *Project Paperclip: German Scientists and the Cold War.* New York, 1971. A fair book on a fascinating topic.

Leahy, William D. *I Was There.* New York, 1950. More involved in political than military matters Leahy influenced plans little.

Lippmann, Walter. *U.S. Foreign Policy: Shield of the Republic.* Boston, 1943. Useful because Lippmann's thinking often reflected the preparedness outlook.

———. *U.S. War Aims.* Boston, 1944.

Lukas, Richard C. *Eagles East: The Army Air Forces and the Soviet Union, 1941–1945.* Tallahassee, 1970.

Matloff, Maurice. *Strategic Planning for Coalition Warfare, 1943–1944.* Washington, D.C., 1959.

Millis, Walter. *Arms and Men: A Study of American Military Policy.* New York: New American Library, 1956. Dated, but still the most imaginative essay on American military history.

———, ed. *The Forrestal Diaries.* New York, 1951. Useful primary source, but the unedited diaries are now open to scholars.

Morison, Elting E. *Turmoil and Tradition: A Study of the Life and Times of Henry L. Stimson.* New York: Atheneum, 1964. Graceful and authoritative, but, except for nuclear matters, has little on postwar planning.

Osgood, Robert. *Ideals and Self-Interest in America's Foreign Relations.* Chicago, 1953.

Palmer, John McAuley. *America in Arms.* New Haven, 1941.

———. *Statesmanship or War.* Garden City, 1927.

———. *Washington, Lincoln, Wilson: Three War Statesmen.* Garden City, N.Y., 1930.

Pogue, Forrest. *George C. Marshall: Education of a General, 1880–1939.* New York, 1963. The first of a superb, exemplary, multivolume biography of the most important military figure of the war, and a valuable general source on the war.

———. *George C. Marshall: Ordeal and Hope, 1939–1942.* New York, 1966.

———. *George C. Marshall: Organizer of Victory, 1943–1945.* New York, 1973.

Polenberg, Richard. *War and Society: The United States, 1941–1945.*

New York, 1972. Valuable survey and interpretation of the domestic side of the war.

Price, Don K. *Government and Science.* New York, 1954.

Quester, George H. *Deterrence before Hiroshima: The Background of Modern Strategy.* New York, 1966.

Reagan, Michael D. *Science and the Federal Patron.* New York, 1969.

Rogow, Arnold A. *James Forrestal: A Study of Personality, Politics, and Policy.* New York, 1963. Valuable as the only biography of Forrestal, but sometimes heavy on psychoanalysis and light on history.

Roosevelt, Elliot, ed. *F.D.R., His Personal Letters: 1928–1945.* 2 vols. New York, 1950.

Rose, Lisle A. *Dubious Victory: The United States and the End of World War II.* Kent, Ohio, 1973. A corrective to revisionism that tries hard but often unconvincingly.

Rosenman, Samuel I., ed. *The Public Papers and Addresses of Franklin D. Roosevelt.* 13 vols. New York, 1938–50.

Ross, Davis R.B. *Preparing for Ulysses: Politics and Veterans During World War II.* New York, 1969. Contains good material on the planning and execution of demobilization and popular responses to it.

Seversky, Alexander P. de. *Victory through Air Power.* New York, 1942. Lively and popular tract of the times for air power.

Sherwin, Martin J. *A World Destroyed: The Atomic Bomb and the Grand Alliance.* New York, 1975. The best book on its topic, stronger on 1942–44 than on 1945.

Smith, Alice Kimball. *A Peril and a Hope: The Scientists' Movement in America, 1945–1947.* Chicago, 1965. Excellent study with a misleading title, since it focuses on atomic scientists rather than all researchers.

Smith, Perry McCoy. *The Air Force Plans for Peace, 1943–1945.* Baltimore, 1970. The basic study of AAF plans, and a guide to AAF archival sources.

Sparrow, John C. *History of Personnel Demobilization in the United States Army.* Washington, D.C., 1952. A dated official account which still contains a wealth of information.

Spykman, Nicholas John. *The Geography of the Peace.* New York, 1944. An academician's warning of future perils to American security.

Tobey, Ronald C. *The American Ideology of National Science, 1919–1930.* Pittsburgh, 1971. Essential for understanding the scientists' mood in World War II.

Truman, Harry S. *Memoirs.* 2 vols. Garden City, N.Y., 1955–56.

Vagts, Alfred. *A History of Militarism: Civilian and Military.* New York: Free Press, 1959. A fine study of how both civilians and officers abuse and misuse military power.

Watson, Mark Skinner. *Chief of Staff: Prewar Plans and Preparations.* Washington, D.C., 1950. Valuable for understanding the army's sense of neglect.

Weigley, Russell F. *The American Way of War.* New York, 1973. Valuable as both history and critique of American military policy.

———. *History of the United States Army.* New York, 1967. The best general history of the army.

———. *Towards an American Army: Military Thought from Washington to Marshall.* New York, 1962.

Wohlstetter, Roberta. *Pearl Harbor: Warning and Decision.* Stanford, 1962.

Articles

The scarcity of scholarly articles in the following list indicates how inadequately scholars have examined military policy. Of those listed, the ones by Adler and Paterson and by Sherwin are critical for understanding American policy toward the Soviet Union, while the two by Kevles comprise the best work on planning for postwar science. Proponents of postwar preparedness churned out dozens of short tracts, of which only some are listed below.

Adler, Les K., and Paterson, Thomas G. "Red Fascism: The Merger of Nazi Germany and Soviet Russia in the American Image of Totalitarianism, 1930's–1950's." *American Historical Review* 75 (April 1970): 1046–64.

Arnold, Henry Harley. "We Must Not Repeat the Mistakes of the Last War." *U.S. Air Services* 29 (1944): 14.

Auerbach, Lewis E. "Scientists in the New Deal: A Pre-War Episode in the Relations Between Science and Government in the United States." *Minerva* 3 (Summer 1965): 457–82.

Baldwin, Hanson W. "Shall We Police the World?" *Sea Power,* March 1944, pp. 6–8.

Bush, Vannevar. "Science and National Defense." *Science* 94 (19 December 1941): 571–74.

———. "Science and Security." *Sea Power,* July 1945, p. 35.

Chambliss, Commander W. C. "Base Nonsense." *U.S. Naval Institute Proceedings* 71 (February 1945): 203–06.

Compton, Arthur Holly. "Science and Our Nation's Future." *Science* 101 (2 March 1945): 207–09.

———. "What Science Requires of the New World." *Science* 99 (14 January 1944): 23–28.

Compton, Karl T. "National Security and Scientific Research." Pamphlet published by the Technology Press, Massachusetts Institute of Technology, n.d. [1945].

———. "Some Educational Effects and Implications of the Defense Program." *Science* 94 (17 October 1941): 368–69.

———. "Technological and Scientific Resources." *Annals of the American Academy of Political and Social Science* 218 (November 1941): 66–75.

Conant, James. "Science and Society in the Post-War World." *Vital Speeches of the Day,* 15 April 1943, pp. 394–97.

Cope, Commander Harley. "When Peace Comes." *U.S. Naval Institute Proceedings* 69 (February 1943): 165–69.

Curzon, Captain Myron W. "Universal Military Training." *Cavalry Journal* 54 (July-August 1945): 69–71.

Eliot, George Fielding. "Science and Foreign Policy." *Foreign Affairs* 23 (April 1945): 378–87.

Fischer, John. "The Future Defense of the U.S.A." *Harper's*, January 1945, pp. 160–67.

Forrestal, James. "Keep the Navy to Keep the Peace." *Sea Power*, July 1945, pp. 21–22.

———. "Will We Choose Naval Suicide Again?" *Saturday Evening Post*, 24 June 1944, p. 9.

Furer, Julius A. "Post-War Military Research." *Science* 100 (24 November 1944): 461–64.

———. "Science Speeds War." *Shipmate*, April 1945, p. 15.

———. "Science Works with the Armed Forces." *Scientific Monthly* 59 (August 1944): 130–32.

———. "Scientific Research and Modern Warfare" *U.S. Naval Institute Proceedings* 71 (March 1945):259–73.

Gillmor, R. C., and Bradley, Follet. "Research for Security." *Aviation*, October 1944, p. 114.

Greene, Fred. "The Military View of American Foreign Policy, 1904–1940." *American Historical Review* 66 (January 1966): 354–77.

Halsey, Lieutenant Ashley, Jr. "A Slide-Rule Formula for a Post-War Navy." *U.S. Naval Institute Proceedings* 70 (April 1944): 371–84.

Hammond, Paul Y. "Directives for the Occupation of Germany: The Washington Controversy." In *American Civil-Military Decisions: A Book of Case Studies*, edited by Harold Stein. Birmingham, 1963.

Hawkins, Brigadier General H. S. "The First Requirement of a Citizen Army." *Cavalry Journal* 54 (January-February 1945): 38–40.

Hopkins, Harry L. "Tomorrow's Army and Your Boy." *The American Magazine*, March 1945, p. 20.

Howard, Frank H. "Summary of Silver Anniversary Forum on the Future of Industrial Research." Pamphlet published by Standard Oil Development Company, n.d. [1945].

Hussey, Rear Admiral G. F. "The Indispensable Material." *Sea Power*, July 1945, pp. 39–41.

Jacobs, Vice Admiral Randall. "The Issue Should Be Decided Now." *Annals of the American Academy of Political and Social Science* 241 (September 1945): 72–76.

Jewett, Frank. "Industrial and Scientific Research for National Defense." *Proceedings of the Academy of Political Science* 19 (January 1941): 151–58.

———. "The Mobilization of Science in National Defense." *Science* 95 (6 March 1942): 235–41.

———. "The Promise of Technology." *Science* 99 (7 January 1944): 1–6.

Johnson, Thomas M. "The Military Essentials for Postwar Safety." *Reader's Digest*, December 1944, pp. 9–16.

Kevles, Daniel J. "Scientists, the Military, and the Control of Postwar Defense Research: The Case of the Research Board for National Security, 1944–46," *Technology and Culture* 16 (January 1975): 20–47.

———. "The Debate Over Postwar Research Policy, 1942–1945: A Political Interpretation of *Science—The Endless Frontier*." Manuscript in author's possession. *Isis*, in press.

Knox, Frank. "Let's Train Our Youth." *Colliers*, 29 April 1944, p. 11.

Koistinen, Paul A. C. "The 'Industrial Military Complex' in Historical Perspective: The InterWar Years." *Journal of American History* 56 (March 1970): 819–39.

Lasby, Clarence G. "Science and the Military." In *Science and Society in the U.S.*, edited by David D. Van Tassel and Michael G. Hall. Homewood Ill., 1966.

Liddell Hart, B. H. "Some Lessons of the European Warfare." *Yale Review*, Spring 1945, pp. 405–26.

McCloy, John J. "Do We Want Permanent Conscription? Yes." *Colliers*, 9 June 1945, p. 114.

———. "The Plan of the Armed Forces for Universal Military Training." *Annals of the American Academy of Political and Social Science* 241 (September 1945): 26–34.

Marshall, George C. "Responsibility of Victory: Strength of Cooperators Tied to the Strength of United States." *Vital Speeches of the Day*, 15 November 1945, pp. 76–78.

Matloff, Maurice. "The American Approach to War, 1919–1945." In *The Theory and Practice of War*, edited by Michael Howard. London, 1965.

Palmer, John McAuley. "General Marshall Wants A Citizen Army." *Saturday Evening Post*, 23 December 1944, p. 9.

———. "How to Solve Our Postwar Defense Problem." *Saturday Evening Post*, 27 January 1945, p. 17.

Patterson, Robert. "Industrial Research and National Defense." Pamphlet published by Standard Oil Development Company, n.d. [1945].

Sasscer, Landsdale G. "The Geography of Peace." *Sea Power*, July 1945, p. 33.

Schaffer, Ronald. "General Stanley D. Embick: Military Dissenter." *Military Affairs* 33 (October 1973): 89–95.

"Scientific Research Is Our First Defense." *Saturday Evening Post*, 25 August 1945, p. 108.

Sheppard, Harry R. "Can We Afford the Cost?" *Sea Power*, July 1945, pp. 29–30.

Sherwin, Martin J. "The Atomic Bomb and the Origins of the Cold War: U.S. Atomic Energy Policy and Diplomacy, 1941–45." *American Historical Review* 78 (October 1973): 945–68.

Smith-Hutton, Commander H. H. "Post-War Problems and the Navy." *U.S. Naval Institute Proceedings* 69 (June 1943): 785–93.

Snedeker, Colonel James. "Our Fighters Discuss Post-War Plans." *U.S. Naval Institute Proceedings* 71 (January 1945): 29–33.

Sunderland, Lieutenant Riley. "Our Future Military Strength." *U.S. Naval Institute Proceedings* 70 (July 1944): 817–28.

"Technological and Scientific High Command." *Fortune*, April 1942, p. 62.

Tompkins, William F. "Future Manpower Needs of the Armed Forces." *Annals of the American Academy of Political and Social Science* 238 (March 1945): 56–62.

Villa, Brian L. "The U.S. Army, Unconditional Surrender, and the Potsdam Proclamation." *Journal of American History* 63 (June 1976): 66–92. An important article, though published too late for this author's use.

Weible, Major General Walter L. "The War Department and the Program for Universal Military Training." *Bulletin of the American Association of University Professors*, Winter 1944, pp. 491–99.

Wilson, Charles. "For the Common Defense: A Plea for a Continuing Program of Industrial Preparedness." *Army Ordnance* 26 (March-April 1944): 285–88.

Woolf, S. J. "Dr. Bush Sees A Boundless Future For Science." *New York Times Magazine*, 2 September 1945, p. 14.

"Yankee Scientist." *Time*, 3 April 1944, pp. 53–57.

INDEX

Adams, Roger, 151
Africa, 46
Air bases: postwar, 42–47, 48–49, 95, 111–12, 166–67, 203–04; in Russia, 169, 173
Aircraft carriers: loss feared by navy, 16, 17; before World War II, 30, 31; in postwar plans, 33, 93, 203, 218
American Legion, 25, 61, 81, 83, 102
Appleby, Paul, 63
Army, United States: in cold war historiography, ix; and post-World War I planning, 1–3; organization of, 13–14; and interservice struggles, 16, 20–21, 48–49, 108–19, 195–98, 207–08, 220–29; fears postwar backlash, 26, 195; strategic plans before World War II, 27–32; and UMT, 73–90 passim; and prewar research, 120–21, 123–24; and mobilization of science, 124–25; and postwar research, 134–50 passim, 152–58 passim; and Soviet Union, 161–62, 181–82, 186–88, 219; and demobilization, 191–94, 217; in JCS postwar strategy, 198–205 passim; and atomic weaponry, 207–08, 212–32; criticized by Truman, 220–21
—plans: initial, 1, 35–39; in *1944,* 94–101; revised at Marshall's order, 101–08; opposed by AAF, 108–19; in fall *1945,* 221–29 passim.
Army Air Forces (AAF): in cold war historiography, ix; starts planning, 8, 15, 17; autonomy in army, 14, 16; and interservice struggles, 16, 17, 20–21, 48–49, 52, 94, 96–98, 108–19, 195–98, 207–08, 219, 221–22, 224, 225–29; postwar plans, 39–47, 54, 94, 96–98, 107, 108–13, 221, 226–27; and UMT, 40–41, 69, 85, 86*n,* 89, 113, 224, 237; on air power as deterrent, 40–43, 46, 52; weaknesses in strategy, 52, 229–32; and Soviet Union, 110, 169, 178, 219; on American interests, 165; on international organization, 167; on Germany or Japan as postwar threat, 168; approves Japan invasion plans, 187; re-

action to atomic weaponry, 207–08, 232; effect of demobilization on, 217; opposes Marshall's plans, 222, 224, 225–26; as viewed by Eisenhower, 228–29
Army Budget Division, 99–101, 107, 109
Army G-1 Division, 107
Army G-2 Division, 14, 54; on Soviet Union, 161, 182, 214, 216
Army G-3 Division, 94, 95, 116
Army Ground Forces (AGF), 8, 96, 97–98, 228
Army Legislative and Liaison Division, 77
Army New Developments Division, 135
Army Operations Division (OPD): importance in army, 12, 15; supports air power, 40, 41, 49; and army plans, 49, 94, 113–14, 118, 119
Army Service Forces, 8, 96
Army Special Committee on the Permanent Military Establishment, 221–22, 226, 228–29
Army Special Planning Division (SPD), 23; established, 8–9; limitations, 9, 10, 11, 12–15; responsibilities, 9–10, 11–12; and navy, 17, 118, 227; and State Department, 24; and civilian groups, 25; and army plans, 35, 91, 94–99, 102, 103–04, 107, 108, 109, 117, 118; and first AAF plans, 41; and UMT campaign, 60, 61, 77, 81; and postwar research, 113, 138, 146, 157; ignores Soviet Union, 168; superseded, 221
Arnold, Henry H. (General of the Army), 109; initiates AAF planning, 15, 17; sketched, 19, 20; and JCS, 21, 197; on future aerial warfare, 47, 112, 195, 229; opposes army plans, 111–14, 115, 227; and postwar research, 131, 132, 150; and Soviet Union, 160, 162, 170, 189; on atomic weaponry, 207, 213, 229; air power doctrine assessed, 229, 230–231
Atlantic Ocean, 16, 34, 46
Atomic bomb, ix, 79, 180; Anglo-American monopoly on, 43, 65, 172, 209; and deterrence, 43, 210–13, 237; development, 124, 125, 126; effect on